A Light Undimmed

Our Lady of Bom Sucesso

A Light Undimmed

The Story of the Convent of Our Lady of Bom Sucesso

Lisbon

1639 to 2006

Honor McCabe O.P.

DOMINICAN PUBLICATIONS

First published (2007) by
Dominican Publications
42 Parnell Square
Dublin 1

ISBN 1-905604-06-8
ISBN 978-1-905604-6-7

Cover design by David Cooke
Index compiled by Julitta Clancy

Printed in the Republic of Ireland
by Betaprint Ltd.,
Bluebell, Dublin 12

Contents

Belém's Monuments; Convento do Bom Sucesso; A Sixteenth Century Wedding of a Noble Couple; Tragedy for Family and Country; Heiress and Bride at fourteen; Bride again at Nineteen; The Gift of a Miraculous Statue; An Unusual Title in the Seventeenth Century; Portugal ruled by Spain; The Countess's noble Lineage; The Countess's Wealth; The Slave Trade; The Countess decides to found a Convent.

The Irish in Lisbon; Daniel O'Daly's early life; The Suffering of the Irish People in the Seventeenth Century; Dominic O'Daly's Project in Lisbon; The Countess of Atalaya learns of this Project; Dominic O'Daly sets out for the Royal Court in Madrid; Young Women's Determination; A Mysterious Visitor; Irish Recruits for the Spanish Army; Licences for the Foundation; The Countess's Will; The Countess as Foundress; The Countess's Dream; Two Religious from São João Convent in Setübal; The Name of Nossa Senhora do Bom Sucesso; Legends concerning the Title; Miracles attributed to Nossa Senhora do Bom Sucesso; Foundation Day; Frei Domingos do Rosário, Diplomat.

Acknowledgments

I would like to acknowledge my indebtedness to many people for their varied help and their interest during my work on this book: Helen Mary Harmey, O.P., the present Congregation prioress and her Council for their interest and support; Geraldine Marie Smyth, O.P., the former Congregation Prioress and her Council for first entrusting me with the research and writing of the Bom Sucesso story; the Community of Bom Sucesso who welcomed me among them and gave me every possible help, in particular, Martinez Murphy, O.P., archivist; my own Community of Nephin Road, Dublin, for allowing me the opportunity to be absent in Lisbon whenever necessary; the publishing editor, Father Tom Jordan, O.P., for his expertise and his patience;

I wish to thank Fr. Ramón Hernandez, O.P., archivist of the Dominican Order, Santa Sabina, Rome, the archivists of the different Dominican convents in Ireland: Rose O'Neill, O.P., Galway, Terence O'Keeffe, O.P., Cabra, Dublin; Dominique Horgan, O.P., the former archivist of the Generalate and Mary O'Byrne, O.P., its present archivist; Maris Stella Mc Keown, O.P., archivist of the Region of Ireland; the readers, Margaret Mac Curtain, O.P., Eibhlín Hegarty, O.P., and Veronica Mc Cabe, O.P., for their time and valuable suggestions; Ana Cristina Ferreira da Costa, Catherine Gibson, O.P., and Edel Murphy, O.P., for material from their respective theses; Giovanna Piscini for material from the archives of the former Propaganda Fide; Monsignor James O'Brien for original material on Dr. Sleyne; my nephew, Timothy Mc Carthy for further material on Dr. Sleyne; Frei Ruí Almeida Lopes, O.P., for varied help; Francisca Sarmento for obtaining maps; Pedro O'Neill Teixeira for information on the Irish Masons; Patricia Lamb for additional material on the Peninsular War and António Cabreras for historical articles on Bom Sucesso.

I would like to thank in a special way the many other Portuguese friends, past-pupils and members of the Bom Sucesso staff who made important contributions to my research, in particular, Isabel Pestana Sarmento for identifying the arms of the Countess; Ana Leonor Nápoles Sarmento for her help; the late Fernanda Gomes da Silva, receptionist; Maria dos Anjos Alves Ramos; Aurea Marques Pereira; Maria da Conceição Pedro and her late husband, António Pedro.

My sincere thanks is also due to the following for artwork, photography and photocopying: Ana Isabel Seruya; Alexandre Pais, Monica Devers, O.P., Malachy Mooney, Pat Hourigan, Frank Miller, Nollaig Ní Laighin; Regis Hegarty, O.P., and Nuno Nunes.

My nephew Jack Mc Carthy deserves a special word of gratitude for his continued technical help in processing the material

Finally, I would like to express my deep appreciation for her invaluable work to Maria de Fátima Menezes who gave so much of her time to reading the whole manuscript, made useful suggestions and verified historical data. Without her painstaking work and continued help the accuracy of historical details would not have been assured

Sister Honor McCabe O.P.
Dublin
January 2007

Foreword

Sister Helen Mary Harmey O.P., Congregation Prioress, has kindly invited me to write the Foreword to *A Light Undimmed*. It is for me a great privilege, and having spent sixty-two years in this beautiful monastery of Our Lady of Bom Sucesso, I gratefully accept the opportunity to express my appreciation of all that I have experienced during these six decades.

As a young sister I was inspired by the spirit in the house, a spirit of prayer and contemplation, of austerity and suffering, but of joy in spite of the lack of material comfort. Most of the Sisters who were here when I entered have passed on. They had lived through several revolutions and other upheavals. Many of us remember the 1974 revolution.

The Second Vatican Council which brought about a deeper understanding of the religious life and its place in the Church opened up for us new frontiers to reach people of other nationalities, and to be engaged in new ministries of prayer, preaching and social solidarity.

This is a book about the story of a remarkable convent, and is truly a marathon work in which the author has woven the histories of Ireland and Portugal with the lives of the sisters from 1639 to the present day. The title of the book is a prophetic expression that the work of prayer, contemplation, study and preaching will continue to flourish in this convent throughout the 21st century and beyond.

Sister Mary Agnes Talty O.P.
Convent of Our Lady of Bom Sucesso
Lisbon

Abbreviations

ANTT	Arquivo Nacional da Torre do Tombo, Lisbon
APF	Arquivium Propaganda Fide, Rome
BSIBSA	Born Sucesso Archives, Lisbon
DAG	General Archives of Dominican, Cabra Congregation, Dublin
DCCA	Dominican Convent, Cabra, Archives, Dublin
DGA	Dominican Convent, Galway, Archives, Galway
M.C.A.	Mother Cecilia's Annals, 1639-1939, Bom Sucesso, Lisbon
S.O.C.G.	Sacrum Officium Congregatioms Generalis, Rome
SSA	Sisters of Sion Archives, Devon England

Preface

Early in the seventeenth century a devout Portuguese Countess, Iria de Brito, had a dream. In her dream she was praying in her private oratory when five women dressed in white came in. They proceeded to light all the candles around the altar and having done so they went out again leaving the candles lighting. Their departure made of the dream a nightmare because of the danger of fire. Startled, the Countess woke up and on realising that it was only a dream she relaxed and duly forgot about the nightmare.

Many years later, when she had generously given over her favourite dwelling place to be a convent for Irish Dominican nuns, she understood the prophetic aspect of this dream. At the opening ceremony establishing the convent, five women received the Dominican habit.

The light that began to shine on 12th November, 1639, has continued to shine down through the centuries in spite of the darkness, at times, of oppression and difficulties of various kinds. This present account is intended to celebrate in a small way the wonderful lives of these great women, some Portuguese and some Irish.

When I was first assigned to Bom Sucesso in the 1960s, I was impressed and inspired by the dedication of the then members of the community to the life they had chosen and the joy which animated them. Where this book is concerned, I would like to pay tribute, in particular, to Mother Cecilia Murray who was annalist and archivist of the convent for many years. When the original annals were destroyed during the 1910 political crisis in Portugal, she painstakingly re-assembled material referring to Bom Sucesso from chronicles and copies of documents in various public and private archives. With this material she accurately re-wrote the annals 1639-1939 and it is mainly from this work together with other documents in the Bom Sucesso archives that I have been able to compose this present history. I have also obtained material from other sources, among them *Arquivo*

Nacional da Torre do Tombo, the Ajuda Palace Archives, Santa Sabina Archives of the Dominican Order in Rome, the archives of the Pontifical Congregation for the Doctrine of the Faith in Rome and a number of public and private archives in Ireland.

However, thanks to Mother Cecilia and other Bom Sucesso archivists, the richest source was in the convent's own archives and much of this documentation has not been previously published. As with all research, the work has been difficult and often frustrating: manuscripts in seventeenth and eighteenth centuries' handwriting that required the help of experts and lengthy research which did not yield the information sought. However, so many people have shown interest in the Bom Sucesso story that it seemed important to share it with a wider readership.

Honor McCabe O.P.

Introduction

Portugal, from a certain point of view, may be considered one of Western Europe's well kept secrets. Every year, its golden beaches attract the sun-loving tourist while its shrine of Fatima draws the pilgrim. However, neither the tourist nor the pilgrim, in general, becomes interested in Portuguese culture and language. Few are aware that, at one time, Portugal's empire stretched from Brazil in the West to Goa in the East and that, even today, its language ranking fifth among the most spoken languages of the world, has given its vocabulary to many other languages. Portuguese *caravelas*, in the sixteenth century, opened up the sea-route to India, thus bringing the riches of the Orient to Europe and many of the place-names on the African coast are still those given by these intrepid explorers.

As the story of Bom Sucesso has been intertwined with the history of the country in which it is situated, it seemed desirable to include a brief account of Portugal's historical events, especially those which directly affected this Irish Dominican convent. For the reader who is well versed in Portuguese history this is not necessary and s/he may only need to glance at the chronology at the back of the book. However, to those readers who are not acquainted with Portugal's historical past the following paragraphs may be of interest in understanding the sometimes tragic story of Bom Sucesso.

PREHISTORIC ERA

The area known as Portugal today has been inhabited from prehistoric times. Archaeological finds show that the group of humans known as *Homo Sapiens* peopled the country some two hundred thousand years ago and there are numerous traces of artefacts from this period. Rich collections of polished stone objects and ceramics from the later Neolithic period also reveal the continuous progress in civilisation in this western part of the Iberian peninsula. Portugal has its own cave drawings near

Montemor-o-Novo in the Alentejo.

SUCCESSIVE INVASIONS

From the eighth century B.C., Portugal, like the rest of the Iberian peninsula, was subjected to successive waves of invasion by land from Indo-European peoples, among them the pre-Celts and the Celts. The latter are responsible for founding Conímbriga, Setúbal and Évora. The *citánia* or hilltop forts date from this time also. Other invaders, such as the Phoenicians and the Greeks came by sea and colonised mainly the coastal regions. Lisbon and Faro had colonies of these Mediterranean peoples.

In 218 B.C., the first Roman legions arrived in the Iberian peninsula during the second Punic war. They found the greatest resistance to their occupation in the courageous stand of the Lusitani, inhabitants of the central region of the future Portugal. Their leader for ten years (147-139 B.C.) was Viriatus. In 80 B.C., the Lusitani tried again to repulse the Romans but by 25 B.C., the conquest of Lusitania by the forces of Octavius Caesar Augustus was considered complete.

With the decline of the Roman Empire, Portugal, like other coastal regions of Western Europe, suffered a series of invasions from Germanic tribes. The most important where Lusitania was concerned were the Suevi who, in the fifth century A.D., settled in the North-West of the peninsula and in part of Lusitania. Towards the end of the sixth century, they were overcome by the Visigoths.

The last significant invasion for the formation of the Portuguese people was that of the Islamic invaders from North Africa. In 711, the Moors disembarked in the peninsula with a view to conquering it. The Moors in this region were mostly Berbers with some Syrians and Egyptians. They were tolerant of other faiths so that both Jews and Christians had freedom of worship.

THE CHRISTIAN RE-CONQUEST

The Christian re-conquest began in 722 when the Christian forces gained a decisive victory over the Moors at Covadonga and by 757, Afonso I of Asturias had recovered a large area of North-West Iberia, including the territory between the Minho and Douro rivers. For five centuries, the land of Portugal was the scene of conflict as the Christian armies tried to win back the territory from the Moors.

Portugal as an autonomous state began its existence in the eleventh century when French knights came to help Christian princes in their conflict with the Moors. Two of these knights from Burgundy, Count Raymond and his cousin Henri of the family of the Dukes of Burgundy, married the daughters of Afonso VI of Leon (1072-1109). This king claimed suzerainty over the various princedoms including the Moorish territory and in 1096, he gave Henri the territory extending from the Minho river to south of Coimbra – *O Condado Portucalense*.

AFONSO HENRIQUES, KING OF PORTUGAL

Henri's son, Afonso Henriques, gained a decisive victory over the Moors in 1139. From then on, he claimed the title King. He continued his advance against the Moors and consolidated his territory as far south as the Tagus. In 1147, he captured Lisbon with help from foreign crusaders. In 1185, the first king of Portugal died and was succeeded by his son Sancho I who captured the Moorish capital of Silves in 1189 but the following year, the territory south of the Tagus was recaptured by al-Mansur the vizier of al-Andaluz. This was the last significant Moorish campaign in Portugal.

During the reign of Afonso III (1248-1279) the territory of Portugal, as it is today, was established. His successor, D. Dinis, in a period of peace, consolidated the frontier, building a number of castles along the border between Portugal and Castile. Agricultural reform was undertaken and many of Portugal's products, such as wine, olive oil, fish and fruit were exported to Flanders, Brittany and England. In 1319, the Order of Knights Templar, being suppressed, at this time, in other countries of Europe, was reorganised in Portugal as the Order of Christ, directly responsible to the king.

THE SECOND DYNASTY

The Burgundian dynasty ended when, in 1383, D. Fernando died leaving his daughter, Dona Beatriz as heiress to the throne and her mother, Dona Leonor as regent. Dona Beatriz had married D. Juan I, the king of Castile and he now claimed the throne of Portugal. However, the people supported the illegitimate son of the king, D. João, Mestre de Avis. At the Battle of Aljubarrota (1385), helped by English archers, D. João won a decisive victory over Castile and ascended the throne of Portugal as D. João I. The famous Abbey of Batalha was built in thanksgiving for this victory.

In 1386, the Treaty of Windsor established an alliance between King João I of Portugal and King Richard II of England. The following year

D. João married Philippa of Lancaster, daughter of John of Gaunt.

HENRY THE NAVIGATOR AND EXPLORATION

While the first dynasty was characterised by the expansion and consolidation of mainland Portugal, the second dynasty would be characterised by Portuguese expansion overseas and the extraordinary feats of exploration undertaken in the following centuries by this numerically small people.

At the beginning, the guiding genius of this movement of exploration was Henrique, D. João's third son, known to history as Henry the Navigator. As Grand Master of the Order of Christ, he used its resources to found, in Sagres, a school of navigation which the leading cartographers and navigators of Europe attended. In 1419, Madeira was discovered, followed by the Islands of the Azores in 1427.

By the time of Prince Henry's death in 1460, the Cape Verde Islands and the west coast of Africa as far as Sierra Leone had been explored. After a short interval, the advance along the West African coast continued until, in 1487, during the reign of D. João II, Bartolomeu Dias rounded the Cape of Good Hope and the hope of reaching India by sea was confirmed. Meanwhile, other intrepid Portuguese sailed west to Greenland and Newfoundland.

VASCO DA GAMA AND THE SEA-ROUTE TO INDIA

In 1497, Vasco da Gama and his fleet left Belém and sailed south and east to arrive in Calicut, India in May 1498. The much-coveted spices from India were brought back to Portugal and Lisbon became the emporium of Europe. The Portuguese monarchy, already enriched by its trade with West Africa, now became the wealthiest in Europe. Meanwhile, Spain had discovered the West Indies in 1492 and, in 1494, had signed the Treaty of Tordesillas with Portugal. By this treaty the two countries divided the world of the discoveries between them with an imaginary line three hundred and seventy leagues west of the Cape Verde Islands.

THE PORTUGUESE DISCOVER BRAZIL

The next great discovery was that of Brazil in 1500 when Pedro Alvares Cabral commanding the second Portuguese fleet to set out for India deviated southwest and disembarked north of present-day Porto Seguro in the country that was, at first, named Vera Cruz (the True Cross). Some time was spent exploring the coast of Brazil and communicating with the indigenous people. Then Cabral sent one of his thirteen ships back to Portugal to tell the king of this discovery and proceeded to India.

The great wealth accruing from these discoveries led to the development of lavish architecture known as Manueline Gothic. The monastery of Jerónimos and the Torre de Belém, the jewel of Lisbon, are the most notable examples of this architecture. Much of the financial expertise needed to govern this wealth was under the direction of Jewish financiers. Portugal had traditionally dealt more tolerantly with the Jews than other European countries but, in 1496, under pressure from Spain, D. Manuel I was obliged to order their expulsion. Many fled to Flanders but some chose to remain as New Christians. The introduction of the Inquisition (introduced with restrictions in 1536) further deprived Portugal of the financial expertise it required for its far-flung empire. By the 1570s the economy was under severe pressure.

PORTUGAL LOSES INDEPENDENCE

The penultimate king of the Avis dynasty, D. Sebastião (1557-1578), ascended the throne at the age of three. His grandmother, Dona Catarina of Austria, acted as Regent from 1557 until 1562 when, his granduncle, Cardinal Henrique became Regent. In 1568, at the age of fourteen, D. Sebastião began his reign. Imbued with the desire to gain glory by fighting the Moors in North Africa, he defied the advice of his courtiers and set off for North Africa where, at the battle of Alcácer Quibir, the Portuguese army was defeated and presumably D. Sebastião was killed. The aged Cardinal Henrique became King until his death in 1580 when Philip II of Spain, as Sebastião's uncle, claimed the throne of Portugal. At the battle of Alcántara, the Portuguese forces were defeated and Philip II of Spain became also Philip I of Portugal.

THE RESTORATION OF INDEPENDENCE

Spanish rule in Portugal lasted until 1640 when the movement know as *A Restauracão* deposed the Countess of Mantua, the Spanish Governor of Portugal and, by popular acclaim, the Duke of Bragança became D. João IV of Portugal. Only in 1668, by the Treaty of Madrid, ratified in Lisbon, did Spain accept the independence of Portugal. However, the economic situation of the country was extremely weak as it had lost many of its trade routes and its traditional allies, the English and the Dutch, had become enemies. Alliance with England was restored through the marriage, in 1661, of D. João IV's daughter, Catherine with England's

19

newly restored king, Charles II.

THE LISBON EARTHQUAKE

In 1697, gold was discovered in Brazil and this new source of wealth enriched the treasury of D. João V who came to the throne in 1706. Portugal's second age of prosperity lasted until the tragic event of the Lisbon earthquake and tidal wave in which, it is calculated that five thousand people perished and as many more in its aftermath. It also destroyed areas in the Alentejo and the Algarve. This catastrophe enhanced the prestige of the King's chief minister, Sebastião José de Carvalho e Melo, later ennobled with the title, Marques de Pombal. He energetically put in place the means of burying the dead, treating the injured and reconstructing the city of Lisbon. He tried to modernise administration but ruthlessly crushed the power of the higher nobility on a charge of attempted regicide. He also had the Jesuits expelled from Portuguese territories and this led to the suppression of the Society.

When, in 1777, Maria I succeeded her father, D. José I as monarch, Pombal was brought to trial, convicted but pardoned, due to his age. Soon, a new threat to the royal families of Europe occurred – the French Revolution beginning in 1789. Due, it is thought, to anxiety engendered by this event the Portuguese queen became mentally ill and her son, the future João VI removed her as Regent.

THE PENINSULAR WAR

With the rise of Napoleon Portugal came under pressure to support his naval blockade of Britain. As England's oldest ally, Portugal could not do this and, consequently, was invaded by the French under General Junot. Prior to this invasion, in 1807, the royal family and Court set sail for Brazil where they remained until 1821. The campaign against Napoleon was left to the responsibility of two British generals, Wellington and Beresford. Twice the French invaded Portugal and twice they were obliged to withdraw. At the third invasion, the French reached the lines of Torres Vedras, defences ordered to be constructed to protect Lisbon. Because of Wellington's scorched earth policy, the French army overcome by starvation left Portugal never to return.

Portugal was now a protectorate of Britain and this was resented by the people. In August 1820, while Beresford was temporarily out of Portugal, officers of the Portuguese army met and drew up a liberal Constitution. King D. João VI was obliged to return from Brazil and accepted the terms of this Constitution. However, Queen Dona Carlota and the King's younger brother D. Miguel refused to take the oath and became leaders of the movement against the terms of the Constitution which included the abolition of privileges for the clergy and nobility. Meanwhile, in 1822, D. João VI's son, D. Pedro proclaimed the independence of Brazil and became its Emperor.

CIVIL WAR

On the death of King D. João VI, D. Pedro refused the throne of Portugal and passed it on to his seven-year old daughter, Maria da Gloria with his brother D. Miguel as regent, provided that he would accept a less liberal charter than the Constitution. Miguel agreed but once in power he reintroduced the old absolutist order. In 1831, D. Pedro abdicated as emperor of Brazil and came to Portugal to defend his daughter's right to the throne. A bitter civil war ensued and in 1834, the liberal movement was triumphant. The religious Orders of men were suppressed causing great distress to many who were old or ill. The convents of women were allowed to continue but forbidden to accept new members.

BEGINNING OF REPUBLICAN MOVEMENT

Throughout the early decades of the nineteenth century, there was constant conflict between those in favour of the Constitution and those who supported the less radical constitutional Charter. In the second half of the century these two factions developed into a two-party political system. The monarchy, however, lost prestige especially when Portugal was obliged to surrender in Africa the territory between Angola and Moçambique. Republicanism began to take root in the army and among the urban poor.

ASSASSINATION OF KING D. CARLOS AND HIS SON

On 28th January 1908, King D. Carlos yielded to his first minister and signed a decree banishing to the colonies those guilty of political crimes. On 1st February, he and his son, the heir to the throne, were assassinated. The reign of his second son D. Manuel II ended with the establishment of the Republic in 1910. The last King of Portugal with the two queens, his mother, Dona Amelia and his grandmother, Dona Maria Pia, went into exile in England. He died there in 1932.

Between 1911 and 1926, the dominant political party was the Democratic Party led by Afonso Costa. However, there was constant political turmoil with consequent negative effects on the country's economy. In those sixteen years, there were as many as forty-five different governments and several military uprisings.

Many believed that only a dictatorship would restore political order. There was conflict within the army as some favoured a return to a monarchy while others favoured a republican government.

0 Estado Novo

Eventually, General Carmona, a monarchist, emerged as president and the Republican constitution was suspended. In 1928, Dr. Antonio de Oliveira Salazar, an economist from Coimbra University, joined the Cabinet as minister for finance and succeeded in balancing the budget. General Carmona had implicit faith in Salazar who became prime minister in 1932. When the ex-king D. Manuel II died that year without an heir, Salazar made it clear that he considered the question of a monarchy closed. He introduced his own brand of dictatorship and entitled it, *O Estado Novo*. Only one political party, the *União Nacional*, was permitted to exist and any political opposition was controlled by the secret police.

Salazar remained in office until 1968 when, because of terminal illness, he was replaced by Marcelo Caetano. The latter endeavoured to introduce a limited democracy in Portugal but the maintenance of the colonies under Portuguese rule had become virtually impossible. Moreover, the younger officers in the army had begun to sympathise with the aspirations to independence of the colonial peoples. India had already annexed Portuguese territories in the sub-continent and conflict in Angola as well as Moçambique was occurring. Internationally, colonialism was outmoded.

Within the army an organisation entitled *Movimento das Forças Armadas* was founded. In February 1974, General Spinola, a high-ranking officer in the army, who had experience of the difficulties in the colonies published a book entitled, *Portugal e o Futuro* in which he stated that it was impossible to maintain the colonies as such and proposed a federalist system instead. The government rejected this and had General Spínola together with General Costa Gomes dismissed from their official functions.

The Flower Revolution

Early in the following month of March, an abortive military coup took place. This was the prelude to the Revolution of the 25th April, known at the time, as The Flower Revolution. The government of Marcelo Caetano fell and its members were deported. In the aftermath of the Revolution, considerable political turmoil ensued for a number of years and, for some time, there was danger of a left-wing dictatorship replacing the Salazarist right-wing one.

During 1975, no fewer than four provisional governments were led by the communist General Vasco Gonçalves. By 1976, the Third Republican Constitution which was both democratic and socialist was approved and General Ramalho Eanes who was trusted by the army was elected President. He was a figure of stability and was anxious to develop links with Africa, Asia and South America. Being re-elected for a second term he remained in office until 1986 when the former socialist prime minister, Mario Soares, was elected, the first civilian president in sixty years. In that year also, Portugal became a member of the European Community and with financial aid consequent on its membership unprecedented economic growth occurred. The PSD (The Social Democratic Party) came to power and they favoured free enterprise as well as privatisation. Opposition to this occurred but in 1991, the PSD was returned to power with a considerable majority.

POLITICAL STABILITY

The decade of the 1990s was characterised by political stability and Portugal played its part in the international scene. The presidency of the EU was held by the Portuguese for the first time in 1992. Lisbon Expo. '98 celebrating Portuguese culture and its contribution to civilisation was highly successful while concern, at this time, for former colonies was of major importance. For decades, Portugal had advocated a referendum in East Timor which, after Portugal's withdrawal in 1974, had been invaded by Indonesia and suffered the genocide of a third of its population. In August 1999, the UN organised the referendum which ended Indonesia's control of East Timor. In the same year, Macau, Portugal's last colony was given back to China. Finally, Manuel Durão Barroso, Portugal's prime minister was elected president of the EU in 2004.

PORTUGAL, REFUGE FOR IRISH RELIGIOUS WOMEN

This is, in brief, the historical background of the country that, since the early seventeenth century, has been the refuge of many Irish exiles, both religious and secular. Our concern is with one specific group - that of Irish women unable to lead a religious life in Ireland due to the penal laws. While seminaries for Irish students for the priesthood were founded in many countries and convents accepted refugee nuns into their communities, Portugal was the only country where one member of its nobility founded a convent specifically as a haven for Irish women who wished to pursue a religious life. Dona Iria de Brito gave her valuable country residence situated adjacent to royal lands in Belém and other property for this worthy cause. It has survived until this century and throughout the ages, its members have shared in the vicissitudes of their adopted country. Founded during the Spanish domination of Portugal, its opening ceremony was honoured by the presence of the Spanish governor in Lisbon.

Throughout the centuries following the Restoration, the Convent of Bom Sucesso was favoured by the kings and queens of the Bragança dynasty. This situation changed in the nineteenth century, when liberalism limited the power of the king and the community shared the hardship of oppression, its members, in 1823, being driven out of their home for one month. However, a new protector was found in the British Embassy as the religious who had come from Ireland were able to claim that they were British subjects. King Edward VII, as Prince of Wales and later as king befriended and visited these sisters.

Today, the restoration of the art work of the Church and Upper Choir – financed by The World Monuments Fund – Portugal and carried out by Junqueira 220 under the direction of Dr Carmen Olazabal and Senhor Luis Tovar Figueira reveals not only the beauty of the many masterpieces but also the generosity of the community's patrons. Without them such valuable work could not have come to Bom Sucesso which, so often throughout its history, was struggling financially.

Many short accounts, some quite inaccurate, have been published in various magazines and some theses have been written on aspects of the convent and church. In this more detailed account I have endeavoured to be faithful to the facts while, because of my own Dominican background, I have also tried to express from the scanty material still available the deep spirituality which inspired these women to lead austere but integrated lives. This spirit of dedication still lives on in the present community and, when I was first assigned there in the early 1960s, the spiritual depth of the then community was a source of inspiration to me. I hope that their story may interest and inspire others in spite of its author's inadequacy.

1

Bom Sucesso Convent
The Setting to our Story

Partimo-nos assi do sancto templo	*Thus, we left the holy temple*
Que nas praias do mar está assentado	*Standing on the seashore*
Que o nome tem da terra por exemplo	*Which bears that city's name*
Donde Deus foi em carne ao mundo dado	*Where God-made- man was born*
Certifico-te o Rei, que se contemplo	*I assure you, O king, if I reflect*
Como fui destas praias aportado	*How I sailed from these shores*
Cheio dentro de dúvida e receio	*Within, full of doubt and fear*
Que apenas nos meus olhos ponho	*That only my gaze reined in*
O freio	

(Luís de Camões: O<small>s</small> Lusíadas, Canto IV - LXXXVII)

Thus, Luís de Camões, the national poet of Portugal, describes the moment in history which made Lisbon's beautiful suburb of Belém (meaning Bethlehem) forever famous. It was from here on the 7th July, 1497, that Vasco da Gama set sail on his voyage of discovery of the sea-route to India. In an earlier century, Henry the Navigator had a hermitage dedicated to the Mother of God where the Church of São Jerónimos now stands. Tradition tells us that it was here he spent the night in prayer before he set out on his voyages of discovery. Hence, the name Belém which replaced the older name, *Praia de Restelo*. Because of the suffering endured by those who took part in these voyages of discovery, the Restelo beach was called *Praia das Lágrimas* (The Sands of Tears).

BELÉM'S MONUMENTS

Today, in Belém, many monuments, some ancient, some modern, commemorate the glorious days of the Portuguese exploration of the seas. The most important of these monuments is the Church of Santa Maria de Belém, popularly known as Jerónimos which has become, over the centuries, a national symbol in memory of Portugal's voyages of discovery. Tradition holds that, as Vasco da Gama's fleet set off in search of the sea route to the Orient, the king, D. Manuel I promised a beautiful church in thanksgiving if the enterprise was successful. This cannot be verified but what is historically accurate is that in 1495 the king had petitioned the Holy See to allow him found a monastery and church for the Jeronimite monks on the site of the chapel dedicated to the Mother of God on the Restelo beach. He wished to establish a pantheon for the second dynasty of Portuguese sovereigns as the church of Batalha was for the first dynasty. Jerónimos, thus contains the tombs of many royal members of the second Portuguese dynasty and these tombs rest on carved elephants, symbolic of India as the tombs of the first dynasty rest on carved lions, symbolic of the African explorations.

With the successful outcome of the voyage to India the king who had already endowed the monastery gave further donations to the building. The foundation stone was laid significantly on 6th January 1501/1502, the Feast of the Epiphany, celebrating the visit of the three wise men from the East. With the second successful voyage to India there were more royal contributions. The church and monastery complex took very many years to build but by the year of the king's death in 1521, considerable progress had been made. Two great architects worked at the design of the church, the cloister and the monastery – Boitac, possibly from France followed by the Basque, João Castilho who was responsible for the magnificent ribbed vaulting of the church's ceiling. The cloister, octagonal in design is among the most beautiful cloisters in the world. In later centuries, many maritime symbols were worked into the stone so that both church and cloister became a monument to the ages of Portugal's exploration of the seas.

Another important monument to the Discoveries is, by contrast, of a much later date – 1960, commemorating the fifth centenary of Henry the Navigator's death. It is in the shape of a sailing ship with the figure of the Infante Henrique at the prow. Some of the most important people of the ages of exploration – the king, the queen, the poet Camões, famous cartographers and explorers – are represented on this ship which is at the water's edge directly in front of Jerónimos. Apart from these monuments, Belém has many former palaces and a modern cultural centre.

Convento do Bom Sucesso

Nestling among these buildings is the *Convento de Nossa Senhora do Bom Sucesso* (Our Lady of Good Success), having a history no less fascinating than that of the area in which it is situated. Founded in

1639 it has continued to survive earthquakes and revolutions so that, when it celebrated its tercentenary in 1939 it was the oldest enclosed convent in Portugal.[1] What is more unusual still is the fact that it is also the oldest Irish Dominican convent in the world. Its history can be described as the story of the collaboration of two peoples in the work of God: one people supporting the other during centuries of persecution and oppression; the other responding to this generosity through the education of Portugal's youth of many generations.

The story begins as early as the mid-sixteenth century when the glory of the discovery of the sea route to India and the wealth accruing from the exploration of West Africa were beginning to wane. Other peoples of Western Europe, among them the English and the Dutch, were starting to compete with the Portuguese for control of the seas and acquisition of this new-found wealth. Moreover, the introduction of the Inquisition (with certain restrictions in 1536 and without restrictions in 1547) deprived Portugal of the expertise of Jewish financiers and withdrew from Lisbon much needed capital for the maintenance of such far-flung enterprises.

A Sixteenth Century Wedding of a Noble Couple

Many noble families, however, enriched by the discoveries in earlier decades continued to enjoy their wealth. One such distinguished family was Ataíde whose eldest member customarily held the title Conde de Atouguia. The holder of this title in the mid-1500s was D. Luís de Ataíde. Not only was he Count by inheritance but he was also appointed Viceroy of India and was to die in Goa in 1580. His sister, Dona Antónia de Ataíde married D. João de Brito, a descendant also of an illustrious family, his mother being Iria of the royal House of Eça (though not in line of succession to the throne). The coat of arms of D. João de Brito and Dona Antónia de Ataíde still adorns the main doorway of the convent, the family's original summer residence.

At first, good fortune smiled on this young couple as they were blessed with four children, two boys and two girls. Cristovão and Lopes began to follow a military career while Francisca de Brito became a religious in the Monastery of Celas. Iria was, at an early age entrusted to the care of her maternal aunt who was first lady-in-waiting to Queen Dona Catarina, the retired regent of Portugal and grandmother to the ill-fated King D. Sebastião.[2]

Tragedy for Family and Country

This young king, fired with enthusiasm to win glory as a Christian knight over Islam, set out for North Africa, never to return. At the Battle of Alcácer Quibir in 1578, the Portuguese were defeated by the Moors and presumably, D. Sebastião was killed.[3] Not only was this a tragedy for Portugal but it was also a personal tragedy for many families in the country. With him perished many of Portugal's youth, among them Iria's elder brother, Cristovão.

The loss of D. Sebastião created for Portugal a crisis of succession which his elderly uncle, Cardinal Henrique offset for two years. At his death in 1580, Philip II of Spain claimed the throne of Portugal and at the Battle of Alcântara defeated the Portuguese. Once again Iria's family was touched by this double tragedy of country and family when her second brother, Lopes, was killed at Alcântara.

Heiress and Bride at Fourteen Years

Iria de Brito was, consequently, only fourteen years old when she became the sole heiress of the House of Brito. Before her fifteenth birthday, her parents arranged her marriage to D. Diogo Forjaz Pereira, the fourth Count of Feira. This was a fortunate arrangement for the young bride. The Count's estate on the Ajuda hill bordering the lands of the Jeronimite monks close to the de Brito estate added considerably to the wealth and prestige of this young couple. Early in their marriage a son was born to them but sadly, he died in infancy. Shortly afterwards, tragedy struck the couple again when D. Diogo was sent on a diplomatic mission to Madrid. During his stay in Spain's capital he was accidentally killed, leaving Iria widowed at the age of eighteen.

Bride again at Nineteen

In 1585, the young widow married again at the age of nineteen. Her second husband was her cousin, D. Francisco Manuel Ataíde, a landowner with the title of Alcaide Mor (Governor) de Marvão, which he had inherited from his father. The latter had also been Portuguese ambassador to France but perished at the Battle of Alcácer Quibir.[4] From 1580 until 1640, Spain ruled Portugal and, though Iria's brother had died defending Portugal against Spanish aggression, neither the de Brito nor the Manuel Ataíde families suffered any diminution of prestige under the Spanish monarchs. The title 'First Count of Atalaia' was even conferred on D. Francisco Manuel by Philip II of Spain in 1583, two years before his marriage.

In 1586, their only son, Nuno Manuel, was born and the family enjoyed a period of tranquillity and prosperity. Tragedy, however, struck again when at the early age of thirteen years, Nuno was killed in 1599 from a fall off a horse. The epitaph on his tomb still today expresses the grief his parents experienced at the loss of their only child:

'Sacred to the memory of D. Nuno Manuel
aged thirteen, only son of the First Count
Atalaya, D. Francisco Manuel and Dona Iria
de Brito, their hope of posterity and dearly
loved on account of his good disposition
and good qualities. Their hope of succession
was disappointed by his death in 1599.'

After this tragedy, the annals tell us, 'the Count and Countess lived in retirement, devoting themselves to spiritual and corporal works of mercy.'[5] It is not stated where they lived during this period but, as the Countess had another residence in Calvário, a district nearer Lisbon, they probably spent the winter months there and moved to Belém when the weather became warm. This was the custom of those families who owned summer residences at the seaside.

The Gift of a Miraculous Statue

It was at this time, prior, perhaps, to the Count's death in 1624, that the story of the miraculous statue of Our Lady of Good Success begins. According to the annals, 'The Countess was remarkable for her great devotion to our Blessed Lady and was anxious to have a statue for her oratory.'[6] Small statues for private devotion were not easily found, and in the Iberian peninsula, it was customary to carve only the head and hands, mounting the head on a block of wood, and adorning it with an appropriate dress. Some beautiful statues of Christ and Mary, dressed in the style of the particular period, still exist in Spain and Portugal. In Bom Sucesso, two life-sized statues of this kind, dating, possibly from the seventeenth century, represent Christ carrying his cross and Mary pierced with the sword of sorrow.

One day, a man wearing the garb of a pilgrim came to the house with a statue of this kind draped in a yellow cloth. When she saw this small statue, D. Iria decided to buy it and sent her servant to ask the price but the pilgrim had disappeared. 'The Countess considered the statue to have been sent by Our Lady herself, as a proof that the devotion the Countess had to her was most pleasing to her Son She dressed the statue in white with a blue scapular and gave it the title, *Our Lady of the Conception.*' [7]

AN UNUSUAL TITLE IN THE SEVENTEENTH CENTURY

This may seem an unusual title in the seventeenth century since the dogma of Mary's Immaculate Conception was not declared until 1854. However, devotion to Our Lady under this title was already popular in Portugal in the seventeenth century. In 1618, the municipal council of Lisbon ordered that on the principal gates of the city an inscription confirming Mary's Immaculate Conception should be engraved in stone. Moreover, in the diocesan synods of Guarda (1634), of Braga (1637) and of Coimbra (1639) the clergy solemnly vowed to defend this doctrine.[8] It is, therefore, not surprising that the Countess should give this title to her statue, especially as it did not have, as yet, a statue of the Infant.

Little else is known of this noble couple between the death of their son in 1599 and that of the Count in 1624. However, two facts about her family give us some idea of Dona Iria's status where Portuguese nobility is concerned. As already mentioned, her aunt under whose tutelage she had lived as a child was first lady-in-waiting at the Court and her uncle was viceroy of India. Moreover, her two brothers had perished defending the Portuguese cause. Nevertheless, like many other noble families they did not suffer loss of status or of property during the Spanish occupation of Portugal (1580-1640). Many noble families of Portugal favoured Spanish rule at this time because they expected that certain advantages might accrue to them should their country be united with a larger power and the King of Spain's promises to the Portuguese people reassured, at least, the negotiators among the nobility.

PORTUGAL RULED BY SPAIN, 1580-1640

The historian, José Saraiva, gives ten principal privileges which Philip II of Spain (Philip I in Portugal) granted to the Portuguese parliament when, in April, 1581, he came to Portugal in order to claim his sovereignty over this country. These include the following:

The king would observe and never alter the traditional liberties, privileges and customs of the Portuguese monarchy;

All Portuguese legislation would remain in force and questions of administration and finance concerning Portugal would be decided by the parliament meeting there;

The offices of viceroy or governor would be held by Portuguese or members of the Spanish Royal family;

All responsibilities in parliament, in administration, justice and the army would be undertaken by the Portuguese; similarly, the Portuguese would be chosen for bishoprics and other ecclesiastical functions in the country;

Portuguese officials would regulate trade in India and Guinea while all import duties and any other limits to the free transport of goods between Spain and Portugal would be lifted;

The language in all official acts would be Portuguese and the coinage would likewise remain Portuguese;

On the other hand, a Portuguese person could be nominated to public offices in Spain.[9]

To the credit of Philip II of Spain, all these conditions were respected throughout his reign. The situation created by these agreements between two neighbouring countries contrasts starkly with that obtaining between two other neighbouring countries – England and Ireland – during the same period of history. From the reign of Elizabeth I (1558-1603), there was constant persecution of the Catholic faith together with the confiscation of the property of those Irish families who tried to defend their religion, their land and their culture until Oliver Cromwell, the Lord Protector of England undertook the total subjugation of the Irish people.

Iria's first husband, the IV Count of Feira, may have been one of those who were willing to accept the sovereignty of Spain in 1580. The annals tell us that he was on a diplomatic mission to the Court in Spain when he was accidentally killed in Madrid.[10] The opposite may, at first, have been true of her second husband. From his title, Alcaide Mor (Governor) de Marvão, a territory on the frontier between Spain and Portugal, not far from Alcântara, we can assume that his family had been engaged in the defence of the frontier. His father, D. Nuno Manuel, II Lord of Atalaia, Tancos, Asseiceira and Alcaide Mor of Marvão had perished in the Battle of Alcácer Quibir in 1578[11]. However, the title, 1st Count of Atalaia (which means watch) was conferred on Iria's husband by Philip II of Spain as the earlier title, Count of Atalaia had lapsed.

THE COUNTESS'S NOBLE LINEAGE

Iria was not only of noble birth but she was also, by right of inheritance a wealthy woman. She would, in time, devote all this wealth to founding the *Convento do Bom Sucesso*. The arms over the door of the convent show that this residence belonged to the de Brito family. The shield is divided into four smaller shields, the first being that of de Brito, the second that of de Ataíde, her mother's family. The arms underneath these two refer to ancestors on her father's line – Manuel Freire de Andrade, her father's maternal grandfather and Iria de Eça her paternal grandmother after whom she was named.[12] De Brito is in Portuguese genealogy an ancient family from the territory south of Braga. In 1033, Aires de Brito gave his estate to the prior and clerics of a monastery which he had founded in the jurisdiction of Vermoím near the river Ave, southwest of Guimarães. His son-in-law further endowed this monastery. Another illustrious member of this family is the Jesuit martyr, São João de Brito. Born in Lisbon on 1st March, 1647, he entered the Society of Jesus and after Ordination went on mission to India. There, he suffered much for the Faith but also had great success in his apostolate. He came back to Europe as a Procurator of the Mission but returned to India where he was martyred on 4th February 1693.

The Ataíde lineage is considered one of the most distinguished in Portugal because of the many illustrious members of this family. Among them was Iria's uncle who was the tenth Viceroy of India. Her mother was the daughter of the III Count of Atouguia. Freire de Andrade is another ancient family, of Galician origin. Two families were so often linked that the two surnames came to be considered as one. The principal Portuguese branches descend from Rui Freire de Andrade who came to Portugal with his two sons, Nuno Rodrigues, later, Master of the Order of Christ and Vasco Freire de Andrade.

The name of Eça has its origin in the royal family of Portugal through D. João, the second son of King D. Pedro I and Dona Inês de Castro. By right of a royal charter in 1360, D. João possessed large territories north of Coímbra and obtained further territory later from his brother, King D. Fernando. He was dispossessed of all these for having assassinated his first wife, Dona Maria Teles, sister of Queen Dona Leonor Teles with a view to marrying his niece, Dona Beatriz, heiress to the throne of Portugal. His eldest son, D. Fernando de Eça, went with him into exile in Galicia. The latter had many wives simultaneously and a great number of descendents but died repentant of his failures and wearing the habit of Saint Francis. Hence, the cord of Saint Francis entwined round the royal arms on the Eça shield.[13]

THE COUNTESS'S WEALTH

On the death of Iria de Brito's first husband his title passed to his brother, D. João Pereira Forjaz who thus became the V Count of Feira.[14] On the death of her second husband, I Count of Atalaia, his title and property were retained by the Countess until her death when the property inherited from her husband passed to his heir – first, his brother, D. Pedro Manuel de Ataíde.[15] However, history allows Iria retain the title, Condessa de Atalaia.

The de Brito property of which the Countess was the sole heiress was considerable. Her will, made at a later date, reveals the extent of this wealth. Not only had she the house and estate in Belém but she owned two residences with estates attached nearer Lisbon, one in Calvário and another in Santo Amaro. She also had extensive property in Golegã, further north in Portugal. The name of this estate was Casal de Barralha and part of its valuable land was a large olive grove the oil from which served as income because the tenants paid their rent partly in money and partly in kind.

Today, little is known of this estate except that the name Barralha is now the name of an area within the town still containing a small olive grove. Its chapel of São João dates from the seventeenth century and is, presumably, that of the estate. The Golegã archives dating from a later time could not give any documentation concerning this property. Consequently, all that can be surmised is that some time after the community's selling it on 18th October 1917[16] the land was incorporated into the expanding town. Today, the town is a tourist attraction, especially famous for its annual horse fair which takes place around the Feast of Saint Martin of Tours, 11th November.

Apart from the estate in Belém which was more extensive than the area occupied by Bom Sucesso today, the Golegã property was the single most valuable estate belonging to the countess. According to her will, the profit accruing from it in money and kind was greater than that of the Santo Amaro estate – twenty-two thousand *reis* and fifteen *alqueires* (bushels) of oil as compared with Santo Amaro's twenty-two thousand *reis*. The nuns who rented the Calvário property from the countess paid twelve thousand, six hundred *reis*. The houses in the Rossio and Calcetaria areas of Lisbon together yielded a further thirty thousand *reis*. Finally, the investments in the *Casa do Paço de Madeira* and the *Casa dos Escravos* which were inherited from her mother gave a further two hundred thousand reis in interest. These two implied investments in the slave trade and this is rather surprising to us today since Iria de Brito was a truly Christian woman.

THE SLAVE TRADE

Slavery has a long history in the Iberian Peninsula, dating back to the Reconquest when Moorish prisoners of war became slaves of their Christian conquerors. Some historians give the need for slaves as one of the motives for the voyages of discovery. Long before the terrible Atlantic Slave Trade, the indigenous people of the Canary Islands were a source of slaves and were brought to Madeira to work in the plantations of sugar cane. As early as 1441, the first African slaves were brought to Portugal.

In Lisbon, they were sold to other European countries but some were retained in Portugal to work mainly as domestic staff. It is thought that these domestic slaves were well treated though they had no rights. Small children were usually sold with their mothers. Otherwise, slaves were denied relationship with other family members. The number in Portugal in relation to the population was small and it is probably the only aspect of the slave trade that Iria de Brito knew.

In 1570, the Lisbon government forbade slavery except in the case of prisoners of war but it was a lucrative trade and was allowed to continue, African rulers even trading their prisoners with the Europeans. By the seventeenth century, the terrible Atlantic slave trade caused unbelievable suffering in the long voyage to the Americas when Brasil replaced Madeira as the major producer of cane sugar.

What is interesting is the declaration which the Countess makes in her will, 'That the patroness of the said Monastery and Church is the Most Holy Virgin, Our Blessed Lady herself under the Most Holy Trinity and, as what concerns herself, the only title she wishes to have is Slave of Our Lady and under this title to help with all her heart and as far as is possible to enlarge the buildings, that she may be able to offer, as a great token of love to Our Lady, this monastery for noble ladies from the most Christian kingdom of Ireland who are desirous of consecrating themselves to God in religion and who have no convent in Spain or elsewhere.' [17]

A tablet on a wall in the sacristy of the present convent indicates that the Countess also had fishing rights in Algarve, the interest from which would be later donated to the construction of the High Altar of Bom Sucesso. The tablet reads,

> 'The Countess of Atalaya, Dona Iria de Brito, foundress of this convent left for her soul two daily Masses in perpetuity and an Office of nine lessons once a month and for the fabric of the sanctuary, she set aside one hundred thousand *reis* in interest from tuna fishing in Algarve, as stated in the deed which is in the archives of the convent.' This inscription dated 1670.

THE COUNTESS DECIDES TO FOUND A CONVENT

For about two years following the death of her second husband, Iria remained in mourning and then began to consider to what use she might put her vast wealth as both her children had predeceased her. She decided to donate her summer residence in Belém to a religious order for a new foundation there.[18] The house was duly adapted in order to make it suitable for a religious community. Nuns of the Jeronimite Order were invited from Castile to begin the foundation. Three sisters of Santa Paula took up residence and a number of young women joined them. The work was progressing favourably but the king's permission was necessary. Unfortunately, or perhaps providentially, as the subsequent history of Bom Sucesso shows, the king refused permission for the foundation and, after three years, the sisters of Santa Paula returned to their convent in Castile while the postulants returned to their parents.[19]

> 'The Countess, whilst resigned to the Will of God regarding the failure of the foundation, made another effort to obtain religious to inhabit 'The Hermitage' as the villa had been called since 1630.'[20]

The *Padres Arrábidos* (Franciscan hermits), were invited to establish an infirmary in the villa. The necessary documents were signed and furniture obtained for the infirmary but again the king's permission was not granted. A set of *azulejos* (decorative tiles) bearing the emblem of Saint Francis preserved still in the convent commemorates this second failure.

When the hope of her ever seeing her foundation come into being was fading, the Countess made the acquaintance of an Irish Dominican named Frei Domingos do Rosário. 'Her gift was accepted in a manner the Countess never even thought of. Fr. Dominic of the Rosary was the instrument chosen by Providence to enable the Countess to carry out her ardent desire to devote her wealth to the service of God and His Holy Mother.'[21]

2

Dominic O'Daly
and the Foundation of Bom Sucesso

Frei Domingos O'Daly was not the first, though perhaps one of the most illustrious of Irish people to settle in Portugal because their presence in Lisbon already had a long history. It dated back to the commercial status of this city resulting from Vasco da Gama's discovery of the sea route to India. In a short while, Lisbon became the emporium of Europe where the much-coveted spices and other exotic goods from the Orient were distributed to various European countries. Irish merchants, especially from the southern counties of Limerick, Cork and Waterford, took advantage of this trading opportunity and some settled in Lisbon from where they traded these oriental products to central and northern Europe. As early as 1462, it is recorded that permission to reside in Portugal's capital was given to four Irishmen, Richard May, Geoffrey Galway and two members of the Lynch family – John and his brother Dominic.[1]

When the Protestant Reformation took place during the sixteenth century, Irish merchants living in Portugal became important for the economy of their adopted country. Being nominally English subjects they could trade with England and other Protestant countries and Irish ships could dock at the ports of these countries when they were closed to the ships of Catholic Portugal. Besides, the Irish living in Portugal did not remain isolated from the people but integrated and even intermarried with the Portuguese. Some Irish families such as Browne and O'Neill are listed in the Genealogy and Heraldry of Portugal while Anderson is described as an Irish family from Dublin a member of whom came to Portugal in the seventeenth century. His son married into a Portuguese family through his wife Dona Ana Bercia da Silveira.[2]

Though Portugal did not have, as France and Italy, the tradition of receiving Irish monks during the early ages of Irish missionary expansion, it became, like these countries, yet another refuge for young Irishmen wishing to study for the priesthood. As early as 1590, the Irish College of Saint Patrick was founded as a seminary for the training of Irish students for the secular priesthood. Its founder and protector is named as Garcia de Melho da Sylva and it was first located in the Jesuit foundation of Saint Roque.[3] Two Jesuits, one Irish, Father John Howling and one Portuguese, Father Pedro Fonseca directed the institution in its early years. It continued its work of training for the priesthood until it closed in 1834.

DANIEL O'DALY'S EARLY LIFE

In 1624, the year of the Count of Atalaya's death, a young Irish priest from Kilsarkan, Co. Kerry, took up residence in the university city of Louvain in Belgium, first, as lector in theology and later as Regent of the small Dominican *studium* or house of studies on that city's Mount César. His name was Daniel O'Daly – in the Order of Preachers, Dominic of the Rosary.[4]

Dominic of the Rosary was the son of Conchubhar Ó Dálaigh, 'rimor and soldier of the Desmonds.'[5] The O'Dalys in the Gaelic tradition were the bards or official poets of the Desmond clan. When, in 1583, the 16th Earl of Desmond was killed, his lands and those of his loyal followers were confiscated by Elizabeth I of England. 'Most of the professional classes – bards, historians and gallowglasses – were dispossessed and the "literati" in particular suffered because they were, in general, ranged on the side of their country, or supported a rebellious chieftain.'[6] Consequently, when Daniel O'Daly was born in 1595, he was born into a dispossessed but by no means crushed family.

Hopes of foreign aid were still high and even the defeat of the Spanish armada in 1588 had not lessened the Irish people's optimism. The victory for the Ulster chieftains at the Battle of the Yellow Ford in 1598 further encouraged this optimism. However, over the O'Daly's of Kilsarkan the shadow of the fall of the Earl of Desmond must have hung heavily. In spite of this and the loss of their ancestral lands, the O'Daly children grew up in a comparatively untroubled atmosphere.[7]

At the death of Elizabeth I in 1603, all the monasteries had been suppressed in Ireland but the Friars and Jesuits were able to help people preserve the Catholic Faith and they in turn were protected by the people, even by lords conforming to Protestantism.[8] When James VI of Scotland, son of the Catholic Mary, Queen of Scots, ascended the throne of England as James I of England, there was hope again in Ireland of greater freedom for the Catholic Faith. However, this was not to be and young men wishing to become priests had to set off to study in one of the Catholic countries of Europe.

Consequently, as Daniel O'Daly decided to enter the Order of Preachers, he was obliged to pursue his studies away from his native country. He was sent first to Lugo in the province of Galicia in Spain where he was received and professed as a Dominican, receiving the religious name Dominic of the Rosary. From there he went to Burgos not far from Calaruega, the birthplace of Saint Dominic, founder of the Order of Preachers. It was a period of intense intellectual activity in the Spanish province of the Order. Secchi, Master of the Order at the time, having made visitation there from 1617 to 1619, declared that the Spanish province was in the foremost rank of the Order. [9]

There in Burgos, Daniel O'Daly was ordained. The date is uncertain, either 1616 when he was twenty-one or 1619 when he was twenty-four. Whatever the date of his ordination and subsequent studies, he was in Ireland by 1623, working in the diocese of Emly. [10] Subsequently, he spent some years, as already stated, in Louvain and when he returned to the Iberian peninsula, he came entrusted with two missions – to ask Philip IV of Spain for financial help for the Friars Preachers of Ireland in Louvain and to obtain authorisation to found in Lisbon a studium or house of studies which would serve as a base for Dominican students from Ireland. [11] For this project, he would later receive considerable financial help from Dona Catarina Telles de Menezes, Lady Barbacena. However, Daniel had another project in mind – that of founding a convent for Irish noblewomen deprived of the opportunity of embracing religious life because of the persecution of the Catholic faith in Ireland. [12]

THE SUFFERING OF THE IRISH PEOPLE IN THE SEVENTEENTH CENTURY

Through Irish émigrés, the peoples of southern Europe were well informed of the harshness of the persecutions and the dire suffering of the Irish people especially under Cromwellian rule (1649-1658). The seventeenth century Portuguese historian, Frei Luís de Sousa, O.P., in his literary work, *História de São Domingos*, (*quarta parte*), gives a graphic description of the reasons for O'Daly's efforts on behalf, not only of young Irishmen wishing to be priests, but also of young Irishwomen wishing to lead a religious life. 'There came continually to the ears of Master Frei Domingos...the cries of Christian Ireland helplessly groaning beneath the scourge of heresy. It dominated and afflicted the five broad provinces that were formerly kingdoms where the Faith flourished and now saw themselves trampled on by sacrilegious apostates who tyrannically tore from their midst their unfortunate children.' [13]

Having founded a College for young Irishmen in Lisbon, Dominic O'Daly turned his attention to the project of founding a convent for Irish girls: 'There now remained for him the greater care of the helpless and afflicted young women of that kingdom (the noblest of its aristocracy) orphaned through the loss of parents that the heretics in cunning and depravity named traitors and whose lives they destroyed, enjoying the aim of extinguishing the Faith with that of robbing their estates. Not being satisfied with lives and property, they exercised on the bodies of those unfortunate people torture inspired by rancour and hatred.' [14]

He gives a detailed account of the forms of martyrdom – public hanging, and the torture of drawing and quartering – current in Ireland at the time; and lists the dangers to young women – the possibility of embracing heresy in order to avoid persecution, the difficulty, almost impossibility, of access to ministers of the faith and the problem of being in the power of heretical relatives.

DOMINIC O'DALY'S PROJECT IN LISBON

On a later visit to Lisbon, Dominic O'Daly told Lady Barbacena of his second project – to found a convent for Irish women who wished to become religious but could not do so on account of religious persecution in Ireland. She was convinced of the value of this second project and promised him four thousand *cruzados* [15] to buy a site for the future convent. With the promise of such a donation the priest was encouraged to press ahead and began to search for future members of the community among the young noblewomen in Lisbon.

One of his Portuguese friends, D. Ruy de Mello de Sampayo, introduced Fr O'Daly to his three daughters. On hearing of the Dominican's hope of founding a convent for the persecuted Irish, D. Ruy De Mello's eldest daughter, Dona Marianna, was fired with enthusiasm for this ideal and promised to be the first to enter the proposed foundation. Her younger sister who had intended becoming a Franciscan, was invited by Marianna to join the new convent. Being in doubt as to what she should do she was advised by Fr O'Daly to place her confidence in God and allow herself be guided by God's Spirit because 'only in God would be found the true light and the way.' [16] While at prayer one night, she saw herself dressed in the Dominican habit but Frei Luís tells us that she did not trust the clear judgment with which she had been endowed. She again consulted not only Fr O'Daly but other Dominican and Jesuit theologians who all agreed that she could accept this vision as advice from heaven. [17]

On the death of their father, the three daughters retired temporarily to the convent of the Order of Saint James in Santos and there they encouraged another young woman to join the future foundation. Magdalena de Silva Menezes was, at first, reluctant to do so but, once convinced she was to be the 'most important collaborator in this undertaking' [18], as the subsequent history shows. Ruy de Mello's youngest daughter, Angélica, was also most enthusiastic for the new foundation. Thus, Dominic O'Daly already had four willing members of the new community but, as yet, there was no site or building for this foundation.

THE COUNTESS OF ATALAYA LEARNS OF THE PROJECT

The historian does not relate how the Countess of Atalaya learned about the Irish Dominican's project or how they were introduced. We can only surmise that, as Iria was well known in this convent of Santos, she told the community about her efforts to found a convent on her estate and they in turn told her about the projected convent for the Irish women. Frei Luís de Sousa simply states, 'Dona Magdalena having heard, by chance, that the Countess of Atalaya wished to consecrate to God an estate with considerable property entered into negotiations with her, having as intermediary the Countess of Sabugal, Dona Luíza Coutinho, wife of the Count of Sabugal, D. Francisco de Castello Branco, Meirinho (Bailiff) mor.' [19] These negotiations were rather difficult because of the Countess's previous efforts at other foundations that had already failed. However, within a short while, these difficulties were resolved and Frei Domingos do Rosário found himself in possession of the site of the future Convento de Nossa Senhora do Bom Sucesso. There still remained the very important issue of obtaining permission from the king of Spain, Philip IV and this had already proved insurmountable when the Countess had tried on two other occasions to make a foundation for religious communities.

FR DOMINIC SETS OUT FOR THE ROYAL COURT IN MADRID

It was the early 1630s when Dominic O'Daly, accompanied by Fr Pedro Yannes, a Spanish Dominican and president of the new college in Lisbon, set out from Lisbon for the Court in Madrid where his companion was acquainted with many of the influential ministers there. Fr O'Daly also carried a number of letters of recommendation to the king.[20] Before his departure some people had tried to dissuade him from undertaking this journey as they considered it fruitless to seek the king's permission when the Countess had already met with refusal on two previous occasions. However, the young, enthusiastic women urged Fr O'Daly to make an attempt because it had been mysteriously revealed to two of them 'that the new foundation would be established and that many religious would enter there; that Master Domingos would see the foundation flourish in perfect observance; that the glorious crowns which the Queen of Heaven and her Divine Son would bestow had been shown to them and that, when five members of the Community had died, he too would pass away'. All this later occurred according to the historian.' [21] Encouraged by this prophecy the two Dominicans set off for Madrid.

YOUNG WOMEN'S DETERMINATION

On their arrival at the Spanish Court, Frei Domingos presented his petition to King Philip IV of Spain and III of Portugal. He received it graciously but passed it on to his Council of State where to O'Daly's great disappointment, it was rejected. Fr Dominic, disheartened by so decisive a refusal, wrote immediately to Dona Magdalena in Lisbon to tell her of the failure of his mission releasing her and her companions from any obligation they had to the foundation. The young enthusiasts replied that they would not be released from their commitment to this project and that they would do nothing until Fr O'Daly returned to Lisbon. Meanwhile, they urged him to continue his efforts to obtain the permission, reminding him of the prophecy which two of their number had received. They placed their hope in heaven because it seemed that it was heaven itself had given this hope. [22]

A MYSTERIOUS VISITOR

Encouraged by the constancy of these young women Frei Domingos made another attempt to obtain the licence, much to the displeasure of the ministers of State. Furthermore, Fr Pedro Yannes, his spiritual guide, advised him to give up this undertaking and return to Lisbon as vicar of the college he had established there. O'Daly made preparations to return to Portugal when, on the eve of his departure, while he was praying in the Church of Saint Thomas in Madrid, a woman of venerable appearance approached him and asked if there was in the community an Irish religious by the name of Frei Domingos do Rosário. On his introducing himself and asking her reason for the question, she replied, 'Padre, remember, as you already know, that obedience to spiritual directors must not be observed to the detriment of the common good and the welfare of others. Deal with the business you have undertaken which will contribute greatly to the service of God.'[23] She then went away without disclosing her identity. Comforted by what seemed to him an intervention from heaven O'Daly turned again to prayer and postponed his departure for Lisbon.

IRISH RECRUITS FOR THE SPANISH ARMY

Meanwhile, the king had important affairs of State to deal with, among them the crisis in his possessions in the Netherlands. He needed reinforcements there to quell a rebellion against Spain and he wished to obtain Irish recruits for this purpose. The tradition of Irish soldiers fighting in the Spanish army in Flanders went back formally to 1587 when the Leicester Regiment of Irish soldiers under the command of the English general, Sir William Stanley, a convert to Catholicism, defected from the English to the Spanish cause. As a sign of their loyalty to Spain, they surrendered the city of Deventer to the Spaniards.[24] Following the defeat of the Ulster rebellion in 1607 and the subsequent flight of the Earls, O'Neill and O'Donnell[25], to Europe many Irish soldiers left their country in order to seek asylum in Europe. They became known as the Wild Geese. Many of those who went to Spanish territories were drafted into the Leicester Regiment in the Netherlands which was renamed The First Regiment of Tyrone and commanded by Henry O'Neill, a younger son of The O'Neill. For about a century, this regiment was under the command of a direct descendant of Hugh O'Neill and 'its valour was legendary.'[26]

Philip IV of Spain needed someone who knew Ireland well and was gifted with the power to persuade young Irishmen to risk their lives in the service of Catholic Spain. The king summoned O'Daly to a number of private meetings and judged that no more suitable person could be found for the purpose of obtaining Irish recruits for the Spanish army. Fr Dominic O'Daly agreed to undertake this difficult mission on condition that, if he succeeded, the king would grant the royal licence for the foundation of the Irish Dominican convent in Lisbon. The king consented and O'Daly set off for Biscay where he embarked for Ireland and after a short sea voyage arrived in Limerick city. [27] According to Frei Luís, Dominic O'Daly completed within a few months his work of recruitment in Ireland while he also tried to interest Irish women in the future Lisbon convent specifically for Irish girls. It is conjectured that at this time Fr O'Daly made the acquaintance of Leonor de Burgo, daughter of the martyr Sir John de Burgo and his wife Grace Thornton. Leonor was living as a recluse in Limerick city.

LICENCES FOR THE FOUNDATION

How successful O'Daly was in recruiting Irishmen for the Spanish army can be surmised from the honours and gifts offered to him by the king on his return to Madrid – a bishopric, dowries for his four nieces are mentioned. However, O'Daly persevered in his one request – the licence for the foundation of the convent in Lisbon. Finally, the king consented and the royal licence was granted. It is dated 21st March, 1639, almost nine years after the Dominican's departure from Lisbon for Madrid.

Frei Domingos did not return immediately to Lisbon. In June he was still in Madrid where he met the provincial of the Dominican Order in Portugal and he availed of this opportunity to obtain the provincial's permission for the foundation. This is dated Madrid, 15th June, 1639.

This second document gives us important information concerning the kind of foundation this new convent would be. It would be one of strict observance according to the rule and constitutions of the Dominican Order; its members would be cloistered, would not eat meat or wear linen except in the case of serious illness; they would observe the choral recitation of the Divine Office and of the Rosary; they would not have open grilles or parlours where they could receive and converse with visitors unless relatives within the third degree of relationship and these only for reasons of charity or the service of God.

THE COUNTESS'S WILL

On returning to Lisbon after some years' absence, Fr Dominic was warmly welcomed by the Countess and the four potential postulants who had waited in hope all these years. On the 15th August Dona Iria made her will in favour of the future community – her summer residence with its adjoining land in Belém, all the silver and vestments for the chapel, property situated in Lisbon and Golegã and a sum of money. She declared that 'the patroness of the said monastery and Church is the most holy Virgin, Our Blessed Lady herself under the Most Holy Trinity.' The only title the Countess wished to have and which was preserved in her heart was 'slave of Our Lady.' [28] She decreed that the high altar would be reserved for the tombs of her husbands and children and that two Masses would be said daily at the high altar for the deceased members of her family. This was rescinded by the Holy See only in the early 1930s. [29] The Office of the Dead which was requested for the same purpose is still said monthly by the present community.

The Countess endowed four places in perpetuity for two Portuguese and two Irish girls. Dona Iria herself would choose the Portuguese subjects and at her death the choice would be made by the archbishop of Lisbon in consultation with the vicar and the prioress. The two Irish girls would be chosen by the vicar and the prioress. These religious would wear round their necks some emblem indicating that they were 'slaves of our Lady.' They would be obliged to offer their spiritual exercises for the Countess after her death. [30]

THE COUNTESS AS FOUNDRESS

Dona Iria wished to live in part of the building given as the convent but her rooms would be outside the enclosure. However, she would take advantage of the privilege accorded by the Holy See to foundresses and would enter the enclosure whenever she wished. Having dealt with all the formalities necessary for a new foundation, the Countess could, it would seem, calmly await the formal opening of her foundation. However, it is at this point that the annals record the number of petitions from religious orders which were made to her for the convent she now intended should be devoted to Fr Dominic's project. [31]

It was very difficult for religious to obtain the royal licence necessary for a foundation and, once it was known that the Countess had received authorisation for her summer residence to be converted into a convent, requests from various orders began to be made. The Jeronimite monks whose land adjoined that of the Countess's estate believed they had prior right, as the nuns of their order were the first to be invited there by the Countess. However, when they were informed of the Dominican mission there they renounced whatever right they felt they had. The nuns of Calvário then made their request followed by Francisco de Gouveia, provincial of the Order of the Most

Holy Trinity, who wanted the property for the nuns of that order known as Trinas. The next applicants were Padres Terceiros de Nossa Senhora de Jesus for the nuns of their order and the Hermits of Saint Augustine used all their influence to obtain it for the nuns of Saint Monica. Finally, the last applicant was Mother Michaella Margarida of Austria, daughter of the Emperor Mathias, archduke of Austria, king of Bohemia and Hungary. On the death of his brother Rodolph, he was elected Emperor and crowned in Frankfurt on 12th June, 1612. Michaella Margarida later built her convent in Carnide and became a Carmelite. She died in September 1663, aged eighty-two. [32]

Throughout this period of preparation, the Countess remained constant in her preference for Fr O'Daly's project. Was it the fact that the royal licence had been given directly to him or was it her conviction that his ideal of establishing a convent for the Irish under persecution was the most worthy of all the petitions presented to her? Was she influenced by the four potential postulants who had shown such great enthusiasm for the Irish cause? As the licence had been given to Fr O'Daly we can only conclude that this was sufficient to assure Dona Iria of the validity of her choice. Subconsciously, she may have been influenced by the dream she had had long before the question arose of giving her property to Dominicans. This dream is already described in the preface but may be worth repeating here.

THE COUNTESS'S DREAM

One night, Iria dreamt she saw five women dressed in white enter her chapel and having lit the candles they went out again. The fear of a fire being caused by the lighted candles being left unattended woke her up and once she realised it was only a dream, she forgot the incident until she saw the first five postulants receive the Dominican habit. The day of their reception into the Dominican Order was also the day of the formal opening of the convent. [33]

TWO RELIGIOUS FROM SÃO JOÃO CONVENT IN SETÚBAL

Before the opening day, however, it was necessary to obtain for the new foundation two religious from an established Dominican convent to train the novices in religious observance. Again, there were difficulties. The first community to be approached was that of the Mosteiro do Sacramento but they felt unable to allow two of their members transfer to the new convent. The Dominican Convent of

São João in Setúbal, by order of the Provincial, Mestre João de Vasconcellos, gave two of their nuns – Madre Anna da Conceição as prioress and Madre Antónia Teresa, as mistress of novices. [34] Since it was the wish of the Countess that Our Lady would be considered the prioress, Madre Anna da Conceição was given the title of vicar *in capite*.

The Name of Nossa Senhora do Bom Sucesso

The name of the new convent had to be decided. Our Lady of Good Success was not one of the most popular titles for the Mother of God in Portugal and Dona Iria had given the name of Our Lady of the Conception to her miraculous statue. It would seem that the choice of Our Lady of Good Success was Fr Dominic's inspiration since the obtaining of the king's licence was considered a miraculous success. In his work entitled, *Nossa Senhora na História e Devoção do Povo Português,* Padre José do Vale Carvalheira states that this title was made popular in Portugal during the frontier conflicts with Spain after the Restoration of Independence in 1640. He mentions one of the earliest shrines dedicated to Our Lady of Good Success near Ribeira da Baságueda close to the Spanish frontier as having been built by the commander of Portuguese forces in the 1640s. Seeing his soldiers outnumbered by the superior Spanish army he promised to build a shrine to Our Lady of Bom Sucesso and the result was victory.

Of the seven Bom Sucesso shrines in the diocese of Guarda the oldest is probably that of São Pedro do Rio Seco again very near the Spanish frontier. This shrine is connected with success at the threshing of corn. Nearer to Lisbon, in the diocese of Setúbal, is the parish church of Cacilhas whose patron is Nossa Senhora do Bom Sucesso. Here, in 1755, the inhabitants terrorised by the tidal wave occurring at the time of the earthquake carried the statue to the water's edge and immediately the cause of their fear ceased.[35]

Was our convent the first shrine in Portugal dedicated to Our Lady of Good Success? We cannot be sure of this but what can be presumed is that it inspired the title for shrines built during the Restoration as Frei Domingos do Rosário played an important role in the court of D. João IV. What may have inspired him was certainly the almost miraculous granting of the king of Spain's licence to found the convent. Or did he remember his time in Louvain when the statue of Our Lady of Pity was secretly brought from Aberdeen and offered to the Archduchess Isabel, Spanish governor of the Low Countries?

When she successfully captured the port of Ostende from the Dutch, the statue was renamed Our Lady of Good Success. [36]

LEGENDS CONCERNING THE TITLE

It was customary in the seventeenth century to have major decisions confirmed by a vision, a divine intuition or a prophetic dream. The choice of the title, Good Success, is no exception to this. Preserved in the convent archives is a letter written by a religious of another convent, Sor Francisca da Cruz whom Fr Dominic had requested to transfer to the new foundation. She was the sister of the Marquês de Montalvão and a religious renowned for holiness in the Convent of the Annunciada in Lisbon. She was refused permission to transfer but, while still hoping that the refusal would be reversed she wrote, at Fr Dominic's request, an account of a dream confirming the validity of the title Bom Sucesso: 'One night when I was in choir, I saw two people going from the grille of the lower choir to the high altar and from there turning to the grille; both were dressed alike and held in their hands beautiful sceptres of silver which I thought were swords because they had beautiful handles; I could not see the face of one of them but of the other I could see all the features and she had a white headdress drawn back from her face and a crown on her head...; this was at night and the Church was as bright as if it were day; it seems to me that this was a dream because I was at a distance from the grille and saw what happened in the Church very clearly and distinctly as if I were awake...; a few days later, Father, you came to ask me if I wished to go to that monastery.'

However, her relatives, the prioress and confessor opposed it and she continues: 'At this I was very upset and one Sister knew of this; one day when I was in choir and crying, she brought me a picture and said: "Don't be upset because I bring you Our Lady of Good Success. Entrust yourself to her; and I turning to look at it saw that it was that person I had seen in the Church. I was amazed and confused but very confident in this Lady that she will bring me to that monastery and still today I do not lose hope that she will give me this grace...; several days later I heard that the monastery was called Our Lady of Good Success at which I was still more anxious to go and serve in this holy place.' [37]

There is no record that this sister later obtained permission to come to Bom Sucesso. In the list of the members of the early communities the name Francisca occurs only once but her life-story is well documented from her early years so that she could not have been the sister who experienced the above dream. The letter serves only to give testimony that the title chosen was divinely approved even if not divinely inspired.

Another legend exists to prove that it was divinely inspired. The sisters assembled in order to decide by lot the title of the convent. They put all the titles of Our Lady from the litany of Loreto in a box and a little child was asked to draw out the title inspired by God. Three times the name Good Success was drawn though not a title contained in the litany. This confirmed for the nuns the divine choice of Nossa Senhora do Bom Sucesso.

The statue of the infant also has its seemingly miraculous story. One day, the chaplain of the convent was walking on the beach nearby and he found the little statue. When he brought it to the community, it was discovered that it fitted between the hands of the statue of Our Lady of Good Success. Subsequently, Our Lady under this title was invoked for the safe birth of children and even today, it is customary in the convent to make miniature cloaks, replicas of the statue's cloak, for mothers to have during pregnancy.

MIRACLES ATTRIBUTED TO NOSSA SENHORA DO BOM SUCESSO

Many miracles are attributed to Our Lady of Good Success and they often refer to provisions at a time of scarcity. Once, when a plague of weevils attacked the wheat in the granary the sisters offered the wheat to Our Lady and reserved a large quantity for the poor. The plague immediately ceased. On another occasion, as there was insufficient wheat, the prioress told the cellarer to give some to the poor. The latter hesitated and when the prioress discovered this she reprimanded her saying, 'those alms were in the name of Our Lady and she will not forget her family.' As the sister was going to distribute the alms, she received a message that a ship had docked with a large quantity of grain for the monastery.

The most picturesque of these miracles occurred in 1662, on the eve of the Feast of Our Lady of the Rosary. Again, the community had neither money nor provisions with which to celebrate this special feast-day. The prioress turned to Our Lady of Good Success, reminding her that she was the lady of the house. While still at prayer she was called to the parlour where, on the other side of the grille, was the captain of a sailing ship. He related that when his vessel was becalmed on the high seas, a pirate ship appeared. Unable to escape, the crew called on Mary and immediately another powerful ship arrived on the scene and put the pirate ship to flight. The sailors realised that it was Our Lady 'the sovereign vessel in whom heaven has traded with earth' [38] who had saved them and they gave the captain alms. It now had to be decided to which shrine the alms should be given. Consequently, lots were drawn between Our Lady of Help and Our Lady of Good Success. The lot fell to the latter and thus the captain's gift was the answer to the prioress's appeal. Probably, the greatest miracle is the continued existence for nearly four hundred years of the convent itself in spite of varied hardships – earthquakes, revolutions, plagues and even warfare.

The king's licence to found the convent had been given in March 1639, the permission from the Dominican provincial in Portugal was obtained in June of the same year and finally, the permission from the archbishop of Lisbon, D. Rodrigo da Cunha was given the 29th August, 1639. There remained only final preparations before the formal opening of the Convento do Bom Sucesso the 12th November of that year.

FOUNDATION DAY

After many years of waiting in hope on the part of Iria de Brito and her friends, Foundation Day finally dawned on 12th November, 1639. History does not tell us what the weather was like but we can presume that a bright sun of Saint Martin's summer shone with hope on the assembled participants of the opening ceremony. The two foundresses, Mother Ana of the Conception and Mother Antónia Theresa of Jesus, accompanied by the Duchess of Mantua, governor of Portugal for the Crown of Castile, entered the cloister. They were followed by a group of distinguished ladies which must have included Dona Iria de Brito, Countess of Atalaya.

Mass was celebrated 'with all solemnity and pomp', [39] and the sermon was given by one of the outstanding preachers of the time, Master Fr Domingos de Santo Thomaz, Dominican and preacher at the Royal Court. Present also were the community of São Domingos, Lisbon, nobles of the Court and a large gathering of the people.

Fr João de Vasconcellos, Dominican provincial of Portugal gave the habit to the first five novices – Dona Magdalena da Silva, daughter of D. Manuel de Menezes, in religion, Sister Magdalena of Christ, Dona Luíza de Mello, daughter of D. Ruy de Mello de Sampaio, in religion, Sister Luíza Maria of the Sacrament. The third novice was Dona Leonor Kavanagh, an Irishwoman, daughter of the Lord of

Pelmonty and Borese, 'an illustrious House of Leinster,' [40] in religion, Sister Leonor of Saint Margaret.

The remaining two novices were both of Portuguese nobility, Sister Leonor of Calvary and Sister Jacinta of Jesus and Mary.

Fr Dominic O'Daly publicly appointed Mother Ana of the Conception, vicar *in capite* and Mother Antónia Theresa mistress of novices and he gave a new statute over and above the Rule and Constitutions. Frei Luís de Sousa summarises this new statute: 'That the Religious would have three hours of prayer divided into Matins, Prime and Compline; after Prime, five mysteries of the Rosary and the Litany of Our Lady in choir, Holy Communion twice a week; that in Advent and Lent, they would take the discipline twice a day, once a day during the period from Holy Cross in September until Rosary Day, except on Holy Days; that throughout Lent, silence would be observed except if attending or visiting the sick; that all would serve in the kitchen; that after dinner grace the community would work there, chorally reciting the psalms while working; that in the cells they would have no more than a board of pine, on it a straw mattress two blankets and a coarse quilt; a cross and a holy water font; that the religious would not ask their parents or relatives for anything of the least value; and if something were sent, it had to be given to the prioress to use it for the community.' [41]

The writer concludes this summary by saying that these and the other statutes laid down by Fr Vasconcellos in his licence were the inspiration for religious observance in Bom Sucesso and continued to be faithfully observed. Thus, we are given an accurate idea of what daily life for the individual sister in the new convent of Bom Sucesso was in the seventeenth century.

The emphasis on some practices of asceticism may seem excessive to us today but it is important to recall that the Iberian peninsula had undergone, in the sixteenth century, an extensive reform of religious life of which the reform of Teresa of Avila was but a part, albeit a very important part. Kieran Kavanaugh, O.C.D., in his introduction to selected writings of John of the Cross states: 'Certain common characteristics marked the spirit of the Spanish reform: the return to one's origins, to primitive rules and the founders; a strict life lived in community with practices of poverty, fasting, silence and enclosure; and, as the most important element, the life of prayer.' [42] All these elements are contained in the statutes laid down at the foundation of Bom Sucesso and borne out in the account of the lives of the early members.

Frei Domingos do Rosário, Diplomat

When, in 1640, the Portuguese people regained their independence from Spain and established the Duke of Bragança on the throne, Frei Domingos do Rosário gave his allegiance to the new king D. João IV of Portugal. This king entrusted the Dominican with various diplomatic missions. It was customary in the seventeenth century for rulers to make use of clerics and religious as ambassadors. This custom had its advantages in that it was less expensive as a religious in particular would not need a costly retinue, would have easy access to royal courts and would be able to stay in one of the houses of his Order, thus further reducing the expense.

In Portugal, in the seventeenth century João IV appointed four such envoys – two Portuguese, Frei Denis de Lencastre and Padre António Vieira and two foreigners, the Englishman Dr. Ricardo Russell and the Irishman Frei Domingos do Rosário. According to Edgar Prestage, Dr. Russell played an important rôle in the marriage arrangement of the Infanta Dona Catarina de Bragança and Charles II of England. In 1662, she left her beloved Portugal for England and only returned, a widow, in 1699.

O'Daly was entrusted with a number of difficult missions on behalf of the king of Portugal. He was in negotiations with Charles I of England and in 1649 with his son, the future Charles II at this time in exile in Jersey. [43] In 1655, D. João IV of Portugal sent Frei Domingos do Rosário to the French court to obtain France's recognition of the independent state of Portugal. He also had to ask for financial and military aid for the new State. A year later, he was appointed accredited Portuguese ambassador at the French court.

Probably the most difficult of all legations which the King of Portugal entrusted to the Irishman was a secret mission in 1650 to Pope Innocent X in order to obtain the nomination of bishops to vacant dioceses in Portugal. The Spanish ambassador in Rome was trying to impede this process and the Pope unwilling to offend Spain hesitated to accede to the Portuguese king's request. However, 'O'Daly continued to play an active part in the protracted dispute between the Vatican reluctant to offend Spain and the independent kingdom of Portugal left without bishops.' [43]

On the death of D. João IV in 1656, Frei Domingos was recalled to Portugal by the Queen Dona Luísa de Gusmão, now Regent, to be her principal councillor. She offered him various rewards for his loyal service – the archbishopric of Portugal's primatial See of Braga or the archbishopric of Goa. He declined all honours but in 1662, in order to obtain financial help for the College he had founded in Lisbon, he accepted the Queen's nomination to the See of Coímbra. However, before his consecration as bishop, he died on 30th June, 1662, and was buried in the Church of Corpo Santo. During the earthquake of 1755, the Church of Corpo Santo was destroyed and the tomb of its founder was buried beneath its ruins. However, the epitaph on the tombstone read: *Hic jacet venerabilis Pater Magister Dominicus de Rosario, Hybernus huius et conventus monialium Boni Successus fundator. In variis legationibus felix, episcopus Conimbricencis electus, vir prudential literis et religione conspicuous. Obiit trigesimo Junii, anno Dominici 1662 aetatis suae sexagesimo septimo.* 'Here lies venerable Father Master Frei Domingos do Rosário, Irish, founder of this and the convent of nuns of Bom Sucesso. Successful in various royal legations, bishop elect of Coimbra. A man outstanding in prudence, letters and religion. He died 30th June in the year of Our Lord 1662 at the age of sixty-seven.'

Edgar Prestage sums up his achievements, 'Of his religious zeal there cannot be two opinions since his foundations testify to this; of his political talent, the diplomatic missions entrusted to him by various sovereigns (are proof).'[44] To the question whether Frei Domingos was ambitious this writer answers in the affirmative but adds that one must believe that 'his worldly affairs were inspired by the desire to be useful to his Order, to his native country and to the Portuguese royal family, his three loves.'[45]

3

The Early Years

THE FIRST YEAR OF THE NEW FOUNDATION

The first year of the new foundation was eventful not only within the community but also in the politics of the whole country. The Countess had decided that she would occupy some rooms adjoining the convent but outside the enclosure. As foundress she would avail of the privilege accorded to foundresses by the Holy See of entering the cloister whenever she wished. However, she did not enjoy this privilege for very long because, only two and a half months after the formal opening of the convent, Iria de Brito died on the 26th January, 1640.

The annalist, Mother Cecilia, observes: 'God had given our holy foundress children and when she needed them most, He took them to heaven. Instead of two God gave her many spiritual daughters. As long as the monastery exists, the family of Atalaya will be gratefully remembered.'[1] She is buried at the Gospel side of the sanctuary and her epitaph reads: 'Here reposes the body of the late Dona Iria de Brito who was Countess of Feira, the widow secondly of the first Count of Atalaya, D. Francisco Manuel. From each marriage God was pleased to deprive of an heir, giving her instead daughters from among the nobility of Ireland for whom she founded this house, endowing it generously. The monastery she placed under the patronage of Our Lady of Bom Sucesso and Holy Mass was celebrated there for the first time on the 13th November 1639. God was pleased to call her soul to the enjoyment of her reward on the 26th January 1640.'

The number of community members increased considerably during the first year of its existence. In March 1640, the eldest and youngest daughters of Ruy de Mello Sampaio received the habit together with two Irish noblewomen, Cecilia of the Rosary and Jane of the Blessed Trinity, daughter of John White seemingly one of the Irish merchants or exiles who had settled in Portugal. Later, in November of the same year, the first five novices were professed and about this time one of the most famous of the early members of the community – not only because of her parents but also because of her personal sanctity – was received. She was Leonor de Burgo, daughter of the martyr, Sir John de Burgo of Brittas and of Grace Thornton, daughter of the Marshal of Munster. Her cousin, Ursula de Burgo was received on the same day. By year's end, there were already five Irish sisters in the community.

THE RESTORATION OF PORTUGUESE INDEPENDENCE

Before year's end also, the political life of the country of their adoption had radically changed. The eventful occurrence of 1640 took place on the 1st December and it is known historically as the Restoration because the throne of Portugal was restored to the Portuguese line of succession in the person of John, Duke of Braganza, grandson of Catherine, daughter of the youngest son of King Manuel 1.

For sixty years (1580-1640), Portugal was ruled by Spain and during this period, in spite of the original promises of Phillip II, Portuguese interests were gradually eroded. Of that period in history known to the Portuguese as *o domínio Filipino,* the historian, J.H. Saraivo writes: 'The incorporation of Portugal and its dominions into the states of Phillip II marks the height of Spain's maritime power in the sixteenth century. According to a phrase of a rhetorician of the period, "the sea was an emerald on the Spanish king's sandal, the sun a topaz in his crown."' [2]

However, this maritime power of Spain was constantly threatened by the growing sea-power of England. In 1580, Francis Drake having circumnavigated the globe returned to his country, his ship laden with treasure acquired from his attacks on Spanish vessels and this piratical activity had the approval of his queen, Elizabeth I.

Where Portugal is concerned, the sixty years of Spanish rule may be divided in two: a) 1580-1620, a period characterised by political calm, improved administration and a reduction in public spending due, primarily, to the absence of a monarchy; b) 1620-1640, a period characterised by a deterioration of the economy especially for the peasants. This is the time of the 'village courts' when many of the nobility went to live in their estates and held court there. The greater part of the profit accruing from the estates was taken by their owners, causing further economic hardship for the peasants. Consequently, there was mass emigration especially to Brazil and Spain. [3]

During the reign of Phillip III, Spain's economy declined: the silver mines of South America were spent and prolonged warfare was gradually using up all the resources of the State. When Phillip IV ascended the throne, Spain's finances were in crisis and this had repercussions on Portugal. In 1623, Portuguese overseas' possessions in the Middle East were captured by the Persians and English while in Brazil, the Dutch took control of its capital, São Salvador da Baia. Two years later it was recaptured by a fleet of Spanish and Portuguese ships. But the cost of this success was levied on the people of Portugal.[4]

At every increase in taxation the people reacted with rioting. The most serious of these popular riots took place in Evora in 1637 and spread throughout Alentejo and Algarve, even to the cities of the North, Oporto and Viana de Castelo. However, for want of leadership this popular rising was spent within a few months and then Spain executed those responsible in Alentejo and Algarve.

During this period, Spanish political policy changed towards a vision of Iberian unity. Many elements of the original agreement with Portugal made by Phillip II were ignored: Spanish nobles were appointed to posts in Portugal while in the provinces recruitment took place for the Spanish wars in Europe. A similar situation started a revolt in Cataluña in June 1640 when a group of harvesters visiting Barcelona on the feast of Corpus Christi mutinied, killing the governor from Castile and burning the public archives.

In order to crush this revolt the Madrid government imprudently ordered the mobilisation of Portuguese nobles to accompany the king in his campaign against the Catalans. This was the immediate cause of the Lisbon rising. A small group of members of the nobility and professionals began to conspire against Spain, among them a former judge, João Pinto Ribeiro, who dealt with the commercial interests in Lisbon of the Duke of Bragança, a direct descendant, through his grandmother, of King Manuel I of Portugal. The aim of this rising was to restore the throne of Portugal to this rightful heir.

On December 1st 1640, forty noblemen entered the royal palace in Lisbon and sought the secretary of State, Miguel de Vasconcelos who was summarily executed. They obliged the Duchess of Mantua, cousin and representative in Portugal of King Phillip IV of Spain, to command the Castilian forces in the São Jorge and Tagus fortresses to surrender without resistance.[5]

Fifteen days later, the Duke of Bragança was proclaimed King

João IV of Portugal. Prior to these events, the Duke had lived in his estate in Vila Viçosa, apparently away from the political life of the capital and he was also trusted by Madrid. Shortly before 1 December, he had been appointed military governor of Portugal. He hesitated to join the conspiracy but the alternative to his kingship was a republic of nobles. He, finally, accepted to be king.

The reaction of the young, fervent community of Bom Sucesso to this momentous political event has not been recorded. The annalist merely states that it did not affect the fortunes of either the College of the Most Holy Rosary or the Monastery of Bom Sucesso.[6] Margaret, Countess of Mantua, had honoured the community with her presence at the formal opening of the convent only a year before. Moreover, she was a close friend of the first Irish member, Leonor Kavanagh who, because of their friendship, received the religious name Leonor of Saint Margaret.

The new queen, however, was Dona Luisa de Gusmão and, due especially to her illustrious surname,[7] she had a special interest in Dominicans. She chose Dominic O'Daly as her confessor and became a most generous benefactress to the Irish Dominican College of the Holy Rosary. Later, the king would send Father Dominic on important diplomatic missions.

King João IV hastened to confirm all existing legislation and to keep at their posts the civil servants of the former administration. Parliament was convoked according to Portuguese tradition. The possibility of warfare with Spain had to be considered but, throughout the reign of João IV, it was confined to activity on the frontier between the two countries.

Meanwhile, in Bom Sucesso the numbers in the community had increased from five novices on the opening day in 1639 to thirteen (including the two sisters from São João de Setúbal) by the end of 1640. After Foundation Day, there is no further mention of Sor Ana de Conceição, the first vicar *in capite*. It is understood that she returned to her former convent once Bom Sucesso was well established, possibly as early as 1644.

BOM SUCESSO RECOGNISED BY THE DOMINICAN ORDER

In 1644, the convent of Bom Sucesso was formally accepted by the General Chapter of the Dominican Order meeting in Rome and this chapter decreed that the convent would be under the jurisdiction of the Master with the Irish provincial as immediate superior. The Irish provincial at the time was the future martyr, Fr Terence Albert O'Brien who, on his way to Ireland from Rome, visited Lisbon. There, he held canonical visitation of Bom Sucesso but we do not have any record of this visitation other than that it took place. In his history of the persecution of the Irish, Dominic O'Daly states: 'It was here in Lisbon that Fr Terence Albert O'Brien received intelligence of his elevation to the See of Emly in the year of Our Lord 1644. He left Lisbon in order to convene the chapter for the election of his successor.' [8] Seven years later this great Dominican endured a martyr's death in the city of Limerick, one of the many Irish Dominicans who set off from Lisbon to meet their death for the faith in Ireland.

TERENCE ALBERT O'BRIEN, MARTYR

O'Heyne gives a detailed account of Terence Albert's apostolic zeal and fidelity to the Dominican way of life, combining this with his pastoral care as bishop in a persecuted church: 'His first care was to combine the Episcopal dignity with the observance of his rule, as the Church at that time, especially in Ireland, was in want of such a champion to zealously help her by his authority, counsel and vigilance.' [9]

At this time the Irish people were undergoing the most severe religious persecution and also confiscation of their estates due to the Cromwellian wars. Oliver Cromwell who came to power in England after the execution of Charles I arrived in Ireland in 1649 with an army of experienced soldiers and proceeded to the massacre of the people of Drogheda. A reign of terror among the Irish ensued and, in the winter of 1649-1650, many towns in the south of the country surrendered rather than endure the fate of Drogheda. When Cromwell left Ireland on May 26th, 1650, the country had been totally devastated and the people driven from their homes. He appointed his son-in-law, Henry Ireton to complete the subjugation of the Irish.

In 1651, Ireton laid siege to the city of Limerick and Terence Albert O'Brien' gave such testimony of his heroic constancy as will be remembered for all time.' [9] Ireton secretly offered him £40,000 and permission to leave the country with safe conduct but 'he firmly resisted, choosing rather to succour the Catholic citizens until death than to have security and riches in another place.' [10]

When the city surrendered, the bishop was arrested and, on the vigil of All Saints he was brought to the market-place where he was executed. His final words to the Catholics in the crowd were: 'Keep the faith; observe the commandments; do not complain of Providence; if you do all this you will possess your souls in peace. Do not weep for me but pray that I may remain firm and unshaken while suffering this cruel martyrdom.' [11]

News of this martyrdom and that of the many Irish Dominicans who had studied in the Colégio do Rosário in Lisbon and subsequently met death for the Catholic faith in Ireland must have contributed to the heroic spirit of dedication characteristic of the young community of Bom Sucesso.

POSSIBILITY OF MOVING FROM THE HERMITAGE OFFSET

At this time, the community had a difficulty concerning the location of the convent and this caused them some anxiety. The grounds of the convent were situated on the banks of the Tagus not far from the harbour bar. The visitor to Lisbon today would not consider the site very close to the estuary because the reclamation of land has set a distance between them. However, in the seventeenth century, the waters of the Tagus reached the walls of the estate as the name of a street beside the convent today indicates: *Rua Praia do Bom Sucesso* meaning simply, the Street of Bom Sucesso Beach.

The nearness to the Tagus estuary meant that the community was in danger of an attack from English vessels. Frei Luís de Sousa explains the problem: 'As the site was so far from the city and so near the harbour bar the religious began to fear that the nearness of heretics' ships which continually came into port (by reason of the contract)[12] could be dangerous as the sanctuary with only two walls between was not well defended.' [13]

The beautiful Torre de Belém with its menacing dungeon did not seem to the community to offer sufficient protection and they began to consider moving to a safer area. However, the annals record that one of the religious besought God to inspire them in their perplexity and in answer she heard a voice saying, 'Here it is to be.' [14] Another person who was held in high esteem by the community wrote to the prioress to advise the sisters not to leave this site as the foundation would not succeed elsewhere. These warnings were accepted as signs from heaven and the building of the enclosure walls was undertaken.[15]

MAGDALENA DE SILVA MENEZES, PRIORESS

In 1645, Magdalena de Silva Menezes, one of the first novices to receive the habit on the 12th November, 1639, was now prioress. She is described in the annals as Fr Dominic O'Daly's first co-operatrix,[16] because, prior to her entering Bom Sucesso, she resided in the Mosteiro das Commendadeiras da Ordem de Santiago in Santos not far from Belém The de Mello girls, possibly after the death of their father, had temporarily settled there also and Fr Dominic was the confessor to that community

Fr Dominic told these girls of his hope of founding a convent for Irish women suffering persecution in their own country. At first, Magdalena intended becoming a Carmelite of the Teresian reform but once won over to Fr Dominic's ideal, she became his most enthusiastic supporter and, to judge from the early accounts of the foundation, she was the leader of the first group of Portuguese women dedicated to the founding of Bom Sucesso who later became members of the community in the first year of its existence.[17]

Maria Magdalena de Silva Menezes was the daughter of D. Manuel de Menezes of the House of the Marques de Marialva and her mother was Dona Luiza de Moura. On her mother's death, she went to live in the Mosteiro das Comendadeiras de San Tiago in Santos where an aunt of hers was a religious.

From her earliest childhood, Magdalena was devoted to spiritual matters and had intended entering the Discalced Carmelite Institute of Santa Theresa when she heard Fr Dominic speak of his ideal. She hesitated in her first project and turned to prayer, begging that God would enlighten her as to what she should do. One night, while absorbed in prayer she was given a vision of Our Lady of the Rosary attended and venerated by Fr Dominic and surrounded by many Dominican women. 'She immediately understood that Our Lady was inviting her to be one of that happy family and, once the difficulties of the new foundation were overcome, she entered there, assuming with enthusiasm the Dominican habit.' [18]

Like other early members of this convent Magdalena was assiduous in acts of mortification and inventive in devising new forms of asceticism so that she 'opened the door to ailments which became her constant penance.' [19] Though the chronicler's eulogy may, at times, seem excessive, an image comes to us over all these centuries of a woman who, as prioress, inspired the other members of her community principally, by her gentleness and the example of her own virtuous life. 'She was zealous without extreme severity, affable without forgetting the interests of her office; and was accustomed to say, with the clear understanding with which heaven endowed her that "for us who govern consecrated families the safest undertaking is charity because it is always necessary to temper zeal.'" [20]

On the death of her brother, Madre Magdalena de Cristo inherited his estate with an income of four thousand *cruzados*. She used this wealth for the construction of the Church and the cloister including the beautiful refectory and dormitories as the increase in the number of the community required.

The foundation stone of the Church was laid on the 20th July, 1645. The Bishop of Targa was invited to perform this ceremony but he was unable to do so and asked Fr Dominic to take his place. The preacher for the occasion was Fr Fernando Sueiro. The statue of Our Lady of Bom Sucesso followed by the Dominican priests was carried in procession to the site of the new church. On the foundation stone were sculptured a star above waves and the letters S.M.M.S.P.N. (*Stella Maria Maris, Succurre piissima nobis*), this in virtue of the proximity of the sea.

THE CHURCH AND SANCTUARY

Maria Magdalena's masterpiece and monument to her memory is the beautiful octagonal church and because of its architectural perfection people have wondered how somebody who was not an architect could have designed it. However, the chronicler merely states that she gave to the professionals (*os officieis*) the idea of the church as it is today.[21] The archaeologist, José Dias Sanches indicates that there were many churches similar in design in the seventeenth century. He writes, 'The simple architecture of the church, octagonal in form with buttresses rounded off with pinnacles and with a cupola overlaid with tiles of two colours, reminds us of the little chapel of Mount Santo Amaro and so many others of that period when the artless decorative motifs did not reveal the taste of the artists of the time.' [22] Many churches and chapels in Lisbon were destroyed in the 1755 earthquake. Consequently, it is difficult to know which church served as model. In Oporto, the church of Nossa Senhora do Pilar is not only octagonal but its cloister is also while in Obidos the Church of San Salvador is similar though of a slightly later date than that of Bom Sucesso.

In the interior of our Dominican church, the dome is supported by columns forming arches over each of the eight sides of the walls. In the recesses formed by these arches are the sanctuary, five altars, the opening to the nuns' choir and the entrance from the convent's patio. On the western side and facing east is the sanctuary with its high altar and directly opposite are the opening and grille of the lower choir with the grille of the upper choir above it. This enables sisters to view the high altar from both the lower and upper choirs.

On the right of the sanctuary is the ornate baroque altar of Our Lady of Good Success. This was formerly the altar of the Holy Cross but for many years it holds the shrine of Nossa Senhora do Bom Sucesso. On the opposite side of the sanctuary is the equally ornate altar of Our Lady of the Rosary containing a life-sized statue of Our Lady with a smaller statue of Saint Dominic. Beside it is the altar of the Sacred Heart, formerly the altar of Saint Patrick at the foot of which Dr. Sleyne, the seventeenth century bishop of Cork and Cloyne, is buried. The next altar was originally dedicated to Saint Gonzalvo but is now that of Saint Joseph. On the other side is the altar dedicated to Saint Anne.

The sanctuary itself is particularly inspiring and contains invaluable works of art. The centrepiece is the large silver- plated tabernacle or, more accurately, the throne containing the tabernacle. Pyramidal in design, it is 2.20m. in height and rests on a base of beautiful black marble, 1.40m. from ground level. This is a very beautiful, well-proportioned work of art, plated in beaten and chiselled silver with a profusion of flower and foliage designs. Inset in these plates of silver are twelve small, almost miniature, paintings of scenes from the Canticle of Canticles. These are oil paintings on copper plates and, though they have suffered from the ravages of time, sunlight and dampness, they are still vivid in colour. They were restored in 2004.

On top of the throne is a space where a crucifix was placed and above it is suspended a wooden carved crown painted silver. The crucifix and original crown disappeared during the Peninsular War. Until Vatican II, this work of art served as a throne for the Blessed Sacrament: during Exposition, the crown was drawn up by a pulley to allow space for the monstrance to be placed on the throne directly under the crown. Stands were set into all the points of the pyramid and lighted candles were placed on them. Flowers and plants adorned the sanctuary and the whole scene was a lavish display to enhance the worship of the Blessed Sacrament. In past centuries, Portugal was known as the land of the Blessed Sacrament and, until abuses crept in, Corpus Christi processions were important public events. Tradition tells us that when these processions passed by the theatre the actors on the stage reverently interrupted their performance. Works of art such as the monstrance (*custódia de Belém*) and the Bom Sucesso throne testify to the devotion of the Portuguese people to the Blessed Sacrament.

Slender, marble pillars form an arch or baldachin over the throne and these, together with side columns support the retable of variegated marble. The walls of the sanctuary are also covered in Arrábida marble of different colours donated by Manuel Cerqueira. In the centre of the retable, directly above the baldachin is a life-size crucifix presented, in 1745, by the Infante D. Manuel, brother of the king, D. João V. It was sculptured by Lourenço Grimaldo Napolitano, procurator of the Franciscan convent in Lisbon. The background to the crucifix is a painting of Jerusalem at a distance from the cross. Both sides of the retable are divided into two levels with niches in which, on the first level, are the statues of Saint Dominic and Saint Francis while in the niches above them are the statues of Saint Thomas Aquinas and Saint Anthony, patron of Lisbon.

Behind the throne is a very large canvas of the Mystery of God being contemplated by the four evangelists. It is the work of the famous Portuguese painter of the seventeenth century, Bento Coelho da Silveira. This was verified a few years ago on the occasion of its restoration.

The Painter, Bento Coelho da Silveira

Tradition attributes the paintings of the Song of Songs on the throne also to Bento Coelho da Silveira who was born in Lisbon on the 14th February, 1620 and died at the age of eighty-eight in the parish of São Domingos on the 3rd March,1708. From 1648, he was a member of the Confraternity of Saint Luke and was appointed Court painter in oils by the regent, D. Pedro on the 10th September, 1678 – eight years after the opening of the Bom Sucesso Church.[23]

Bento Coelho da Silveira was a prolific artist but did not always sign his paintings. Though we are certain that he painted the large canvas at the rear of the sanctuary we can only, so far, depend on the strong tradition that attributes them to him and on the internal evidence given by the brightness of the colours in each of the twelve paintings. A similar work of his is in the Seminary of Penafirme.

The Resurrection depicted on the Tabernacle Door

The tabernacle door itself contains in beaten and chiselled silver the scene of the Resurrection, thus completing the triple mystery of

Christ's Passion, Death and Resurrection. The risen Christ radiating light and surrounded by clouds rises from his tomb. Crowned and wearing a mantle over his left shoulder he holds in his left hand the standard of the cross while he raises his right hand in triumph. Of the four soldiers guarding the tomb two are awake but surprised to the point of incredulity, the third is half-asleep and the fourth slowly waking up. To the left of Christ but further back the three Marys are on their way to the tomb and behind them in the distance is the city of Jerusalem. To succeed in portraying this scene in such detail on metal is craftsmanship of the highest degree.

While there is agreement about the author of the paintings, there is a certain doubt about the name of the silversmith who produced not only the tabernacle door but also all the throne's other plates with their intricate designs. The annals simply state that all this silverwork was accomplished by a famous seventeenth century silversmith named Evano[24]. However, among the very many artists in this craft in Lisbon at the time the name Evano has not, as yet, been located. 'The truth is that we are in front of one more work of Portuguese art with no author attributed to it.' [25]

How much input did Madre Magdalena de Cristo and her community have in the artists' inspiration? We do not know but we can surmise that they took a lively interest in the progress of the work. The Song of Songs applied figuratively to the relationship between Christ and the human soul was part of their spirituality emphasised by the writings of Saint John of the Cross particularly in *The Ascent of Mount Carmel* and *The Spiritual Canticle*. However, the complete set of paintings seems to point more to the Church as figuratively the bride of Christ, guardian of Baptism and the Eucharist and teacher of the Christian way while religious persecution as part of the Christian life is prominent in the paintings. Thus, this tabernacle/throne is not only a work of art but mystically a mirror of the Church's life, especially in the historical context of the suffering of the Church in Ireland at the time.

The Cloister

'The cloister is sober and its smooth simple stones exhale a conventual perfume which the odd whirling round of the century of speed has not yet reached; where the life of humanity is as calm as that of the flowers; where a living, wholesome light penetrating our spirit purifies it like a hidden retreat, appropriate for a contemplative meditation on the whole work of creation coming from the Creator's hands.'[26] So, wrote the archaeologist, Sanches describing, in the mid-twentieth century, the cloister of the Bom Sucesso Convent. This was the important addition made to the original hermitage in the last decades of the seventeenth century. Few of the first members would have known the peace above depicted as its building was not complete until 1688. Between 1645 and the early years of the eighteenth century the cloister, refectory and sleeping quarters for the increasing number of sisters were constructed adjoining the original summer residence donated by Dona Iria de Brito.

Sanches continues his eulogy, 'This beautiful cloister where the rays of the sun impart a happy smiling life from the first hours of morning until it hides behind the flanks of the Sintra ridge is divided into two floors.'[27] Some of the expense for the construction of these buildings was paid for by a member of the Inquisition, Manuel Cerqueira. He contributed sufficient money to cover the cost of an infirmary on the upper floor of the cloister and workshops on the lower floor. He also had the walls of the Church's sanctuary covered in marble and the former two grilles of the upper and lower choirs were installed also at his expense. The tablet on a wall in the former infirmary (now a classroom) states that he had other works done as well, including, probably, the punishment cell for dissident religious, situated on the ground floor beneath the infirmary: 'Manuel Cerqueira Campos, official of the Holy Office had built, out of devotion, this infirmary, workshops on the ground floor, pointed grilles, the covering of the sanctuary and other works. He put this tablet here so that future generations may commend his soul to God. The year of 1688.'

The cloister itself is rectangular with arches enclosing a small space which contains flower beds and a fountain. Both the columns and the masonry surrounding the fountain were originally covered in blue and white tiles but the ravages of time have depleted their beauty. From the veranda, one can see the belfry with its cupola also covered in blue and white tiles. Again, Sanches has a poetic reference to the belfry that 'looks at the sea, bosom of the *caravelas* which with Good Success brought to the fatherland a new fatherland.'[28]

The largest and possibly the most beautiful room of the convent is the refectory. It measures 21.3 x 12 metres and its walls are partially decorated with seventeenth century tile-work (*azulejos*). It is dominated by a very large oil painting of the Last Supper in a lavishly carved frame. The ceiling is of painted wood with the inscription, 'It is better to pay attention to the reading than to the food.' At the other end of the refectory from the painting is a raised pulpit for the reader during the meals which were, otherwise, taken in silence. This pulpit was approached by steps in the adjoining servery.

THE UPPER CHOIR

On the second floor directly above the choir and chapter room is the Upper Choir. It presumably was part of the original summer residence and consequently, was adapted as a choir in the early years of the foundation. Its ceiling is, like the refectory, painted with floral and leaf designs. Above the grille is a beautiful mural of Our Lady giving the Rosary to Saint Dominic. Over the entrance is another mural depicting Saint Michael, the Archangel. The walls are adorned with large paintings of the life of Christ and midway on either side of the choir are two shrines dedicated to Christ carrying his cross and Mary as Mother of Sorrows. The ante-choir has also a mural over the entrance to the choir and two altars, one of which has a polychromatic statue of Saint John the evangelist in contemplation and the other a large statue of Saint Patrick of less artistic value. All the artwork of the Upper Choir was restored in 2004.

MAGDALENA DE CRISTO AND QUEEN LUÍSA DE GUSMÃO

Magdalena de Silva Menezes was not only a good administrator who courageously undertook the building of the church and a large part of the cloister, she was also a very wise woman who was consulted for her good advice. She was the friend and confidante of the Queen of Portugal, Dona Luísa de Gusmão who often visited the convent in order to converse with its prioress. This friendship must have meant that the prioress's counsel was reciprocated by the queen's interest and support in the building projects of the convent, possibly in the choice of artists and architects.

In the convent's archives a sheet in Spanish with its title in Portuguese purports to be Queen Dona Luísa's thoughts on her choice of residence when she would retire from the Court. It refers to Bom Sucesso as her preference because of its spacious grounds and because of her desire to have a view of the sea. Moreover, she has great affection for Saint Dominic as she considers herself a member of the same Gusmão family as he. However, on account of Bom Sucesso's nearness to the harbour bar, in time of warfare, it would be the first convent to be attacked. Again, when her daughter, Queen Catherine of England, retired to Portugal, the same reason prevented her from choosing Bom Sucesso as her place of residence while her palace of Bemposta was being built. Thus, from the early years of its foundation, it was a much favoured convent especially by the Queens of the Bragança dynasty.

4

The Spirituality of the Community
Twelve Scenes from the Canticle of Canticles

Why, it may be asked, the choice of *The Song of Songs* as the biblical text illustrated on the tabernacle of the church in a convent of enclosed, contemplative nuns? Bridal imagery to describe the union of the human soul with God is an ancient tradition. In the Old Testament, God's loving relationship with the people of Israel was often analogically described in terms of the relationship between a bridegroom and his bride. Prophets such as Hosea, Isaiah, Jeremiah and Ezekiel, metaphorically describe Israel's infidelity to God's covenant as adultery while they try to win the people away from the fertility cults of neighbouring tribes back to the covenant that God had made with them. In her commentary on this theme in the Old Testament, Catherine Gibson writes, 'The definitive factors in establishing Israel's identity remained the Exodus and the Covenant, and bridal or marriage imagery remained a useful linguistic method of expressing the relationship and commitment resulting from these two constitutive realities.'[1]

The inclusion of *The Song of Songs*, an *epithalamium* or nuptial song, purporting to celebrate the betrothal of Solomon and his Shulamite bride, only merits a place in the Bible if understood as an allegory depicting the union of God/Christ with the human soul or the Church. Bridal imagery is used also in the New Testament particularly as a figure of the relationship between Christ and his Church. In Mt 9:15, Christ likens himself to the bridegroom, 'surely the bridegroom's attendants cannot mourn as long as the bridegroom is with them.' In Jn 3:29, John the Baptist speaks of the Messiah as the bridegroom, 'It is the bridegroom who has the bride and yet the bridegroom's friend who stands there and listens to him is filled with joy at the bridegroom's voice.'

Many of the Fathers of the Church used this metaphor also to describe both the union of Christ with his Church and of Christ with the individual soul, whether man or woman, but Origen, in his commentary on *The Song of Songs*, may be said to have created the tradition within Christian mysticism. Rowan Williams, Archbishop of Canterbury, defends Origen's application of the metaphor both to the individual and the Church, 'Origen's concern with direct experience may give a rather individualistic colouring to his thought. Yet the whole of the commentary on the Song of Songs moves back and forth between the corporate and the individual, the Church and the soul, and there is never any pretence that the experience of the particular soul is independent of that of the Church as a whole.'[2] Something similar is attempted by the artist in the twelve paintings inset in the Bom Sucesso tabernacle.

Medieval spiritual writers, such as Bernard of Clairvaux, continued the analogy between the union of the soul with God/Christ and that of the bride and groom. In Dominican spirituality the use of bridal imagery is common. Catherine of Siena experienced a mystical marriage with Christ in 1366/67, when she was about twenty years of age. And Meister Eckhart describes the Incarnation and Redemption in terms of Christ's marriage with the human race: 'When God created the soul, he created it according to his highest perfection, so that it might be a bride of the Only-Begotten Son. Because he (Christ) knew this he wanted to come forth from the secret treasure chamber of the eternal Fatherhood, in which he had eternally slept.... This is why he came out, and came leaping like a young hart (Sg. 2:9) and suffered his torments for love and he did not go out without wishing to go in again into his chamber with his bride. This chamber is the silent darkness of the hidden Fatherhood.'[3]

At the beginning of the twentieth century, a renewed interest in mysticism began to develop within the Christian churches of Western Europe. While the Anglican Evelyn Underhill was writing her work, *Mysticism*, the Spanish Dominican, Fr Juan Arintero was studying mystical theology and this resulted in his work entitled *The Mystical Evolution*. In 1918, he completed his commentary on *The Song of Songs* and in the Introduction to this work he states, 'With great vividness it represents or symbolises, in the form of a human betrothal between Solomon and the Shulamite, or between a shepherd and a young shepherdess, and through the tender love that exists between them, the ineffable loves of Christ for his Mystical Bride, the Holy Catholic Church and for the Most Blessed Virgin...the example for all holy souls, revealing to us the ineffable mysteries of the spiritual betrothal that the Divine Word wishes to celebrate with all such souls.[4]

In this work, recently republished, the writer has taken quotes from a great number of spiritual writers who interpreted the mystical meaning of the Song of Songs and I include some of their comments applicable to the paintings in Bom Sucesso's tabernacle.

That the spirituality of the early members of the Bom Sucesso community was influenced by this tradition is borne out by the death-bed scenes of many of these sisters. They were full of joy at the thought of their approaching death as a bride looks forward to her wedding. Today, with the universal renewal of interest in Spirituality, the age-old allegory of *The Song of Songs* applied to the spiritual life and its nuptial interpretation becomes relevant again.

The actual positioning of the paintings on the front of the three-tiered tabernacle/throne highlights the tradition of bridal imagery in mystical theology and thus refers directly to the vocation of contemplative Dominicans. The inscriptions on the three paintings in the foremost position are the quotations from *The Song of Songs* traditionally applied to virgins. The two largest paintings, one on the front of the first/lowest tier of the tabernacle and the other directly opposite in the back panel are the most prominent and refer principally to the Church in its roles as praising God and preaching the Incarnation of the Son of God.

FONS HORTORUM

Fons Hortorum, the centre front of the lowest tier, refers to *The Song of Songs*: 'She is a garden enclosed, my sister, my promised bride, a garden enclosed, a sealed fountain...well of living water' (4:12-15).

The scene is a large garden with trees and, in the background, a mountain. The figure seated on the left foreground is the bride and she is playing on the harp. She is attended by three women, the daughters of Jerusalem. Her gaze is directed to the sky where, among the clouds, two cherubim hold a scroll with the music or words of a song composed, as it were, by angels. The figure on the right of the picture is the lover leaning on his wooden staff listening to the heavenly music while a cherub calls his attention to the harpist and two other angels watch behind him. The scene of the enclosed garden represents the beauty of virginity but it also represents the Church in its liturgical role. The fountain on the left of the painting is a symbol of baptism and the red roses growing beside the group of women represent martyrdom.

Concerning this verse, Arintero quotes St Lawrence Justinian, 'These words ...are rightly applied to the soul who, carefully examining her interior life, corrects her faults, washes away her stains...and guards and subjects her senses; so that Wisdom can come and dwell in her as in His own mansion. The Church is also an enclosed garden for the faithful, filled with flowers and fruits which are the various and good works of her children. The fountain which waters this garden is the doctrine of salvation enclosed in Sacred Scriptures which, because of the hiddenness and profundity of the meanings they enclose, are like a sealed fountain.' [5]

SIC DILECTUS MIHI...

The corresponding painting at the back of the tabernacle refers to Sg. 5:16, *Sic dilectus mihi...*'Such is my love, such is my friend, Daughters of Jerusalem.'

This painting is placed directly under the silver door of the tabernacle and its caption is the concluding phrase of the beloved's description of her lover's qualities. The bride is turned to her women companions but she points to her lover on the right. Like the first panel it refers especially to the Church but, whereas the former picture depicted the Church's role as praising God through the liturgy, the present painting represents its preaching role concerning Christ This is further emphasised by the fact that the beloved is in a standing position and holding the staff of authority in her hand.

Arintero's commentary on this caption refers mainly to the individual soul who, once converted, seeks to draw others to faith in and commitment to Christ He writes, 'Thus the loving soul praises Him and seeks to tell everyone about Him, and tries to win for Him as many souls as she can, working with zeal, and almost without realizing it, in the very enterprise that a short while before, lacking faith in herself, she had been so unwilling to undertake. In this way the Lord triumphs over this innocent resistance, and brings everything to redound to the greater good of His chosen ones.' [6] This painting is specifically relevant for members of the Order of Preachers.

Veni Sponsa mea...

Front paintings: On the second tier in the centre front, *Veni Sponsa mea...* (Sg. 4:8): 'Come from Lebanon, my Bride / Come from Lebanon, come / You will be crowned from the top of Amana / From the top of Shenir and Hermon / From the dens of lions, From the mountains of leopards.'

This is the Bridegroom's invitation to the Bride and in the religious sphere it is the call of Christ to the individual soul. In this scene the bridegroom on the left of the picture holds in his left hand a golden crown decorated with a garland of red and white flowers, symbols of martyrdom and virginity. These he offers to the bride coming down a hill towards him.

Arintero explains the symbolism of the presence of wild animals as indicative of the trials that the committed Christian must undergo. When these paintings were being produced, the Church in Ireland was experiencing a severe persecution of the Faith and this accounts for the emphasis on martyrdom so prominent in many of these works of art. He writes, 'This is one of the passages in which the mystical sense of the divine Song, the sense truly intended by the Holy Spirit most visibly transcends the matter of the symbol; that is the King's betrothal represented by it, which could be attributed to a human agency. For it is inconceivable that Solomon could invite his queen to win such a crown as this.

'The Lebanon spoken of here is not the famous mountain in Phoenicia but...one of the royal sites near Jerusalem where it is known that the monarch built a country house for his bride, the daughter of the king of Egypt.... He calls her so as to crown her, not with flowers but with piercing thorns, glorious trophies which, like Him, she herself must collect on the rough and dangerous heights of Amana, of Shenir and Hermon where many terrible wild animals have their lairs. How clearly does this daring image which could never have occurred to a worldly lover convey the extremity of love the Son of God has for souls and likewise the degree of love He demands of His brides in contributing to His work of salvation.'[7]

Fructus ejus dulcis...

The front panel on the third tier of the tabernacle, appropriately in the highest position, has the painting which portrays the result

71

of the union of the bride and groom. *Fructus ejus dulcis...*(Sg. 7:14). The bride speaks, 'The mandrakes already yield their scent / At our doors there are all kinds of fruit / The new and the old, my beloved / I shall keep them for you.'

Arintero, 'The mandrakes seem to symbolize the active life that is rich in good works, as though saying that these works now yield a very sweet scent. Thus, these are all symbols of the fertility that accompanies this holy soul, and of the perfect faithfulness and purity of intention with which she proceeds. In her presence everything flourishes, everything exhales a fragrance and yields abundant fruit, giving great glory to God.[8]
He concludes, These brilliant images give an excellent picture of the immense good accomplished in the world by the apostolate and works of devotion of souls truly united with Jesus, communicating to others what they have contemplated and bearing everywhere the message of peace.'[9]

Thus the three front paintings emphasise the progress of the soul towards union with God. The fruit of this union between Christ and the human soul or the Church is an increase of grace for the whole human race. The first painting stresses the turning of the soul to God through prayer and self-denial, the second portrays the call of Christ to a deeper commitment and the response of the human soul. This culminates in the Divine union which is most fruitful for others. The two largest paintings represent the double role of the Church of praising God and preaching the Word. With no obvious sequence, the remaining paintings on the sides of the tabernacle represent specific aspects of the soul's journey to God.

PROSPICIENS PER CANCELLOS...

On the right front panel the caption under the painting reads *Prospiciens per cancellos...* (Sg.2:9)

'My beloved is like a gazelle, like a young stag / See where he stands behind our wall / Looking in through the windows / Peering through the lattice.'

Verse 8 of chapter 2 begins the description of the second phase of progress towards union with God – the illuminative way when the mysteries of Faith illumine and give joy to the soul. There is an awareness of the presence of Christ guiding and directing the soul. This presence is described specifically as the Divine gaze.

Arintero quotes St Teresa (Comment. II) concerning this: 'Behind the wall of this body, He is looking with my eyes and speaking with my tongue and so on. I also feel beside me, outside, the company of Christ the Man in an intellectual way, not by picturing Him in any way in the imagination but by attending to the fact that He is always gazing at me and accompanying me wherever I go...' [10] Arintero's own comment on this passage also merits quotation: 'Here it is clearly shown how quickly God comes to console His own souls, to cheer them with His visit, especially in times of affliction and tribulation. If He ever flees or turns away from the soul, His love, He does so imitating the way of these gracious little animals, the gazelle and the stag, which from time to time turn their heads around.'[11]

NE SUSCITE...

In the right back panel of the first tier, the painting has the caption, *Ne suscite...,* which refers to the refrain closing the first, second and fifth poems of *The Song of Songs* (Sg. 2:7; 3:5; 8:4)

'I adjure you, O daughters of Jerusalem, /By the gazelles or wild does / Do not stir up or awaken love / Until it is ready.'

In the scene, the bride is asleep and the bridegroom addresses her companions. The spiritual interpretation is that her sleep is symbolically the experience of mystical contemplation when the soul is completely absorbed in God.

Commenting on this prayer of deep contemplation Arintero states, 'He (Christ) earnestly charges them not to waken her until it is time, for she accomplishes more by being like this, more even for the good of her neighbours, than all she could possibly achieve through great work and labour in active life. For it is here that she gains strength and receives knowledge and skill; it is here that she pleads with God for the conversion and advancement of souls and acquires the ability to attract, win, soften and change hearts; and finally, it is here that she enters into the Spirit of Divine Love so as later to exhale everywhere the sweet fragrance of Jesus Christ with which to win countless hearts to Him.'[12]

Referring to the final repetition of the verse, the same writer states, 'In order to be productive, this sacred ministry must always be accompanied by the exercise of prayer where lights and blessings are received from on high in great abundance. Just as the body, so also this life of great spiritual activity needs to be refreshed with food and rest....The great saints, however busy they are or however demanding their apostolate, never abandon this absolute essential of prayer, this better part which consists in the contemplation of the Supreme Good.'[13]

ACERVUS TRITICI

The painting in the left back panel of the first tier has the caption, *Acervus tritici,* referring to Sg. 7:2.

'Your body contains a heap of wheat / Surrounded with lilies.' This is here applied as an obvious reference to the Eucharist of which the Church is the repository. In the centre a heap of wheat is surrounded with lilies. On the left, the bride holds in her left hand a slender staff, symbol of authority. The bridegroom also has a staff in his hand and his right hand is raised in a gesture of blessing.

Arintero writes, 'This wheat symbolizes the Holy Eucharist which is the mystical Bread of Life and the precious wheat of the chosen which the Holy Virgin grew and prepared for us in her pure breast.... Thus, it is surrounded with lilies not only in the Virgin because of her immaculate purity, but in all those who worthily receive it as true nourishment for their souls.... There is a superabundance for all, symbolized by the heap of wheat or granary....The Eucharist, indeed, intimately unites the Christian with Christ and, setting the copy against the model, it produces a wonderful impression in the soul, stamping her with new features of divine filiation and bringing her to be more and more closely patterned on the Saviour.'[14]

FULCITE ME FLORIBUS

The painting in the front left panel of the first tier has the caption, *Fulcite me floribus,* referring to Sg. 2:5.

'Sustain me with flowers / Comfort me with apples, For I am sick with love.'

According to Arintero, the word translated as flowers means in Hebrew a perfume box or flask of wine. The sickness referred to is the soul's longing for God and in this pain of desire she is sustained by the example of the Crucified Christ Arintero writes,

'She strives to sustain herself with the flowers of virtue and fruits of good works to please the bridegroom.... In practising these through love of her Spouse, she begins to spend herself with ardour and zeal to the great benefit of her neighbours, thus producing precious fruits of good works that will comfort, strengthen and sustain her, and she will gain more and even greater gifts and consolations.'[15]

PASCE HODOS TUOS

The four paintings in the side panels of the second/middle tier stress mainly the progress of the individual soul, though one of the paintings, which refers to Sg. 2:15, is traditionally interpreted as a reference to the persecution of the Church. Beginning with the front panel on the left, the painting has the caption, *Pasce hodos tuos*, Sg. 1:8.

'O loveliest of women / Follow the tracks of the flocks / And take your kids to graze / Close by the shepherds' tents.'

This is the advice given to the shepherdess when she asks her shepherd lover, 'where will you lead your flock to graze, where will you rest it at noon that I may no more wander like a vagabond beside the flocks of your companions' (Sg.1:7). The spiritual interpretation of this stanza is that, at the beginning of the soul's search for God, she seeks guidance as to how best she can proceed. The advice is to follow the well-worn path of prayer and self-denial that all the great saints before her have followed. 'Follow the tracks of the flocks, not of the lost...but along the holy, pure and narrow way of abnegation and justice (Is 35:8-9) which is the only way to life and true rest (Mt 7:13-14). Follow the footsteps of the saints and all my faithful servants, those happy sheep who hear my voice and follow me and to whom I give eternal life and whom no one will ever steal from me. (Jn 10: 27-28)'[16]

PASCITUR INTER LILIA

The the painting in the back panel of the left side has the caption, *Pascitur inter lilia,* (Sg.2:16).

'He pastures his flock among the lilies / Until the day breathes / And the shadows flee.'

In this painting, the lover is seated, holding his staff in his left hand while with his right hand he raises a piece of bread to his lips. At his feet is a stretch of water on the margins of which lilies are growing. On a large stone to his right is a white cloth on which is laid a loaf of bread. The beloved standing on the left of the picture addresses the daughters of Jerusalem while pointing to her lover. This may be interpreted as the Church's role to preach Christ in the Eucharist

Gregory of Nyssa comments, 'He is a wonderful shepherd for he does not pasture his sheep with hay but with pure lilies. He does not want his flock to feed from the coarse pastures of the world....But whoever lives by the Spirit of God is not only freed from corruption but also becomes one spirit with him...converted into the very nature of this divine food.' [17]

E NOBIS VULPES PARVULI

The caption for the painting in the back panel, right side of the tabernacle reads, *E nobis vulpes parvuli*.

'Catch us the foxes / The little foxes / That ruin the vineyards / For our vineyards are in blossom.'

Traditionally, this verse has two interpretations according to the great spiritual writers. One interpretation considers the little foxes that cause havoc in the vineyards as imperfections which the individual soul must correct while the other views these little foxes as the heresies which cause havoc within the Church.

The scene depicted in this panel is of a vineyard in the foreground and on either side an angel is busy trying to tie up small foxes. Behind, to the left the bride and groom are seated side by side on a low wall and behind them again, the daughters of Jerusalem regard the scene. On the right, two more angels carry a small fox each around their necks.

Regarding the first interpretation, Arintero states that Christ 'charges his ministers to catch the little foxes of certain disordered attachments or affections or other little defects that pass unnoticed but which, unless they are quickly eradicated, will gradually and secretly ruin her changing her from his chosen vine and garden of his delights into a true desert.'(Is 5:6; Jer. 12:10-11).

The second interpretation is a symbolic reference to dangers to the Church because of heresies particularly where the Eucharist is concerned. It may be interpreted in this context as referring to the religious persecution in Ireland and the proscription of the Mass. Oliver Cromwell who came to power in England wreaked havoc among the Catholic population. 'According to many Fathers (Origen, Augustine, Gregory, Cassiodorus, Bede etc.,) these little foxes or jackals...represent the heresies that destroy the Saviour's vine; therefore, he charges his apostles, prelates, preachers and doctors to catch these little foxes.' [19]

SUB CAPITE MEO...

The painting in the left front panel of the middle tier has the caption, *Sub capite meo*. This is the penultimate verse of the first and last poems of *The Song of Songs* (Sg. 2:6 and 8:3).

'O that his left hand were under my head / And that his right hand embraced me.'

The painting accurately illustrates this verse as the bride is seated on grassy ground, supported by her bridegroom whose left hand is under her chin and whose right arm is round her neck. The daughters of Jerusalem on the left of the picture are in an attitude of wonder and awe while the angels on the right are each absorbed in prayer and adoration. The left hand is interpreted as representing the persecutions and afflictions of the Church or the individual soul and the right arm the peace of Christ that fills the Church or the soul.

Commenting on the same verse in Sg. 8:3, Arintero writes, 'This is spoken by the holy soul as she is caught up into a much higher rapture than what she experienced in the other stages of contemplation. She no longer loses the use of her senses as formerly nor does she suffer abandonment or aridity or other similar trials.... His left hand here represents the sufferings of Christ in which the soul is now made to participate so that, united to him in his passion and death, she may cooperate with him in his apostolic work for souls and in making reparation to the Divine Majesty. His right hand represents the exalted delights she now receives from this embrace which, as St John of the Cross says, 'tastes of eternal life and pays every debt.'[20] This verse is also applied to Our Lady and the Infant Jesus in her arms where the Holy Child has his right arm round his mother's neck and his left hand grasps the collar of her robe.

These paintings together with the Upper Choir paintings of gospel scenes indicate to us that the spirituality of the Bom Sucesso nuns was deeply rooted in the Bible. As Dominicans, their search for the Supreme Truth would be mainly by way of contemplation, especially of Christ's mysteries. Consequently, the liturgical celebration of the principal feasts of the Church and the Rosary were important means to deeper contemplation. We know from the extra ordinations laid down by Fr Dominic O'Daly that the choral recitation of the Prayer of the Church or Divine Office occupied a considerable part of the daily timetable while the Sisters were also obliged to the saying of the Rosary in choir.

The convent was founded in the Iberian peninsula at a time when the reform of religious life was in full vigour following, in particular, the Teresian reform of the sixteenth century. Bom Sucesso was established only seventy-seven years after the first foundation of discalced Carmelite nuns made in 1562. The relaxation of primitive rules that occurred after the plague of the mid-fourteenth century had taken quite a while to redress but, from the mid-sixteenth century, religious orders, especially in Spain and Portugal, returned to their original asceticism. According to Richard Woods, O.P., 'The movement towards stricter observance among the mendicant orders was the last and perhaps the major influence on the revival of spirituality in Spain at this time. The Franciscan Observantist movement led by Saint Peter of Alcántara, a friend and close adviser of Saint Teresa was matched by the preaching and writings of the Dominican Luís de Granada.'[21] Considerable evidence exists of harsh and, from a more modern viewpoint, excessive ascetical practices in the lives of the early members of the Bom Sucesso community.

The fact that the reason for the convent's foundation was the persecution of the Irish Church inspired a certain spirituality of martyrdom. Many Irish Dominicans of the Colégio do Rosário, founded by Dominic O'Daly, returned to Ireland to meet their death for the faith. Within a short time of its foundation twenty-nine of its former members had suffered martyrdom so that it came to be known as the College of Martyrs. This must have influenced the community of Bom Sucesso who would have known many, if not all, of these Dominican martyrs. Moreover, the presence in the community of Leonor de Burgo, the daughter of a martyr, was a further incentive for the sisters to practise a form of asceticism akin to martyrdom.

The Early Members of Bom Sucesso

We are fortunate in having brief accounts of the lives and spirituality of eighteen of the early members of the community – nine

Portuguese and nine Irish. The first of these accounts tells the story of Madre Antónia Theresa de Jesús who, by order of the Portuguese provincial, left her convent of São João de Setúbal to become the first mistress of novices at Bom Sucesso. She was thirty-four years of age at the time. She never returned to Setúbal and died in Bom Sucesso ten years later on 13th October, 1649.

According to the chronicler, this sister was an outstanding model of penance. 'Her spirit was not content with the rigours of the monastery's statute; when the taking of the discipline with the whole community was over, she withdrew to continue hers with so much cruelty that, afterwards, however much she tried to conceal, it showed.'[22] She also wore a hair shirt and her fasting was more strict than that ordained by the Constitutions. Most of the time she had only a plank for a bed and her habit was so worn that it scarcely protected her from the cold until she was obliged by obedience to accept a less patched but coarser one.

Antónia Theresa's prayer was continuous. 'The whole time was for her time for prayer'[23] She became prioress and is considered the first prioress of Bom Sucesso since Madre Ana de Conceição was called vicar *in capite*. As prioress, she redoubled her efforts at charity to all the sisters in the community. An interesting story is told of this sister's wisdom while she was prioress. Four young girls arrived from Ireland with the approval of the Irish provincial to take the habit in Bom Sucesso. However, as many Irish girls were applying to the convent at this time, the religious, with insufficient resources to support them, hesitated to receive these young women.

One day when Madre Antónia Theresa was in the choir at prayer after Communion, she was graced with an intuitive vision. She saw seated in the novices' places the four Irish girls, each wearing the Dominican habit. She accepted this vision as a sign from heaven and, first, informing Madre Magdalena de Cristo and then the whole community, she gave the habit straightaway to Inês do Rosário. She was unable to receive the other three girls because she died shortly afterwards.[24]

One other incident during her time as prioress is a further example of Antónia Theresa's intuitive gift or, perhaps, the practical awareness of another member of the community. She was accustomed to go down the garden to pray and, on one occasion, she was so lost in contemplation that she did not notice the time passing away. When she realised where she was, it was already night and she became frightened. She turned to prayer and asked that the most obedient sister would come to her. Turning round she saw one of the sisters standing beside her and on asking her why she had come the sister replied that she had been washing delft in the pantry when she felt urged to go to the garden to accompany the prioress to the house. The name of that sister was Leonor do Calvário.

When, in 1649, Fr Dominic O'Daly was about to set out for France on a diplomatic mission for the king of Portugal, D. João IV, Antónia Theresa asked to be relieved of the responsibility of prioress but Frei Domingos evaded the issue and set off, leaving her in office. She felt this deeply and said to her sisters: 'Now that Father Vicar has not wanted to release me, God will release me in some other way.' A few days later, she met with a serious accident and was close to death. Madre Magdalena de Cristo asked her if she wished to receive the Sacrament of Reconciliation but she replied that, by the mercy of God, she had nothing to confess and was waiting only for the final hour which was so important. The enthusiasm with which she awaited death was evident in spite of the pain she was enduring. On 13th October, 1649, the first prioress died at the age of forty-four, ten years after the foundation of Bom Sucesso.[25]

Leonor do Calvário

Leonor do Calvário, already mentioned in the life-story of Antónia Theresa was Portuguese and came from Vila Nova de Tancos, a small village in the north of Portugal. She was of noble birth but was left an orphan when quite young. The Countess of Atalaya brought her to her home and treated her as her own daughter. In her youth she was remarkably beautiful and consequently had many offers of marriage but she refused all of them as she wished to choose religious life instead. However, the Countess could not bear to part with her and this problem was only resolved when Bom Sucesso was founded. Leonor was one of its first novices, finally fulfilling her life's ambition at the age of fifty.

Leonor do Calvário, though of noble birth, wished to live the life of the humblest member of the community and when the sisters intended electing her prioress, she went from cell to cell begging them, on her knees, not to elect her for this office. When advanced in years she became invalided, as the chronicler states, since 'heaven wished to give her the crown of endurance.'[26] She was devoted to Saint Barbara and died on her feast-day as she had always requested.

JACINTA DE JESÚS MARIA

The last of the five novices received on the opening day of the monastery of Bom Sucesso was Madre Jacinta de Jesús Maria who, having had to care for her mother, came to religious life late, though she had wished to lead a cloistered life from her earliest years. Her outstanding characteristic was love of neighbour, which she practised to a heroic degree in her office as infirmarian. Like Leonor do Calvário, Jacinta de Jesus Maria had the same unwillingness to be prioress and the sisters were obliged to excuse her from this office. She had prayed that she would not cause her sisters trouble at the close of her life and her prayer was answered. Towards the end of Mass one day, she met with an accident and was carried to the infirmary. She died shortly afterwards, having received Communion at the Mass she had attended.

LEONOR DE SANTA MARGARIDA

The first and only Irish woman to receive the Dominican habit on the opening day was Leonor Kavanagh, daughter of the Lord of Pelmonty and Borese (Borris?, Co. Carlow), Ireland – in religion, Madre Leonor de Santa Margarida. Like Leonor do Calvário and Jacinta de Jesús Maria, she was no longer young. She was the widow of *Domhnach an Spáinneach* and mother of adult children, who, after the death of her husband, left Ireland and settled in Castile. There, Dominic O'Daly met her living in retirement. She was a friend of Margaret, Countess of Mantua, cousin of the king of Spain, who, at this time was governor of Portugal in the name of the king of Castile.

The Countess of Mantua attending the opening ceremony of the convent asked the provincial, Fr Vasconcellos, if she could have Leonor's beautiful hair, not because it was beautiful but as a kind of relic, out of her esteem for her friend.[27] Leonor in turn took the name of Saint Margaret in honour of the Countess. In spite of illnesses which already troubled her, Leonor of Saint Margaret lived her new form of life to the edification of all so that she was unanimously elected mistress of novices and later prioress. She lived to an advanced age and died on 21st March, 1669, after almost thirty years of religious life.

Catharina do Rosário

The clearest description of the dominant spirituality of the community is given in the short account of the life of Leonor de Burgo, in religion, Madre Catharina do Rosário. She was the daughter of John de Burgo, Lord of Brittas, and of Grace Thornton, who was the daughter of George Thornton, Marshal of Munster. In 1608, prior to Leonor's birth, her father had already suffered martyrdom in Limerick city for the Catholic faith.

On the death of Elizabeth I of England in 1603 and the accession of James VI of Scotland to the throne of England, hopes were high in Ireland that the persecution of the Catholic faith would come to an end. It was thought that the new king, being the son of the Catholic Mary Queen of Scots would not pursue Elizabeth's policy of persecution. Consequently, the young Lord of Brittas invited, in 1608, three Dominican priests to celebrate a solemn Mass in his castle on Rosary Sunday.

Unfortunately, news of the celebration of this Mass reached the Lord President of Munster who sent soldiers to surround the castle. The priests and Lord Brittas took refuge in the tower of the castle, managing to escape after a while and wander in the woods. Intending to set sail for the continent Lord Brittas was hiding in a house in Carrick-on-Suir when he was betrayed. He was captured, tried and condemned to death. Before his execution, he asked his wife that their unborn child be dedicated to Saint Dominic. In the spring of 1609, Leonor de Burgo was born and was brought up under the influence of the friars of the Rosary.

On the death of her brother who had been educated in Castile, Leonor became heiress to the house of Brittas and pressure was put on her to renounce her intention of following the Dominican way of life and consent to marry one of her many noble suitors. She refused and was relegated by her family to a house in Limerick city where she had neither light nor a bed to lie on.[28] Here, tradition tells us, Dominic O'Daly met her and told her about the Bom Sucesso project. He approved of her intention and that of her cousin, Ursula de Burgo, to join the Dominican Order and before leaving for Castile, he put them under the direction of the Irish Dominican provincial. The two girls then went to live in the house of a lay Dominican where they could lead a religious life in secret.

Here, they remained for about two years until, in 1640, they set out for Lisbon and entered Bom Sucesso where 'Sor Catharina began to breathe freely as in the centre of her spirit.' [29]

In Bom Sucesso, Leonor de Burgo advanced rapidly in the spiritual life, practising rigorous penances and praying constantly. To her sisters in the community she seemed to live continuously in the presence of God. Moved by this some religious asked her what her method of prayer was. She replied that she knew nothing about methods of prayer but she prayed the Rosary and that for a long life one mystery was enough to contemplate. 'Thus, profound was the contemplation she experienced.'[30]

In 1651, Leonor de Burgo fell gravely ill and a sister seeing her suffer so much suggested that she ask for relief from Our Lady of the Incarnation to whom she had great devotion and whose feast-day would be celebrated within three days. Sister Catharina replied, 'Great will be my misfortune if, on the feast of the Incarnation, I shall not be with my Lord.'[31]

She asked for and received the sacraments and a few hours before her death, she requested that a handkerchief be dipped in perfume and given to her. With this she washed her face and hands. The prioress joked her about this, 'What a good religious of Bom Sucesso with a perfumed handkerchief.' To this Leonor replied: 'Indeed, Mother, if worldly people use perfume for the world, what wrong do I do to wish to go perfumed to my Spouse?'[32] She continued soliloquising with Christ and Our Lady of the Rosary and, as her voice began to tire, Leonor said goodbye to all her sisters with great joy as one who was on her way to Paradise. She died as she had predicted on the 25th March, 1651, the feast of the Incarnation. She was buried in the Choir but six months later when her coffin was being transferred to the Chapter room, it was partly opened and emitted the perfume of flowers. Her body also was as flexible as if she were alive.[33]

This account of the life of one of the early members of the Bom Sucesso community illustrates another aspect of the spirituality of the sisters – the extraordinary devotion to Our Lady principally as Mother of God and Lady of the Rosary.

MILAGRISMO

One of the characteristics of seventeenth century literature in Portugal was what is known as *Milagrismo* – a method of explaining every event as having a divine origin or inspiration. Numerous monastic chronicles of this particular century contain endless accounts of unusual occurrences interpreted always as divine interventions. Not only was this common in the chronicles of religious houses but it is to be found in secular writing also.

It is important to remember this as we read the accounts of the early members of Bom Sucesso and the so-called miracles attributed to them. The date of publication of the Dominican chronicle by Frei Luís de Sousa is 1678, a date which is quite close to the date of the Convent's foundation. It contains accounts of events which were often interpreted as miraculous by the sisters who witnessed them.

However, these miracles or answers to prayer are useful for another reason in that they throw light on the way of life of these sisters and the society in which they lived. Wheat had to be unloaded from ships and flour milled in the Bom Sucesso windmills. Landed property had to be cultivated or rented out and revenues collected. A strict discipline of private prayer as well as liturgical ceremonies had to be maintained. The actual work was not done by these noble ladies but the different enterprises required a staff of skilled workers while the ultimate responsibility lay with the prioress and community. Several legal documents in the Bom Sucesso archives testify to the difficulties these sisters had, over the centuries, with tenants neglecting their obligations or a government trying to confiscate their property. Very often, these difficulties were solved through prayer.

The life-story of Luíza Maria do Sacramento is one example of a miraculous interpretation of every event in her life beginning with her birth. She was the third child of D. Ruy de Mello de Sampaio and Dona Maria de Azevedo. Her mother had suffered much in giving birth to her older children but had little difficulty at Luíza's birth – attributed, not to the fact of its being the third birth, but to divine intervention. At an early age, she had a vision of heaven where two of her siblings already deceased invited her to join them. The vision ended before she had time to respond to them.

While still young she began to practise severe penance and, probably at the death of her father, retired with her two sisters to the monastery of the Comendadeiras de Santiago in Santos. There, she spent whole nights in prayer and, when overcome by sleep, she rested her head on her bed for a few hours. When she entered Bom Sucesso, her penance was such that the prioress obliged her to restrain it.

Maria Luíza was always anxious that the convent of Bom Sucesso would advance in monastic observance. One night, at prayer beside the tomb of Madre Antónia Theresa, she asked her to plead for the community and raising her eyes to the shrine of Our Lady of Bom Sucesso, she clearly saw the former prioress at prayer.

On the eve of the Feast of the Annunciation, 1651, Luíza came out from Matins, suffering from a fatal fever but, as Catherina do Rosário was dying, she went to assist her. On the following day, she received Holy Communion and spent the whole day in prayer in the choir. She was then obliged to go to bed. Frei Diogo Artur, vicar of the community had come into the convent because of Catherina and seeing Luíza lying on her bed of two planks he turned to her sister, Marianna and said, 'What account will I give to God, I who have the same obligation as this servant of God.' On leaving Luíza's cell he said to the prioress, 'I very much fear that, on the Day of Judgment, you will be our judges.'[34] Luíza died shortly afterwards.

Marianna de Mello, Luíza's older sister whose father D. Rui de Mello de Sampaio had wished her to marry also entered the monastery of Bom Sucesso. Already practising exercises of piety she willingly embraced the austerities of the Dominican Order. She had outstanding devotion to the Blessed Sacrament and brought a beautiful monstrance with other valuables to adorn the altar. She lived many years after her sister's death but, in 1668, she had an accident and when the prioress told her that the doctor had said she should receive Viaticum, she gave thanks to God. She died on 4th May of that year.

Two examples which might be considered typical of *milagrismo* are given in the life-story of Brigid of Saint Patrick, an Irishwoman. According to those who knew her, she was gifted with extraordinary sincerity and frankness. Her life was a continuous prayer and her penance, like that of her sisters, was severe. In honour of Saint Rose of Lima to whom she had great devotion she wore a crown of thorns under her veil. She worked in the kitchen and when the food was scarce, she blessed it in the name of Saint Patrick and consequently, there was more than enough for everyone. She also had the gift of prophecy and when asked how she knew of events before they happened she replied that she had dreamt about them.

Once, a fire broke out in the cloister and was threatening to engulf the monastery when Sister Brigid of Saint Patrick earnestly turned to prayer. A great bird of unknown species flew in and flapping its large white wings extinguished the flames. On another occasion, when she was very ill she lost her appetite but told one of the sisters that she would like some partridge. Her companion said that if she could obtain one, she would buy it for her. However, Brigid replied that God would provide it if it were God's Will that she should recover. On the other sister's going out to one of the kitchen-gardens of the monastery, a partridge fell at her feet. She stewed it and brought it to Brigid who thanked God for the miracle and having eaten some partridge began to recover. 'Wonder of wonders! Still attested today by the companion to whom it happened.'[32]

A similar type of miracle explains why, even to this day, a statue of Saint Anthony stands at every fountain or tap in the cloister. One day, it was discovered that there was no water in the tanks and in such a large estate as the convent possessed this was a serious matter. When there was no hope of obtaining water by ordinary means, the prioress turned to Saint Anthony and, putting his statue outside on a window sill, she told him that it would have to stay there until the tanks were full of water. The following morning, there was a plentiful supply of water throughout the estate.

Exaggeration and superstition apart, one cannot but admire the simple, deep faith which inspired awareness of God's presence and care in the ordinary needs of daily life. The eighteenth century had yet to dawn when rationalism would prevail over faith and the scientific revolution would lead to the exploitation of the earth. We are recovering something of the earlier centuries' appreciation of the organic universe and, hopefully, we will attain also a deep and informed faith.

5

Other Ministries

While the principal ministry of the Bom Sucesso community, in the early centuries, was prayer, they also served the Church in a number of other ways.

Pupils in the early Years

In the seventeenth century, it was customary for young women, prior to their marriage, to spend some time in a convent where individual tuition, mainly on Christian values, was given by the nuns. An oral tradition in the convent holds that the Bom Sucesso community engaged in this ministry also but there is no written record of the number or names of those who availed of this facility. Very often they were younger relatives of the sisters and, in Bom Sucesso's case also, Irish girls whose parents had settled in Portugal.

John Baptist Sleyne

In 1703, the community was called upon to give hospitality to one of the most prominent Irish bishops who had arrived, penniless, in Lisbon. His name was John Baptist Sleyne, bishop of Cork, Cloyne and administrator of Ross. He had been deported from Ireland where he had already spent some years in prison because of his defiance of the Bishops' Banishment Act of 1697.

The biography of this Irishman is fairly typical of the kind of life led by so many priests and bishops of Ireland during the penal days. He was born in Cloyne in 1639 but we do not know where his early education took place. As a young man, John Baptist Sleyne went to study at the Sorbonne in Paris where he was to have a distinguished academic career. At the age of twenty-two he obtained his Master's degree and, at the early age of twenty-four, he was ordained priest by special privilege of Apostolic Indult because of his youth.[1] After ordination he continued at the Sorbonne and, in 1670, was awarded the doctorate in theology. He returned to Ireland where he served in the diocese of Cloyne .

In 1679, Dr. Sleyne went to Rome where he was appointed professor of Moral Theology at the College of Propaganda Fide. He was to spend fourteen years there, lecturing and acting as agent for Bishop Creagh of Cork and Cloyne. Through this work in particular, he remained in touch with the Church in Ireland. In 1692, on the transfer of Dr. Creagh to the Dublin diocese, Dr. Sleyne was appointed Bishop of Cork and Cloyne. He was ordained bishop In Saint Isidore's, Rome on 18th April 1693 by Russano, Cardinal Forbin Janson/Giansone and, one month later, he left Rome on the difficult journey to Ireland.

A letter of Bishop Sleyne's in the archives of the Sacred Congregation of Propaganda Fide and dated 5th March 1694 contains the information that he had arrived in his diocese the previous month. He had already begun his Episcopal ministry for which he now requested that he be given the administration of Ross also. This had been intended by the Sacred Congregation and consequently, its secretary, Monsignor Cybo was requested to obtain this concession as soon as possible.[2]

However, the Ireland to which the bishop had returned was in a worse state than the country he had left in 1676. In the meantime, the island had become the battleground for two kings fighting for the throne of England. Many Irish had been killed and many more who had fought for the Jacobite cause had gone to France to continue to fight in the Irish Brigade. Writing to Rome, the newly ordained bishop of Cork and Cloyne describes Ireland as 'this deplorable country' and appeals for a prompt remedy for this poor, desolate people.[3] In his cry for help one can still sense the anguish of this dedicated man at the sad state not only of the Catholic Church in Ireland but also at the impoverishment of Irish Catholics.

AN ENTHUSIAST FOR GAELIC CULTURE

Dr. Sleyne was not only a pastor anxious to reorganise the dioceses under his jurisdiction but he was also a man of learning and an enthusiast for Gaelic language and culture. 'In the grim aftermath of the Boyne disaster, this Bishop of Cork and Cloyne was the first Munster prelate of note to personally promote the Irish language and culture.'[4] Not far from Carrigtwohill, Carrignavar had its *Cúirt Eigse* (literary circle) which kept a love of Gaelic literature alive. The bishop generously provided copies of manuscripts, among them, Seathrún Céitinn's *Eochairsciath an Aifrinn,* and *Foras Feasa ar Éirinn* and he lent many of his own books to those interested in Gaelic culture.

REORGANISATION OF THE CHURCH IN IRELAND

The work, however, to which Dr. Sleyne devoted the greatest possible energy was the reorganisation of the Church in Ireland, particularly, the restoration of the hierarchy through the ordination of bishops. He consecrated Maurice Donnellan for Clonfert in 1695, William Daton for Ossory and Richard Piers for Waterford in 1696 and in 1697, Patrick O'Donnelly for Dromore, Michael Rossiter for Ferns and Edward Comerford for Cashel.[5] He also ordained priests for many dioceses in the country but his own diocese of Cork was served, at this time, by priests ordained in France. Between 1693 and the year of his death in Lisbon in1712, the number of ordinations for which he was responsible was thirty-eight.

THE BISHOPS' BANISHMENT ACT

Unfortunately for the Catholic Church, the Bishops' Banishment Act of 1697 considerably curtailed Dr. Sleyne's work of restoration of the hierarchy in Ireland. Two of the bishops he had consecrated about two years before, William Daton of Ossory and Richard Piers of Waterford, went into exile in 1698. That year, because he did not obey the Act of Banishment, John Baptist Sleyne was arrested and imprisoned in the South Gate Gaol of Cork city. A letter in the Vatican archives describes his imprisonment as being *con gran stretteza* [6] Nevertheless, he was able to say Mass and to fulfil his Episcopal duties by ordaining priests. He also had contact with his literary friends one of whom composed a eulogy of the bishop, thanking him for reviving the spirit of poetry.[7]

On 27th July, 1702, Dr. Sleyne and Peter Morrough, his vicar-general, were arraigned for exercising their ecclesiastical functions in contravention of the Act of 1697 and on 8th August, Joshua Dawson, Secretary of State at Dublin Castle sent to the mayor of Cork a warrant for the transportation to Portugal of the titular bishop of Cork. However, this deportation order was not carried out and in October of that year, Bishop Sleyne wrote an appeal to Count Wratislaw, Imperial ambassador in London.

He feared that he would be sent to a remote English colony because he states, 'it is decreed that after so long imprisonment and hardships your petitioner shall be banished to some islands he knows not in this rigorous winter season and in the time of war.'[8]

DR. SLEYNE'S APPEAL AGAINST DEPORTATION

Dr. Sleyne appealed to the Austrian ambassador in London because Queen Anne might not have been aware of this harsh sentence of deportation imposed on him and he wished the ambassador to represent this issue on his behalf to her majesty. 'If your excellency, out of your tender regard to God's cause and the Church, should interpose with her majesty in this thing and oppose this cruel sentence, it is in the power of her majesty and her lieutenant to prefer the petitioner to spend the few days he has yet remaining in his native country, either in or out of prison.'[9]

The bishop's anxiety about being transported to an unknown island was well founded because, exactly fifty years before, the most severe ethnic cleansing of Ireland had taken place under Oliver Cromwell. On 24th August 1652, 'There was put into operation the most thorough and ruthless transfer of the Irish people to overseas colonies ever undertaken by any English leader.'[10] The proclamation issued on that day gave power to the English commissioners in Ireland to seize and transport anyone of whatever rank considered dangerous to the Commonwealth. Where the Catholic clergy were concerned, Cromwell was ruthless. During his campaign in Ireland, many priests were killed and many more were transported across the Atlantic to work on the sugar plantations of the Caribbean. It was awareness of the hardships endured on these plantations that caused Bishop Sleyne to write to the Austrian ambassador in London.

This petition seems only to have precipitated the deportation of the bishop because, when the Lords justices read the Queen's order in Dublin, Secretary Dawson wrote to the mayor of Cork complaining that on the previous 8th August he had sent an order to the then mayor and sheriffs of Cork 'to cause the said titular bishop to be putt on board the first ship that should be bound from Corke to Portugall…but no account having ever been sent up of the execution of that order, or any reasons been given why the said bishop was not transported, their Excellencies have commanded me to write up to you for an account of that matter.'[11]

The mayor's reply is rather amusing in the explanation he gives and it indicates that there was considerable reluctance on the part of those involved to comply with the order of deportation. Alderman Dring, the former mayor, 'had received the orders referred to but could find no ship going to Portugal.' Mayor Whiting confessed that he had met with the same difficulty because, 'though he had agreed with several ships to take Dr. Sleyne all pretended to be 'forced to sea unawares' so that the bishop is in 'as bad a condition to be transported as formerly.'[12]

On 30th January, 1793, Lord Rochester, Lord Lieutenant of Ireland wrote to the Lords of Council in Dublin, stating that he had presented the situation of the bishop to the Queen at the Cabinet Council and received her majesty's command 'that your own order of the 8th August last…be put in execution.' He added that 'some particular directions must be given to the mayor of Corke to be more diligent in observing your orders, for that by his own account to Mr. Dawson, it was taken notice of her, his reasons were very slender for not having done as he was directed.'[12]

Deportation to Lisbon

Some time towards the end of February, 1703, the deportation of the bishop took place and Dr. Sleyne himself wrote, on 27th March of that year, to Cardinal Giansone (Janson), Prefect of Propaganda Fide, giving an account of his deportation and arrival in Lisbon. This letter explains to the Cardinal who had ordained him bishop his reasons for remaining in Ireland in spite of the Act of Banishment, 'I resolved then to abandon myself wholly to Providence and to continue as best I could my Episcopal functions and after a success greater than I dared promise myself God permitted at last that I should be imprisoned in my Episcopal city and I remained in this state for five years, most of the time confined to bed.'[13] He describes the harshness with which a troupe of soldiers carried out the deportation without regard for his age or ill-health.

On arrival in Lisbon, however, there was some consolation because he was visited by the French ambassador 'who, as a worthy minister of so great and pious a monarch came to offer me his residence and all that was within his power.'[14] However, the Irish Dominicans in Lisbon assumed responsibility for him and the Bom Sucesso community generously gave him hospitality in their chaplain's house on the grounds of the convent. A few days later, he was received in audience by the king of Portugal and his aunt, Queen Catherine of Bragança, widow of King Charles II of England. They were 'extremely moved by the state in which they saw me and by the account I gave them of the situation in which the Catholic religion in Ireland is at present, so contrary to what the agents of England at this court try to tell them.' [15]

AN IRISH BISHOP IN EXILE

Even in exile John Baptist Sleyne was working for the Faith in Ireland because he now asks the Cardinal if he would obtain the fullest powers possible for marriage dispensations needed by the bishops still in Ireland. If his Eminence sends these to him in Lisbon, he will be able to forward them perfectly safely to the bishops. Finally, he asks for some financial assistance for himself from Propaganda Fide, reminding the Cardinal of the fourteen years he spent teaching Moral Theology there and he is confidant that they will not forget him in his present need.[16] He was not forgotten because, on 11th June, 1703, Propaganda sent him financial help through the Nuncio in Lisbon.[17]

For the remainder of his life, (1703-1712), Dr. Sleyne lived in the chaplain's house on the grounds of Bom Sucesso. The annals of the convent record, 'The community gave him a warm welcome and placed at his disposal some rooms in the chaplain's house in the patio. His Lordship resided there for nine years in the company of the Irish Dominican chaplain and a Portuguese priest, Padre Mateus Gomes.'[18] The annals also record that in 1709 'His Holiness, Pope Clement XI sent a letter to the king of Portugal, D. João V, recommending Dr. Sleyne and Fr. Anthony O'Carroll to his majesty as deserving all the aid that could possibly be given them.'[19] The financial aid both from the Church and civil authorities seems to have been considerable because 'His Lordship, having received substantial aid, helped the nuns to defray the expenses of the Capella of Saint Patrick in return for their hospitality.'[20] This capella or altar was only completed about 1703, the year of the bishop's arrival in Lisbon. Likewise, Padre Mateus had the capella of Saint Gonçalo decorated and he is buried at this altar.

RESIGNATION AND DEATH

Dr. Sleyne continued as Bishop of Cork and Cloyne and Administrator of Ross for a number of years but on the 4th December,1707, he appointed Dr. Donatus McCarthy his vicar-general for Cork and Cloyne and Dr. John Kenneally vicar-general of Ross. On 22nd January 1712, he signed a petition to have Donatus Mc Carthy his coadjutor with the right of succession. On the same day, he resigned his See of Cork and Cloyne and his administration of Ross.[21]

Dr. Sleyne died at Bom Sucesso on 16th February, 1712, and his funeral ceremony was carried out with great solemnity by the Irish Dominicans. He is buried in the Church of Nossa Senhora do Bom Sucesso at the altar which he financially helped to decorate. Originally the capella of Saint Patrick, this altar was re-dedicated to the Sacred Heart in 1897, past pupils having presented the statue.[22] It is a beautiful and peaceful resting place for one who had lived and zealously worked for the Faith during most turbulent times in his country. It is also an historical monument to his memory.

THE CONFRATERNITY OF THE HOLY ROSARY

In 1704, the community allowed their Church to be a centre of further devotional activity in honour of Our Lady of the Rosary. The Confraternity of the Most Holy Rosary, principally for the laity, was founded there on the 20th July, 1704. The opening paragraph of its Constitutions indicates that the Confraternity was in conformity with the Dominican Order's regulations for such an association. 'In the name of the Father, Son and Holy Spirit. These are the constitutions that I, Frei António Serqueyra, religious of the Order of Preachers, lay down in this Church and monastery of Bom Sucesso, having founded the Confraternity of the Most Holy Rosary in virtue of a patent of the Most Reverend Father António Cloche, Master General of the Order, which begins, *Quemadmodum Christianae Perfectionis*, drawn up on the 4th August, 1697, I having been nominated for this (purpose) by the Reverend Prior Provincial, the Master, Frei João Baptista de Marinis. 20th July, 1704.' [23]

The first section of these Constitutions shows the democratic nature of the confraternity because 'in the first place, we ordain that persons of whatever state and condition may enter this confraternity by having their name inscribed in this book without being obliged to pay anything.' [24]

Membership required that those enrolled in the confraternity would recite, each week, one rosary of fifteen decades – an entire rosary on one day or five decades on three days. Thus, they would obtain the indulgences granted for membership and would share in the prayers and works of the Order of Preachers. However, if they omitted the saying of the rosary they would not sin but would not enjoy the privileges of membership. Every first Sunday of the month, a candlelight procession was held around the church and those taking part had a rosary beads in their hands.

On the first Sunday of October, the principal feast of Our Lady of the Rosary was observed with the greatest possible solemnity – sung Mass, preaching, exposition of the Blessed Sacrament and finally a procession. Another important celebration took place on the first Sunday of May or June, depending on whether there was an abundant supply of roses, because, on this day, the blessing of roses took place. These blessed roses were then distributed to members of the confraternity and to 'other Catholics who would use them in their infirmities and keep them as precious relics because by means of them, this Lady has worked many singular wonders.' [25]

In order that these feasts and the service of Our Lady might be maintained throughout the year, elections of a judge, secretary, treasurer, procurator and administrator took place on the evening of Rosary Sunday or any more convenient day.[26] However, in spite of this careful organisation, 'after a short while it languished whether for want of fervour or funds or both the chronicle does not record.' [27]

Some years later, it was re-established due to the indefatigable efforts of a layman who had great devotion to Our Lady of the Rosary and he succeeded in enrolling many members. The king himself, D. João V, became *juíz perpétuo* and contributed annually a sum of money. Because of the king's membership, it could now have the title, *Real Irmandade* (Royal Confraternity). Other members of the royal family were enrolled and the community allowed the monthly meetings to take place in the chaplain's house. A plot of ground was also given for the burial of poor members.[28]

In 1726, the prioress, Mother Antónia, daughter of the Count of Atalaya, became the first member of the community to be enrolled in the confraternity. In the following year twenty-four sisters became members. Their other involvement was their prayer, in particular, their solemn chanting, every November, of the Office of the Dead for the deceased members of the confraternity. For this they received a donation of two *escudos*. This annual solemn chanting of the Office of the Dead was maintained until 1750 when the members decided instead to have forty Masses for the dead said during the year. [29]

In 1729, the council of the confraternity requested more land for the burial of its poorer members. This was granted on condition that it would not inconvenience the resident chaplain[30]. During the remainder of the eighteenth century, the members continued to maintain a high standard and to celebrate 'with great pomp and solemnity all the feasts throughout the year.' [31] The names of some of the directors in the latter part of the century are recorded in the annals: Fr. Dominic Mc Donnell followed in 1766 by Fr. Martin Horan until his death in 1777 when Fr. James Bradley succeeded him. Free burial was given to poor members and vaults for this purpose which were situated outside the sacristy continued to be used until 1865.[32]

THE CONFRATERNITY OF SAINT ANNE

Early in the eighteenth century also, a request was made to the community for permission to found another confraternity in the church. This was the Confraternity of Saint Anne which was formally established there in 1734. This confraternity had membership mainly from the nobility, among others, descendants of the Countess of Atalaia. They were enrolled as 'slaves of Saint Anne' and the altar of Saint Brigid in the Church became that of Saint Anne. Today, on this altar, the realistic statue of Saint Anne teaching her daughter, Mary, is a memorial to the members of this confraternity which flourished until 1875.[33]

6

Portugal in the Eighteenth Century

By the early decades of the eighteenth century the main buildings of the monastery as we know it today were complete and the community could more peacefully live out their commitment in an atmosphere conducive to prayer and contemplation. José Dias Sanches describing the cloister states, 'This lovely cloister unknown to many people, where the sun's rays timidly rest but smile during summer, is among the most beautiful corners of my country where one would wish to spend the rest of one's life.'[1] Corresponding with this peaceful state of religious life is the prosperity of its adopted country.

In the last decade of the seventeenth century, gold in large quantities was discovered in Brazil and when Pedro II's son ascended the throne of Portugal, in 1706, as João V, he began a reign which coincided with the acquisition of this new found wealth. In 1699, the first consignment of this precious commodity arrived in Lisbon inaugurating literally a golden age for Portugal.

Royal palaces and residences for noble families were built and churches were lavishly adorned. Trade increased and the gold of Brazil contributed to the development of the trade not only of Portugal but that of Europe in general. Art and architecture flourished in Portugal as it had done when the Indian spices were brought to Lisbon during the reign of Manuel I. A cultured elite created interest in learning and founded libraries. Unfortunately, there was little advancement of education or even literacy for the whole population.

Through this wealth the king could afford to be generous as he was to Bishop Sleyne and Fr Anthony O'Carroll. He earned the title, *The Magnificent* and aimed at having a Court similar to that of France's Louis XIV. Where relationship with the Holy See was concerned, he obtained certain privileges, such as the title of Patriarch for the Archbishop of Lisbon and, in 1747, the title of *Rei Fidelíssimo* for himself and his successors.

Iria de Brito, Countess of Atalaya portrayed as Our Lady of Sorrows.

Coat of Arms of Brito family (left), and Foundress's Coat of Arms over main door of convent.

Jeronimos Monastery – engraving 17th century.

Mother Teresa
Staunton

Mother Brigid
Staunton; oil painting
by Marianna Russell
Kennedy aged 13 in
1843 (page 125)

Prioress and Community –1880s?

Novices 1927. Back row: Srs Alphonsus Davis, Hyacinth White, Emmanuel Davis; front row: ?, Sr Rose Niall

First Communicants 1925

Group 1890s; profession of Sr Raymond Farrelly with Sr Alberta, left, and Sr Columba. Sr Pius Carroll, prioress, is standing directly behind Sr Alberta

King Edward VII of England leaving Bom Sucesso, 1903

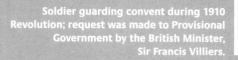

Soldier guarding convent during 1910 Revolution; request was made to Provisional Government by the British Minister, Sir Francis Villiers.

Treslado do Auto da posse q. se tomou do Casal da Golegã
por esse Conv.to de N.S.ra do Bom Successo em o d.o
Mes de Julho de 1642

1642

Saibão quantos este publico Istrumento de posse dado, e pa-
sado em publica forma por mandado, cautond.e de justiça
virem q. no Anno do Nascim.to de nosso S.or Jesu Cristo de
mil e Seis Sentos e Corenta e dous Annos, aos dezanove dias
do mes de Julho do ditto Anno nesta Villa da Golegã nas
Cazas da morada de mim Tabaliam, pareceo D.or fran.co Castano Proc.dor q. dise ser das freyras do bom Successo da Cid.e
de Lx.a de Bellem, e por elle me foi aprezentado Sua Carta
executoria de posse, pasada em nome de Sua Mag.de e asina-
da pello D.or Diogo Lobo P.to Corregedor da Corte do Cível, e
C. ella me aprezentou Sua Procurada das D.tas Religioza, e
querendome C. a dita Carta desse dar posse do Casal da baralha C. suas terras, e olival e Ademas pertencente ao dito Cazal q. foi da Condessa da Mallaya Donna Iria de Brito, e
querendome Sua posse tras dar a dita posse, e logo en Tabalião
C. Andre Pinto Alcayde Somos a barulha aonde esta o dit
Cazal q. des Clara Brancha, e outra Sim C. o dito Proc.dor Der
fran.co Castano, entramos nas terras do dito Cazal, e elle deme
posse delle dandolhe terra, eramos das Oliveiras, e tudo pello
dito Alcayde lhe foi dado na Sua mão, andando pello dito
Cazal e terras delle de Sua parte parte p.a aquila apegando
C. Seos pés, e da Ley Somos as Ademas outro Sim termos desta
Villa aonde estão huns dattos de terra q. Clamos as Ademas C.
mais Sua Courela de terra de doze estis de Largo, ou os na
Cerg.a Sor, entramos nellas nas ditas terras, e tal os q. se Clama as
Ademas e o d.o Alcayde lhe dau terra na mão delle Proc.or e andou
pellas d.as terras, e Ademas elle Proc.dor de Sua parte p.a aquela,
apegando tudo C. Seos pés, e C.o estas Solemnid.os e mais q. o di-
reito em tas Casos Concede, e outorga a posse C. o d.o Alcayde ao
dito Proc.or D.er fran.co Castano do dito Cazal C. Sen Olival e
Ademas e envisto na d.a posse dandolhe de tudo posse Real, actual

Document (above) dated 14 May 1823. Decree of suppression of the monastery of Bom Sucesso and the command to the prioress and community to transfer to the convent of Rei Salvador, Lisbon. (page 117)

Document stating that the king, D. Manuel II accepted to be Judge in Perpetuity of the Royal Confraternity of the Holy Rosary like his predecessors.

Letter dated 1916, written by Pere Hyacinthe Cormier, former Master of the Dominican Order. He was beatified by Pope John Paul II in 1995. (page 158/9, 169).

High altar and details of Tabernacle

SONG OF SONGS (12 panels) – See Chapter 4: The Spirituality of the Community, page 67

Fons hortorum (page 69)

Sic dilectus mihi ... (page 70)

Veni Sponsa mea ... (page 71)

Fructus eius dulcis ... (Page71)

Prospiciens per cancellos ... (Page 72)

Ne suscite ... (Page 73)

Acervus tritici (Page 74)

Fulcite me floribus (Page 74)

Pasce hodos tuos (Page 75)

Pascitur
inter lilia
(Page 75)

E nobis
vulpes
parvuli
(Page 76)

Sub capite
meo ...
(Page 77)

Community Mass: Srs Bernadette Pakenham, Michael Forde, Martinez Murphy, Nuala McKinstry, Colm McCool; front row: Srs Teresa Faherty, Alicia Mooney.

Mass at high altar: Fr Gus Champion with Srs Colm McCool, left, and Nuala McKinstry.

With Lay Dominicans in Chapel.

Altar of Our Lady of Bom Sucesso

Our Lady of Bom Sucesso

Church ceiling

Our Lady's altar

Our Lady's altar with with paintings
of Dominican saints above.

Cristo dos Passos

Our Lady of Sorrows

Presépio/Crib

Flight into Egypt (page 77)

St Joseph's altar with Dominican saints above

Visitation (page 77)

THE IRISH COMMUNITY IN LISBON

By the eighteenth century the Irish community was well established in Lisbon and continued its tradition of military service to its adopted country. In 1712, when, before the peace of Utrecht had been signed in the war of the Spanish Succession, Spain invaded Portugal, Brigadier General Hogan defended Portugal so that the Spanish army was obliged to retreat. He became influential at the court and he as well as his brother John married women connected with the Bragança family. [2]

Denis Hogan, came to Portugal in 1724 and was appointed cavalry officer because of his uncle John's service.[3] He was obliged to appear before the Inquisition as he had become a member of the Irish Masonic Lodge in Lisbon. Usually, the Irish in Spain and Portugal had nothing to fear from the Inquisition because they were regarded as persecuted Catholics. However, when news reached Portugal that Pope Clement XII had issued a Bull condemning Freemasonry, Catholic members of a Masonic lodge were under suspicion.

According to the testimony given by Hugo O'Kelly to the Inquisition, the Irish lodge of Lisbon was founded there at the end of 1733 or the beginning of 1734. Its title was *Casa Real dos Pedreiros Livres da Lusitania*. It was not attached to the Grand Lodge of London and numbered among its members mostly Irish Roman Catholics resident in Lisbon.

THE IRISH MASONIC LODGE

In a well documented work, *História da Maçonaria em Portugal,* Vol.I, the names of twenty-four members of the Irish Lodge are given. Of these, fourteen are described as Roman Catholic and Irish and one as Irish and Protestant. The list is of interest in giving information about the Irish then living in Lisbon:

Patrick Brown, aged forty, from Waterford, a ship's captain
Charles Carroll, aged fifty, from Leinster, a businessman
James Dillon, Dominican, resident in Corpo Santo
Thomas French, aged fifty-four, from Galway, businessman
Denis Hogan, aged thirty, from Tipperary, cavalry officer
William Kelly...............................ship's captain
Patrick Kennedy, Dominican, resident in Corpo Santo
Joseph Lynham, Dominican, ship's chaplain
William Noonan.............................doctor
Hugh O'Kelly, aged fifty-five, infantry officer

> James Thomas O'Kelly, aged fifty-two, from Dublin dance master
>   & attendant to the Infante D. António
> Michael O'Kelly, aged thirty-four, from Dublin
> James Smith, Irish Protestant, dance master
> ....Smith, Catholic, doctor
> James Tobin, Catholic, ship's captain

Of the remainder, three are described as Catholic but their nationality is not given – Charles Carti, John Jelly and James Naccart, Two Protestants from Scotland, three English Protestants and one Hungarian Catholic complete the membership.[4] Once it became known that the Pope had condemned Freemasonry, the Irish lodge was closed. However, Irish influence, particularly in the army, continued and this is also reflected in the number of Irish women born on mainland Europe who entered in Bom Sucesso at this time.

THE BOM SUCESSO COMMUNITY AND THE ORDER OF PREACHERS

Two aspects of the Bom Sucesso community which characterize it particularly during the eighteenth century are its relationship with the Order of Preachers and its connection with members of the royal families of Europe.

Where jurisdiction is concerned the community was directly under the Master of the Dominican Order and consequently, ordinations dealing with the government of the convent in spiritual matters were often issued from General Chapters of the Order. In 1706, at the General Chapter held in Bologna, the Master of the Order issued three decrees dealing with the vicar of the monastery, the confessors and the number of religious in the community:

> 'We ordain as it was ordained by the Most Rev. Marinis and confirmed by His Holiness Pope Alexander VII that the rector of the Lisbon College and the vicar of the Monastery of Nuns of Bom Sucesso of the same city of the aforesaid province be always Irish Religious.
>
> We ordain as it was often ordained for the Order, that the Confessors of the said monastery be not continued beyond two years, without the special permission of the General of the Order and that they be always Irish Religious, taken from the more mature, and from those well versed in the Irish, English and Portuguese languages.
>
> We declare that the number forty regulated by the Most Rev. de Marinis and confirmed by His Holiness Pope Innocent XI must be

understood as referring to the Irish nobles, including, however, the four places of the Foundress; and that the exceptional and extranumerary Portuguese who are received into the Monastery under the title of special dowry in no way be prejudicial to the said number of forty Irish.[5]

In regulating for the number of Irish sisters in the community in 1706 the General Chapter emphasises the reason why the convent was founded almost seventy years before – for Irish noblewomen who could not lead a cloistered life in their own country. It may be asked, then, why the confessor would need to be well versed in Portuguese. Apart from the small number of Portuguese sisters, some of the Irish were daughters of émigrés who had settled in Portugal and, consequently, would have Portuguese, at least, as their second language. Again, in 1725, the General Chapter of the Dominican Order legislated for Bom Sucesso when it decreed once again that 'the monastery be subject to the Irish province.' [6]

Between 1740 and 1745, five novices were professed. Their families were all Irish but lived in Lisbon and their mistress of novices, Mother Iria Victória Tuomy, was Irish but born in France.[7] One of the novices, Magdalena Van Zeller, of Irish-Belgian descent, who lived in Lisbon brought a considerable dowry to the convent. In his *Hibernia Dominicana* de Burgo states, 'Sister Magdalena Van Zellar helped the monastery which was heavily in debt by a very ample dowry; that is on entering the Order she gave £625 sterling and on her profession day (1740) another £625. She arranged, moreover, that the monastery should receive another £625 on the day of her death; she received the interest on this annually but used it rather for Divine Worship than for the support of herself.' [8]

Of course, the papal nuncio also could and did exercise his jurisdiction as when, in 1715, the then papal nuncio, Vicentius Bichius, permitted a married woman whose husband also wished to enter the religious state to become a member of the Bom Sucesso community as a tertiary sister. In granting Antónia Frances Balthasar dos Reis dispensation to enter Bom Sucesso he stated, 'We dispense and grant these favours , notwithstanding the Constitutions, Statutes and customs of this Monastery or the Order or anything else to the contrary.' [9]

SUCESSO COMMUNITY'S LINKS WITH ROYALTY

From its foundation the Bom Sucesso convent had close links with royalty. It was virtually a *convento real* though not founded or originally endowed by the Crown. In 1639, as already stated, the

Countess of Mantua, representative of the king of Spain in Portugal attended the opening ceremony. A year later, when the throne of Portugal was restored to the Portuguese people, the queen, Dona Luísa de Gusmão, who claimed descent from Saint Dominic's family, became a frequent visitor and often brought her daughter, Catherine of Bragança, the future wife of Charles II of England. On the death of her husband in 1656, Dona Luísa became regent and remained so because of her elder son's disability.

In 1662, Dona Luísa was overthrown in a *coup d'état* within the palace which was led by the Conde de Castelo Melhor. The government was given to her elder son D. Afonso VI. Later, due to the intervention of members of another political faction, this king was dethroned, imprisoned and replaced by his younger brother, D. Pedro II. Dona Luísa had wished to retire to Bom Sucesso where her friend, Madre Madalena de Cristo was prioress but she was afraid because of Bom Sucesso's nearness to the harbour bar.[10] This connection of the Bom Sucesso community with the Bragança dynasty continued down to the reign of the last king of Portugal.

Throughout its history, members of Europe's royalty and nobility visited Bom Sucesso. On 4th February, 1669, Cosimo de Medici, son of the Grand Duke of Tuscany, Fernando de Medici, on his visit to Portugal, was received by the community. Shortly afterwards, in 1670, he succeeded his father as Cosimo III.

In 1683, Queen Francisca Isabel, the French wife of D. Pedro II, the younger son of Queen Luísa de Gusmão, continued the royal tradition of visiting Bom Sucesso. Her first marriage to Dona Luísa's elder son had been annulled on the grounds of his impotency. As already stated, D.Afonso VI was deposed and D. Pedro II acted as regent until his brother's death in 1683.

In 1685, Charles II of England died and his wife, Catherine of Bragança, made arrangements to return to her native country. In order to accommodate her, the Count of Aveiro vacated his *Palácio* in Belém and went to live in the *Palácio do Correio Mor* adjoining the grounds of Bom Sucesso. The queen arrived in Portugal in 1693 and lived in different residences until the building of her own palace, *O Paço de Bemposta*, should be completed. Between 1700 and 1701, she lived in the *Palácio de Belém*, the first queen to occupy it.[11]

The queen's lady-in-waiting, the Countess of Fingal, accompanied her to Portugal. The annals record that this lady with her daughter visited Bom Sucesso in 1693 and again in 1700 when she came to say goodbye before leaving Portugal.

Meanwhile, in 1699, Queen Catherine visited the convent she had known as a child. When she died in 1705, she bequeathed 2000 *cruzadas* to the community.[12] Her nephew, D. João V was also a generous benefactor to the Irish clergy and religious. In 1709, when Fr Anthony O'Carroll was returning to Portugal from Rome, the then Pope, Clement XI sent a letter to the king recommending Dr. Sleyne and Fr O'Carroll as 'deserving all the aid that could be given them' and the king generously responded.[13]

In 1736, the queen of Spain, Dona Isabel Farnese accompanied by her daughter, the Infanta Marianna Victória, came to Mass in the Church of Bom Sucesso.[14] They were guests of the Portuguese royal family in Belém. The princess later married D. João V's son who ascended the throne of Portugal in 1750 as D. José.

In 1745, the Infante D. Manuel, the brother of D. João V, offered a magnificent crucifix to the Bom Sucesso community. 'By order of D. Manuel it was sculptured by Fr Lourenço Grimaldo Napolitano, procurator of the Franciscan convent in Lisbon.'[15] The Apostolic Nuncio, Monsignor Lucas Melchior Tempi, archbishop of Nicomedia, blessed the crucifix and officiated at its installation on the altar of the Holy Cross. This crucifix was later transferred to the recess above the baldachino in the sanctuary when the shrine of Our Lady of Bom Sucesso was moved to the former altar of the Holy Cross. The prioress at the time of the presentation of the crucifix was a member of the Atalaya family. The inscription on the back of the crucifix reads: *Offerecido pelo Infante D. Manuel por sua devoção, sendo Prioreza a Ex. Senhora Sor Maria Antónia. Ano de 1745.*[Devout gift of Prince D. Manuel, the prioress being Her Excellencey Sister Maria Antonia, 1745]

Another member of the Atalaya family was Cardinal Patriarch of Lisbon about this time. In 1752, Fr Thomas Milo de Burgo, regent of studies at the College of the Most Holy Rosary, Lisbon, wrote a book entitled *A Catechism, Moral and Controversial*. In presenting this book to the Patriarch, Joseph Manuel, Count of Atalaya, the author paid tribute to the piety of the Atalaya family 'which began and increased that celebrated sanctuary of religion and sincere piety, the *coenobium* of nuns commonly known as of Bom Sucesso founded by them and endowed in favour of the noble and poor ladies of Ireland who confided to the pious protection and safe keeping of the ancestors of your Eminence, left their native land to preserve the precious deposit of faith and to consecrate themselves to God.' [16]

THE EARTHQUAKE OF 1755

On a height overlooking the commercial centre of Lisbon today stand the ruins of the beautiful gothic Church of the Carmelites begun by D. Nuno Álvares Pereira in 1389.[17] It is the memorial to the tragic event which struck Lisbon in 1755. This was an earthquake of great seismic intensity and the worst natural disaster to occur in Europe since the Black Death of the fourteenth century. It took place on 1st November, 1755, at 9.45 a.m., just as the people were assembled in the churches to celebrate the feast of All Saints. It was felt in various regions of Portugal, especially in Algarve but the death toll in the capital was greatest. According to the historian J.H. Saraiva, 'The information of the period is contradictory and varies between 6,000 and 90,000 casualties; the more authoritative calculations fix the number at 12,000. No other event in the history of Portugal has had such widespread and sorrowful repercussions on Europe.'[18]

About 10,000 buildings were destroyed and these included the royal palace on the waterfront in the centre of Lisbon. Dating from the sixteenth century it had been enlarged and enriched during the reign of João V. The Opera House which had been opened a few months before was ruined. Among other palaces demolished were the palace of the Dukes of Bragança which contained treasures and records of the reigning dynasty and the palace of the Marquis of Louriçal which housed a famous collection of manuscripts and ancient books. The royal library containing seventy thousand volumes and important manuscripts as well as the libraries of the Dominicans and Franciscans were destroyed by the earthquake or by the resulting fires which could not be extinguished for several days. One exception to this mass destruction was the National Archive of the Torre do Tombo because its elderly director succeeded in having its contents rescued and taken to the safety of the precincts of the Castelo de São Jorge.[19]

The earthquake was accompanied by a tidal wave (*tsunami*) which swept over the buildings on the waterfront further adding to their destruction and the loss of life. Not only the royal palace on the waterfront in the city centre but the Irish Dominican College of the Holy Rosary and the Church of Corpo Santo adjacent to the palace were thus doubly affected by this tragic event. Six Irish Dominican priests lost their lives, among them Fr Thomas Milo de Burgo who was celebrating Mass in a private oratory when the earthquake occurred. According to the historian de Burgo, 'At the elevation of the Sacred Host, the earth trembled.... Not wishing to leave the Holy Sacrifice unfinished he remained, not even time to consecrate the chalice, the oratory walls fell, the celebrant was buried beneath the ruins.'[20] The Bom Sucesso annalist concludes her account with the observation, 'The remains of our founder, the great Fr Dominic O'Daly had a second burial, this time, not an honoured place in the Church he had built but beneath its ruins.'[21]

The community of Bom Sucesso was much more fortunate though the force of the earthquake was felt in the convent and the surrounding area of Belém. The heavy grille of the upper choir fell, badly damaging the floor beneath but two sisters who were near it at the time escaped injury. Similarly, the sister who was ringing the bell was unharmed when the belfry gave way.[22] There is a tradition in the convent that the two shrines of Christ carrying his cross and of Mary, Mother of Sorrows which stand opposite each other in the upper choir came together with the force of the tremor and then went back to their usual position. 'The community attributed their preservation from harm to the protection of Our Lady of Good Success.'[23]

The Brigittine community of English sisters was not as fortunate as that of Bom Sucesso. 'During three days, the nuns feeling it unsafe to remain in the convent all went down to the low garden, to be as far from the building as possible and stayed there night and day. One sister had the courage to enter the building and fetch all the eatables she could find.'[24] Included in this letter in the archives of their Devon convent is an appeal for help made by these sisters to friends in England following the earthquake. It reveals the desperate plight of the survivors in the aftermath of this disaster, 'we have neither house nor sanctuary left wherein to retire; nor even the necessaries of life; it being out of the power of our friends and benefactors here to relieve us, they having undergone the same misfortune and disaster; so that we see no other means of establishing ourselves here than by applying to the nobility, ladies and gentlemen of our dear country.'[25] Here again, the Bom Sucesso sisters were more fortunate because the king, D. José I, graciously donated sufficient money to cover the cost of repairing all the damage done to the choir and convent. By 1758, according to Padre João Baptista in his work, *Mappa de Portugal,* the repairs were already completed.

The royal family also had a miraculous escape. The king and queen with their daughters had spent the summer and the first months of autumn at their summer residence, the Palácio de Belém. On November 1st they were still in residence there because the weather had been excessively mild and the temperature, unusually high for that time of year. 'On that day, the activity in the palace was normal; nothing would lead one to foresee what would follow. Shortly after 9.30, the earth began to tremble. The building began to sway as if it were a boat. Panic followed amazement and then running. Minutes later, all were in the gardens, the queen, the king, the princesses, ladies-in-waiting, servants. And in the midst of shouts and tears, was distinctly heard the roar of the sea which first retreated, revealing the seabed and now advanced towards the land in gigantic waves.' [26]

Three days later, the queen Dona Mariana Victória sent by special royal courier a letter to her mother, Queen Isabel of Spain, to re-assure her of the safety of the royal family 'before any false news would cause you anxiety.' [27] She then relates their experience and reaction when they felt the 'most horrible tremor, we fled out of doors with great difficulty because we could not keep ourselves on our feet.' The queen went by the arab steps, the king by another way while the princesses stayed in the oratory and joined their parents later. 'Since then, we are in tents in the great garden. They say that the first tremors lasted five minutes but I think they lasted longer. When we were in the garden we felt another very strong tremor but not as strong as the first. Now, from time to time, shocks are felt but (they are) much lighter, thank God.' She then tells her mother of the state of the capital. In Lisbon almost everything was in ruins and to add to their misfortune fire was consuming a large part of the city; and she continues, 'Our palace on the waterfront was half in ruins and what remained has been burned together with all it contained but the women were saved. … There are horrible disasters and universal desolation. I humbly beg you to pray God for us that He may continue His mercy towards us and spare us if it be His holy Will.' [28]

For several months, the royal family lived in tents in the great garden as the king had been so traumatised by the earthquake that he was afraid to live in a large stone building such as the Palácio de Belém. At the end of November, the queen wrote again to her mother, 'The king wishes to build a small palace of timber beside our Belém residence…Some people are advising the king to go to Mafra where the palace was not damaged but he does not wish to do so because he thinks he cannot now be far from Lisbon and he is also afraid of being in such a large, high building; so, I think we shall stay for some time yet in the tents; they are good enough but one feels the cold.' [29]

Some months later, the royal family moved to the estate bought by D.João V from the Count of Óbidos, which was situated on the summit of the Ajuda hill above the grounds of the Palácio de Belém. Here, some buildings were improvised as a temporary royal residence until the timber palace should be built. Begun early in 1756 and finished five years later, this timber palace did not have a long history. On 10th November, 1794, less than forty years after its inception, it was destroyed by fire. Today, visitors to Lisbon may wonder at the existence of two palaces, the Palácio da Ajuda and the Palácio de Belém, one on the summit of the Ajuda hill and the other almost directly below it in the village of Belém. After the earthquake, the king, D. José I, never again lived in the Palácio de Belém and similarly, his daughter, Dona Maria I who succeeded him as sovereign did not return there when the timber palace was destroyed by fire.

BOM SUCESSO, A FLOURISHING COMMUNITY

At the time of the earthquake, the Bom Sucesso community was flourishing.[30] In a contemporary document, the names of thirty-seven sisters are recorded for the year 1760. They range from Sister Eugenia McCarthy, eighty-five years of age and sixty-two years professed down to Sister Teresa Moroch, twenty-two years old and four years professed. The only member of the community who may not have entered in 1755 was twenty-three year-old Mary McDonnell, a novice.[31] Of these thirty-seven sisters twelve were Portuguese and a thirteenth was Portuguese from Latin America. Of the Irish five had been born in Europe, mainly Portugal. In this document, Sister Magdalen Van Zellar is listed as the daughter of Irish parents and one sister, Mariana Oath, who was born in Lisbon is described as the daughter of an English father and a Swedish mother. The two senior sisters, the Irishwoman, Eugenia McCarthy and the Portuguese, Antónia de Santa Clara (daughter of the Count of Atalaya), would have known some members of the earliest community and consequently, were able to transmit the spiritual tradition of the founding sisters.

Between 1760 and 1770, no records of life in Bom Sucesso are so far available but in 1770, it is recorded that Dr. Burke, Dominican bishop of Ossory, visited Lisbon and found the community flourishing. There were thirty-one nuns in that year and in the seven years between 1773 and 1780, a great increase in vocations occurred. Thirteen novices entered and the community now numbered forty-four. This was a period of calm before the tide of ant-religious feeling set in train by the French Revolution was to overwhelm many countries of Europe. In 1790, came the decree suppressing religious orders in France and many French Dominicans took refuge in Spain. The Portuguese Dominican province of priests and brothers was flourishing – 727 religious *in toto,* of whom 543 were priests, 117 brothers and 67 students [32] – while Corpo Santo had only eighteen members and they were very poor. Between 1794 and 1795, Dr. Luke Concannon, at one time socius of the Master of the Order and later first bishop of New York, gave money to Corpo Santo and the interest from this money was given to his relative in Bom Sucesso.[33]

THE FRENCH REVOLUTION'S EFFECT ON PORTUGAL

The events in France threatened not only religious life but the royal houses of Europe felt its effect also. 'The news of the French Revolution that reached Portugal, the forecast on the way the world was going and the future of its institutions were not of the kind to give peace and calm to the Court.' [34] In 1792, possibly as a result of the fear engendered by the French revolutionaries and their treatment of the monarchy in France, the queen of Portugal, Dona Maria I, gave signs of mental illness which proved to be progressive. Consequently, her son, D. João, assumed royal responsibility, but only in1799 did he become officially regent of Portugal.

Thus ended the eighteenth century – a century that had begun for Portugal with the golden age of the reign of D.João V, the Magnificent when Brazilian gold enriched the royal coffers and most of the land around Bom Sucesso was acquired by the crown. However, 'One of the lasting features of the golden age was a legacy of public works. In Coimbra the university library was rebuilt with the most ostentatious gilt decorations. The Bragança family seat out in the plains beyond the river was rebuilt to palatial standards. The city of Lisbon commissioned engineers to build a huge Roman-style aqueduct to bring fresh water from the hills on 200-foot stone pillars astride the valley.' [35]

THE MARQUÊS DE POMBAL

The tragedy of the 1755 earthquake, however, changed the course of Portuguese history and brought to power the Marquês de Pombal whose despotic rule led to the diminution of influence on the part of the nobility, the expulsion of the Jesuits and the adaptation of the Inquisition from being a Church tribunal judging heresy to a State tribunal condemning those accused of treason. In 1758, Pombal used this State tribunal to condemn for treason and execute a large number of the nobility whose power and influence he feared.

In order to do so, he used as pretext an assassination attempt made one night when the king was returning from a rendezvous with the young countess of Távora. Shots were fired at the royal coach and the king was injured. It is not certain if this assassination attempt was against the king or one of those who accompanied him. What is certain is that the incident was used by the Marquês to destroy with the utmost barbarity all the members of the most important noble families of Portugal who might pose a threat to his despotism. *O chão salgado* with its obelisk in Belém, commemorates the event and marks the site where the executions took place, not far from the Bom Sucesso convent. Among the principal innocent victims were not only members of the noble houses of Aveiro and Távora but also of Atougia to which Dona Iria de Brito, through her mother, had belonged. The annals do not record the effect on the Bom Sucesso community that these executions had but as they occurred within a short distance of the convent and were followed by the total destruction of the palácio de Aveiro adjacent to the palácio de Belém, the religious could not have been unaware of this tragedy. Moreover, given their long tradition of connections with the Portuguese nobility, it is probable that they knew many of the victims.

As Pombal continued his administration, the king became little more than a figurehead while his first minister endeavoured to introduce the political ideas of the Enlightenment. With the expulsion of the Jesuits which led finally to their suppression by the Pope, 'Pombal little suspected that he was setting a long-term precedent for a much wider and more revolutionary dissolution of monasteries in Portugal itself.' [36] However, another reign – that of Dona Maria I – would end before numerous political disturbances would totter the monarchy and endanger the Church.

7

Presence

Sometimes a shaft of sunlight through a shutter
Is enough to reassure
Or the birdcall in the olive tree
The woodcut in the floor
Or the certain curve of river in some light
The open-armed Christus in the night
Sometimes it is the feel of foot on flagstones
Or the air
At batlight
Or the sound of all this silence on the stair
All times it is the echo of a prayer
A Presence I would call it
And I find it everywhere
(*Maria Mackey, O.P.*)

At the dawn of the nineteenth century, 'the sound of all this silence' was shattered in Bom Sucesso when, with the arrival of the French in the Tagus estuary in 1807, 'a cannon ball actually fell into the cloister and the panic-stricken fled to the granary which, being vaulted was considered safe.'[1] However, the decade prior to this event had already been difficult for the sisters, due to a lack of vocations and also financial problems. The last Irishwoman had entered in 1795 and many members had died, reducing the community to twenty-six.

WOLFE TONE AND THE UNITED IRISHMEN

The political situation in Ireland was not conducive to the nurturing of religious vocations. The French Revolution of 1789 inspired Irishmen with the ideal of winning independence from Britain and founding a republic in Ireland. One of the great leaders of this movement was Theobald Wolfe Tone (1763-1798). Following the example of France and the United States, his dream was to separate Ireland as a republic from England and to unite Irish people of all religions – Catholic, Protestant,

Dissenter – in this struggle for freedom. To achieve these aims Tone with Thomas Russell founded the Society of United Irishmen in Belfast on 18th October, 1791, James Napper Tandy joining on 9th November. At first, the majority of its members were Protestant but soon Catholics joined in large numbers. When, in 1793, war broke out between England and France, this society was declared illegal and Tone, in order to evade arrest, went to the United States.

In February 1796, he left his family there and came to Paris in order to persuade the French Directory to send troops to Ireland with the purpose of attacking England from there. The Directory finally agreed to do this and in December 1796, a fleet of forty-three vessels with 15,000 soldiers under the command of General Lazare Hoche set sail for Ireland. The weather was so bad that the ships had to remain offshore on the south-west coast of Ireland for more than a fortnight. Finally , the French expedition had to return to France without landing in Ireland.

On 24th May 1798, the signal for the Irish insurrection was given with the stopping of the mail coaches from Dublin. The Ulster Rising began on 7th June under the leadership of Henry Joy Mc Cracken. Two days later, Henry Monroe, a Protestant draper from Lisburn, led the Rising in Co. Down. After a week of fighting the Ulster Rebellion was put down by British troops and the leaders were executed. The Wexford Rising, however, has become the most famous as it posed the greatest threat to British rule in Ireland. Here the Irish freedom fighters had some victories but were finally defeated at the Battle of Vinegar Hill on 21st June 1798.

Two months later, on 24th August, 1798, a second French expedition under the command of General Humbert landed at Kilala Bay, Co. Mayo. The thousand French soldiers were joined by men from the whole of Connacht. Initially they were successful but were defeated by a larger British force as they marched to Dublin. For a third time, the French attempted to help by sending a final expedition to Ireland in September, 1798 with Wolfe Tone, as a French general on board the flagship, the Hoche. This force of 3,000 men, like the first, never landed. After a fierce, naval battle off the coast of Donegal the French were defeated and Tone was arrested. He was brought to trial in Dublin and sentenced to death for treason. He asked but was refused a military execution but on the morning set for his execution, he attempted suicide, dying from his wound on 19th November, 1798, one of 30,000 men who lost their lives for Irish independence in one year alone.

NAPOLEON'S RISE TO POWER

While, in the aftermath of the French Revolution, Irish freedom fighters looked to France as their ally and hope in their political struggles, Portugal came to regard France as the aggressor during Napoleon's meteoric rise to power. The Iberian peninsula played a crucial role in his final defeat but the Portuguese people suffered greatly from three French invasions.

In March 1796, Napoleon took command of the French army and during a campaign of fourteen months was victorious, returning to Paris in the Autumn of 1799 and seizing power together with two consuls. Five years later, he crowned himself Emperor on18th May, 1804.

The Portuguese Court had factions both in favour of and opposed to France while the prince regent, the future D. João VI, tried to steer a neutral course in an effort to save his people from the ravages of war. By 1807, Portugal and Sweden were Britain's only allies on mainland Europe. Consequently, in order to destroy the power of England Napoleon had to subdue Portugal. On 12th August, 1807, representatives of France and Spain (France's ally at the time) issued an ultimatum to the prince regent – Portugal must abandon its traditional alliance with Britain, seize all British ships and imprison British subjects.[2] Before an answer was given, Napoleon sent General Junot with an army of 30,000 men from Spain to Portugal, reaching Lisbon on 29th November 1807.

Prior to this date, *The Monitor,* the official journal of the Empire, had announced that the Bragança dynasty had ceased to reign in Portugal. When the British ambassador in Lisbon showed this to the Prince Regent, the royal court including not only the royal family but also many nobles, rich merchants, the upper departments of administration, judges of the higher courts and royal attendants set sail for Brazil.[3]

Before leaving for Brazil the Prince Regent had recommended that the French army would be peacefully received. Consequently, it crossed Portugal without encountering any resistance, either official or popular. According to Saraiva, for some, Junot was coming as a liberator, 'It was the Revolution which, with him, was arriving at last in Portugal. That is an aspect which should be underlined: the French invasions were the first episode of the conflicts between absolutism and liberalism in our country.'[4]

This peaceful reception did not last very long because the people deeply resented Napoleon's invasion of their country and the behaviour of Junot's soldiers. The Bom Sucesso annals sadly record what the community underwent at this time. 'The French soldiers under Junot encamped near the convent and the officers lost no time in visiting it. The Church was pillaged, the beautiful silver cross which surmounted the tabernacle was taken. All the silver and gold plate belonging to the Rosary Confraternity was removed except the crowns on the statues on the Rosary altar. The nuns had concealed all their valuable treasures belonging to the sacristy in the garden just outside the refectory.[5]

The people of Portugal, though ill-equipped to fight experienced French armies, were willing to risk their lives in order to win back their country's freedom. They also resented the presence of the French because of their ability at living off the countryside. 'Soldiers were taught to cut, thresh and mill grain and were adept at discovering hidden food and wine. Veterans could live well anywhere in central Europe without receiving supplies from France.'[6] These two factors – pillaging the country's valuables and despoiling the people of their food – increased the Portuguese people's resentment of Junot's forces. 'Junot and his army soon found that they controlled only a few fortified towns and the ground on which they themselves stood.'[7]

THE ARRIVAL OF ARTHUR WELLESLEY

Spain had also revolted and the Junta of Galicia had appealed to Britain for help. On 14th June, 1808, Arthur Wellesley was formally appointed to command a force already assembled in Cork, Ireland. The Galicia Junta, however, did not require troops but arms and when Wellesley arrived in Coruña to consult with them, they advised him to take his army on to Portugal to fight the French there. Leaving Coruña, he sailed to Oporto, arriving there on 24th July. The Junta of Oporto headed by its aged bishop, D. António de Castro was accepted as the Supreme Junta of all free Portugal and Wellesley was very well received by them. The following day, he (Wellesley) sailed south to the mouth of the Tagus to consult with Admiral Sir Charles Cotton, the senior British naval officer in the region. It was agreed that the British force would be landed at the mouth of the Mondego where Coimbra students had won back the small fortress of Figueira de Foz and handed it over to Admiral Cotton.

Between the 1st and the 5th August, Wellesley's troops and equipment were landed while General Spencer's forces, arriving from Gibraltar, disembarked during the following three days. The first battle of the Peninsular war was fought and won by the British before the village of Roliça on 17th August, 1808. Four days later, the French attacked the British and Portuguese forces at Vimeiro but suffered such a defeat that on the following day, General Junot petitioned an armistice. The definitive agreement was signed by Wellesley at Sintra on 30th August. The English undertook to transport the French army with all its baggage back to France, and Lisbon was given over to Wellesley without a fight.

WELLESLEY AND THE BRIGITTINE SISTERS

With the British occupation of the Portuguese capital, religious houses were to endure further suffering. The Brigittine community of English sisters, in the face of the plundering of convents by the French, was alarmed, and decided with the Nuncio's permission, to retire to England for some time. Consequently, in 1809, the majority of the community sailed for England. However, one of their number, Sister Anthony Allen Gomes, was terminally ill and could not travel. Her brother, Father Allen, of the English College in Lisbon promised to support the sisters who would stay to care for her. Six other sisters were willing to remain in Lisbon but, with the arrival of the British forces, they were to suffer at the hands of their compatriots. The following account of the demands made on them by Arthur Wellesley, later the Duke of Wellington, was sent by the Brigittine sisters in England to Bom Sucesso many years later: 'The nuns who remained in Lisbon underwent for a time many privations; the convent being converted into a hospital for the sick and maimed of the Duke of Wellington's army; Sister M. Rose Low and her little community were obliged to leave the convent and go to Bom Sucesso, a Dominican convent of Irish nuns who received them with the greatest cordiality.'[8]

This account reveals one instance where Wellington deserves his title, the *Iron Duke*, 'When the English arrived to drive the French out of Portugal the General demanded the use of the convent. The sisters pleaded that they were only a few nuns with one in a dying state; but he said that he cared more for one of his soldiers than for all the nuns together, so the community had to leave and they carried the dying sister on a litter.'[9]

The English Brigittines stayed in Bom Sucesso for a number of years and there Sister Anthony Allen Gomes died on 16th January, 1811. She had spent fifty-five years of her life in religion and most of these were peaceful. However, she had begun her religious life in Lisbon on the very day of the great Lisbon earthquake of 1755 when her community had to spend several nights in tents in their garden. The last years of her life were passed in the turmoil of the Peninsular War. She died outside her own convent and was buried in the Chapter Room of Bom Sucesso among Dominican sisters.[10]

The War in Portugal

The battles of Roliça and Vimeiro were significant in that they were the first victories over Napoleon's forces on mainland Europe but the war in Portugal was far from over. During the winter of 1808-1809, Sir John Moore was left in command of about 30,000 British troops in northern Spain and was obliged to retreat to Astorga. Here, in a good defensive position, he might have engaged in battle but 'Napoleon was in personal command with some of his best troops and subordinate generals; without question the Emperor wanted a battle. To have fought under such conditions a hundred long miles from safety would have been foolhardy.'[11] Napoleon personally pursued Moore as far as Astorga and there he left Soult in command while he returned to France. The French pursuit of the British continued and on 11th January, 1809, the advance troops reached Coruña for embarkation. Early on the 16th, Soult attacked and Moore was fatally wounded. Sir John Hope took over the command and embarked his entire force leaving Soult and his exhausted men in control of northern Spain.

General Soult, having reorganised his army after Coruña, advanced into northern Portugal and took Oporto on 29th March, 1809. General Lapisse had an infantry division at Ciudad Rodrigo and Marshal Victor had a large army at Mérida. Both were ready to join Soult in the conquest of Portugal and all three together outnumbered the British by more than two to one. This was the situation Sir Arthur Wellesly came into when he was formally appointed to command in Portugal on 6th April, 1809. Reaching Lisbon on 22nd April he decided to attack Soult before Victor and Lapisse could join forces with him.

Beresford had reorganised the Portuguese army so that Wellesley could now place one infantry battalion of Portuguese soldiers in each of the five British brigades. On 12th May, the Anglo-Portuguese army took Oporto while Soult had to retreat north into Spain. Wellesley's campaign had lasted less than two weeks and, although no major battles were fought, the French losses in men and artillery were considerable.

While Silveira was left to guard the northern frontier, the main army marched south to deal with General Victor's force. On 3rd July, 1809, the British crossed the frontier into Spain where the hard-won battle of Talavera took place on 28th July. Wellesley was given the title 'Viscount Wellington of Talavera' and on 16th September, for the first time, signed his dispatch 'Wellington.' [12] Meanwhile, in August, the British army moved back to Badajoz in order to obtain food supplies from Elvas in Portugal.

Northern continental Europe was by now under Napoleon's control and he could turn his attention to the conquest of the Iberian Peninsula. The Spanish army suffered two major defeats in September and this meant that only Portugal and the British stood against a total conquest by Napoleon of the European mainland. Consequently, Lisbon had to be defended and Wellington went there early in October 1809 in order to organise a system of fortifications around the city and its environs later known as the Lines of Torres Vedras.[13] 'The citadel of Torres Vedras and similar stone castles in other towns were re-enforced with earthworks.... Thousands of men worked diligently under supervision on this vast project for more than a year before the Allied army made use of it.'[14]

THE THIRD FRENCH INVASION

Portugal was now to endure a third French invasion under General Massena who had taken Ciudad Rodrigo on the Spanish border by 10th July 1810. He crossed into Portuguese territory and attacked Almeida on 26th August. Due to an accident, the very strong cathedral which contained very many tons of gunpowder blew up killing five hundred Portuguese. Almeida surrendered. 'With its surrender, Massena assumed that he had nothing between him and Lisbon but the Anglo-Portuguese army.'[15] The French army numbered 65,000 and were led across the northern route from Almeida to Coimbra. Wellington concentrated his army on the Bussaco ridge and there on 27th September 1810, the Anglo-Portuguese forces defeated the French.

In spite of this, Massena outwitted Wellington, finding a way around the Bussaco ridge en route for Lisbon. The British commander was obliged to retreat south to behind the fortifications known as the lines of Torres Vedras. Here, they had plentiful supplies while, due to Wellington's scorched earth policy, Massena's army had difficulty in finding sufficient food and were at the mercy of unfriendly inhabitants. In March, reinforcements from England landed at Lisbon and the French general, his army depleted by hunger, disease and a hostile people decided to begin his retreat from Santarém. Wellington pursued until Massena and his army left Portuguese soil and reached their base in Salamanca on 11th April, 1811.

These military campaigns in Portugal from 1807 until 1811 caused severe suffering and deprivation to the people of the country and the Bom Sucesso sisters had their share in this hardship. Not only had they to endure the pillage of their church by the French but Wellington also made demands on them, billeting his soldiers in the church and stabling horses in the buildings on the patio. According to the Brigittine annals, '…-the English brought their horses into the church and used the courtyard as stables but did not expel the nuns from their cloister.'[16]

Because of the unsettled state of the country the Bom Sucesso sisters were afraid that they would have to leave Lisbon. Their property in Golegã most probably suffered from Wellington's scorched earth policy and plundering by the French stationed in nearby Santarém. It could not have yielded its usual produce. They thought of going to Brazil since the Prince Regent had promised to protect them.[17] However, once Portugal was finally set free and the threat of invasion ended, they gave up this idea.

The Brigittine sisters also were able to return to their convent. Referring to this time the annals of the latter record, '…the community recovered all or part of the landed property belonging to it and were, comparatively, in easy circumstances.'[18] It is not stated in either annals when Wellington vacated the Lisbon convents. It may have been as late as his final offensive in Spain in May 1813. Prior to this, he had wintered in Ciudad Rodrigo just inside the Spanish-Portuguese frontier but might still have used Lisbon especially for the sick and wounded.

POLITICAL CRISES OF THE 1820S

By December 1813, the Allied forces had penetrated the Franco-Spanish frontier and the Peninsular War could be said to have ended. The Bom Sucesso annals observe, 'when the Peninsular War ceased, the community enjoyed peace for some years but it was just the calm that precedes a storm.'[19] The domino effect that the ideology of the French Revolution had on so many countries now affected the Lusitanian world, first in Brazil and then in Portugal. From 1808, Brazilian trade progressively achieved independence from Portugal whose exports had been almost totally channelled to Brazil and whose imports came mainly from there also. Influenced by the war of independence in North America, the Brazilians aspired to a similar political status and finally achieved it in 1822.

Meanwhile, the absence from Portugal of the royal family in Brazil was resented in the mother country once the Peninsular War was ended. In Lisbon, government was in the hands of a governing Junta which depended on the instructions it received from the royal court in Rio de Janeiro. Furthermore, though the war was over, the English army had remained in Portugal and numbered almost one hundred thousand men under the command of Marshal Beresford. According to a report sent, in 1820, by the governing Junta to D. João VI, king since his mother's death in 1816, the army was costing the state 75% of its revenue. The historian, J.H. Saraiva sums up the state of Portugal at this time: 'The situation of Portugal in 1820 was one of crisis in all sections of national life: political crisis caused by the absence of the king and organs of government in Brazil; ideological crisis born of the progressive diffusion in the cities of political ideas which considered absolute monarchy an oppressive and obsolete regime; economic crisis resulting from the economic emancipation of Brazil; military crisis due to the presence of English officers in high posts in the army.'[20]

On 24th August, 1820, while Beresford was in Brazil seeking an extension of his mandate, revolution broke out in Oporto against the British occupation of the country. It soon spread to Lisbon and leaders of both cities met in Coimbra in order to draw up a moderate agenda, asking for the departure of the British, the return of the king with the court and the re-establishment of the Brazil trade.[21] Leaving Brazilian affairs in the hands of his son, D. Pedro, King D. João VI returned from Rio de Janeiro to Lisbon in 1821.

The revolution of 1820 which resulted in the surprisingly radical Constitution of 1822 was anti-clerical and, as the Church was the one institution that reached out to all the people many of whom were illiterate, there was conflict. The clergy declared the revolution 'the enemy of the throne and the altar' and the archbishop of Lisbon was obliged to go into exile in France because of his opposition to some of its agenda.

THREAT OF EXPULSION FROM BOM SUCESSO

Once again the sisters of Bom Sucesso became the innocent victims of the country's political situation, suffering, this time, from political decisions of the anti-religious and so-called liberal programme. In the convent archives a record containing copies of documentation and eyewitness accounts of the events of 1823 where Bom Sucesso was concerned reveals something of the sufferings of the sisters but also their heroic efforts to save their convent. The first official document dated 6th February, 1823, and signed by a local magistrate courteously asks that the prioress would furnish an inventory of all property situated outside the city. As Belém was outside the city of Lisbon at that time, this inventory would have to include not only the estates of Ameixoeira and Golegã but also the extensive land on which the convent itself stood.

Another document dated 5th February, 1823, comes from the office of the Secretary of State for Justice Affairs and is signed by the secretary of the local magistrate's office in Belém. In tone much less deferential than the foregoing document, it states that the king has ordered the magistrate to draw up immediately an inventory of all the property and goods belonging to the six religious houses of Belém. All members of each community must be present on the day of the magistrate's visit and the letter carries the threat of punishment should the religious conceal their ownership of any property.[22]

On 20th April, the Secretary of State for Justice Affairs notified the prioress that the Convent of Nossa Senhora do Bom Sucesso was to be suppressed and the communities of the three Dominican houses of Bom Sucesso, Rei Salvador and São João Baptista de Setúbal were to be congregated as one community in the convent of Rey Salvador. The sisters could not accept this and sent an appeal requesting that the three communities be accommodated in Bom Sucesso.[23]

The refusal to this request came promptly on the 6th May, signed by the Secretary of State himself and with the king's seal. It explained that the important purpose of the Law for the Reform of Regular Orders would not be fulfilled if the religious were to come together in Bom Sucesso. 'Once vacant, the government can dispose of it according to its prudent judgment.'[24] The reason given is because of the state of disrepair the house was in. However, the document continues that it was a matter of indifference to the government which convent was retained or suppressed once the reduction of the number of religious houses was achieved 'without detriment to religion, the State or the same religious bodies.'[25] There follow seven decrees:

1. I ordain that the religious of Nossa Senhora do Bom Sucesso de Pedrouços and of São João Baptista da villa de Setúbal be united and incorporated with all their rights, both active and passive, into the Community of Rey Salvador in Lisbon.

2. I ordain that as soon as the religious of the three convents are together, the whole community enter into Chapter and elect canonically in secret scrutiny a superior; at whose election shall preside an ecclesiastic authorised by the Ordinary to whom the elected superior and all the community will offer obedience and produce the competent document to be sent to my royal presence.

3. I ordain that to the goods of the Convent of Rey Salvador be assigned all similar property of the two convents of São João Baptista da Villa de Setúbal and Bom Sucesso de Pedrouços not belonging to the National Treasury or other public entity, except the enclosure and lands attached of these two convents which are vacated for the nation.

4. Surrendered also for the Nation are entitlements to interest, capital in the Treasury, policies of loans, old or new, credits of these entitlements, incomes, pensions and every and any loan that the Treasury or any Customs or other public department paid to the said three convents.

5. Similarly surrendered to the Nation the tithes of Benfica, Salvaterra de Magos and the three estates of Olivais connected with the support of the parish priest of the parish of Salvador established in the church of the same convent; these tithes are, at present, paying 200,000 reis annually which the said parish priest has to collect.

6. There belong still to the united community of Rey Salvador the active debts of these three houses which are not connected with the Treasury or other public departments and thus, whatever their nature, remain the responsibility of the passive entities.

7. I ordain that the same community elect as its confessor a secular priest authorised by the Ordinary and that the religious who are presently their confessors or chaplains return to the nearest convent of their Order.... The same religious, if they are administrators of the income of any of the above-mentioned three convents must immediately give an account of this to the superior and community united in the Convent of Rey Salvador, handing over to her all titles, books, papers and moneys under their control and having recourse, if necessary, to the district authorities to ensure the legality of the same accountancy.'

Signed: José da Silva Carvalho, Secretary of
State for Justice Affairs with the seal of the king.
Palácio de Bemposta, 6th May, 1823

Thus, the Government, in the name of the reform of religious orders would obtain the wealth accruing from the sale of the buildings and land of the suppressed houses. For the individual member of the Bom Sucesso Convent, added to the loss of her home, was the difficulty of having a confessor who might not understand Irish or English.

Bom Sucesso's Appeal to the King

The sisters concerned were not going to surrender their beloved Bom Sucesso without using every means in their power to retain it. They decided to make a personal appeal to the king especially as the good relationship between Bom Sucesso and the Bragança dynasty had a very long history. A deputation of eight sisters set out for the royal palace of Bemposta. The names of these eight sisters are given and reveal that all but one were Irish born or of Irish descent – the prioress, Maria de Jesús Cunha, the sub-prioress, Bridget Staunton, Catherine Concannon, Ana O'Neill and her sister Cecília, daughters of João O'Neill who had settled in Portugal, Júlia Joyce, Margaret Dorran and Teresa Staunton. 'On their way to the palace and on their arrival, they excited the greatest sympathy, the guards lowering their arms in token of respect. Murmurs could be heard, such as, "the poor exiles from their country, let them pass."' [26] Without any difficulty they were admitted to the audience chamber where the king graciously received them and the prioress presented their petition.

In this document they accept the suppression of some convents in conformity with the Decree of 24th October, 1822 but hold that, by suppressing Bom Sucesso, the government infringes this very decree which states that the convent with the largest number of members and in a good location should be preserved. This should be Bom Sucesso situated outside the city and in an area 'where it can be more useful to the people.' Its ruinous state (the government's argument against Bom Sucesso) can be easily repaired and, besides, this is similar to the condition of Rey Salvador which is in the centre of the city and in a hollow. If the members of the commission that examined Rey Salvador had come to Bom Sucesso, they would have to confess (if they were impartial) that Bom Sucesso had far better facilities and better workshops than Rey Salvador.

However, the members of the commission did not wish to make this inspection and allowed themselves to be influenced by persons who were obviously bribed by a neighbour and enemy of the convent. The sisters do not hesitate to name him – Francisco António Ferreira – who had declared a living war (*viva guerra*) against the community and put in motion every means to obtain the suppression of the convent. The reason for this is that in obedience to the Decree of 24th October, 1822, they could not rent out to him some land he wanted while, at the same time, they offered it to him *gratis*, promising never to disturb him.[27]

The bribery of the commission's members is evident in the evaluation of the convent which was valued at a much lower price than its worth; it was valued together with some storehouses which are separate buildings – all this to satisfy the bribes and pledges of their neighbour and enemy.

The ruinous state of the convent should not be an obstacle as the damage is only in the roofs and can easily be repaired because the petitioners commit themselves to do the repairs in a short while. If his majesty does not deign to accept this request, the sisters ask that they be allowed to stay in Bom Sucesso not as in a cloister but as in a college of education for girls since they have this already and their religious houses in Ireland are doing likewise. They would also pay the State a rent or even stay in some houses nearby for the same purpose and administer their property according to the clauses directed to that end.

If, however, none of these petitions be granted, the Irish sisters would prefer to return to their native land and their homes rather than bury themselves alive in the hollow of the convent of Salvador. They request his majesty to give them some alms for their support as ordained by the decree of 24th October, no. 37 for secularised religious. The petitioners being foreigners ought to be considered as such and ought all to receive this gift. 'May your Majesty, because of your supreme piety attend to these requests which your petitioners bring to your royal presence. Signed: Sister Maria de Jesús, prioress.' [28]

The king promised to do all in his power in favour of this just claim[29] but the royal power was no longer absolute according to the Constitution of 1822 which supported the principle of national sovereignty – the only true sovereign is the nation, not the king. The nation elects its representatives and consequently, the second principle upholds parliament's supremacy over royal power. The king has only the authority that parliament, the nation's representative, allows him to have.[30]

AN APPEAL TO THE BRITISH AMBASSADOR

The sisters realised that their efforts to appeal to the king were fruitless. They returned to their monastery rather discouraged but the Irish sisters now decided to appeal to the British ambassador, Mr. Ward. The community was virtually unknown to the British authorities as it had always enjoyed a very good relationship with the Portuguese monarchy and, consequently, had not needed the services of the British embassy.[31]

Mr. Ward sent his consul to enquire into the matter and his opinion was that the nuns had no alternative but to obey the government. Nevertheless, the ambassador consented to present another petition to the king.[32] It is humbler in tone, using such phrases as 'prostrate themselves at the royal feet of your majesty' and omitting reference to their neighbour and enemy. They now explain the origin of the convent's foundation as a reason why it could not become the property of the National Treasury. They repeat the other reasons – the lack of facilities in Rey Salvador, the number of sisters in Bom Sucesso exceeding the number of the other two communities together. Other reasons given are those mentioned in the first appeal – Bom Sucesso's situation outside the city and its very good facilities sufficient for the reception of the other two groups.

Finally and most importantly, they are foreigners who have always enjoyed the favour of the legitimate sovereigns of this kingdom. 'Is it possible that they will not be granted this favour from the greatest of these monarchs who unites in himself all the virtues shared by his predecessors.... A sovereign so worthy of eternal memory will not refuse justice to those who request it with so much humility...and especially when this request claims the protection due to vassals of an ally such as the king of Great Britain.'[33] Only five sisters – those born in Ireland – signed this petition. They were the sub-prioress Bridget Staunton, Anna Margarida Dorran, Honoria da Santa Anna O'Flynn, Júlia de São José Joyes and Teresa Staunton. 'They beg your Majesty to deign through your great clemency to consent to what they ask with the brevity that their sad circumstances demand.'[34]

EXPULSION FROM BOM SUCESSO

In a last effort, they sent a third appeal to the king through the Commission for the Reform of Convents. It was all to no avail. The refusal came on 20th May, 1823 and on 23rd, they were obliged to leave their beloved Bom Sucesso. 'On this day, the saddest in the history of the monastery, the Holy Sacrifice was offered at a very early hour and the Blessed Sacrament removed. At 10 a.m., the officials arrived and announced that carriages would be provided to convey the nuns and all their personal belongings to Rey Salvador.'[35]

The officials then removed all valuables – paintings, statues, furniture – while the community helplessly witnessed this interference with their property. Each member was obliged to take an oath that she had nothing but personal belongings. The sacristan who had packed some vestments with her personal property had to ask a servant to return them to the sacristy before her turn came to take the oath.[36]

At 5 p.m., the carriages were ready for their departure but before they went beyond the enclosure door, the sisters all declared they would not leave without the statue of Our Lady of Bom Sucesso. This concession was granted them and the prioress carried it in her carriage, drawing back the curtains so that the people could see and venerate the statue of Our Lady of Good Success. 'So great was their veneration for Our Lady's statue that, as the carriages passed slowly through the streets, everyone fell on their knees; even the soldiers lowered their arms, such was the spirit of religion and piety that reigned in Portugal at that time.' [37]

On the sisters' arrival at Rey Salvador, the officials expressed displeasure at the attention their journey through the city had attracted. They even insinuated that the nuns had wanted to stir up a revolt. Given their unwillingness to leave Bom Sucesso and the many efforts they had made to have the government's order revoked, it is quite likely that apart from offering their statue for veneration, they were also appealing to the people for their sympathy and support. At Rey Salvador they were graciously welcomed, not only by the community there but also by the sisters of São João Baptista de Setúbal. It was from this convent that, at the foundation of Bom Sucesso in 1639, two sisters had come to train the first novices.

Nobody realised on that fateful day of 23rd May, 1823, that their exile would not last very long. Possibly, due to the prayers of all those who had suffered from the so-called liberal constitution of 1820, the enthusiasm for the wonders it would develop was waning, while the clergy and nobility, fearing the loss of their privileges, were opposed to it. The Queen, Dona Carlota Joaquina, was totally against it and her younger son, Infante D. Miguel took up the counter-revolutionary cause. On 27th May, 1823, in Vila Franca, he proclaimed a *coup d'état*, asserting, 'it is time to break the iron yoke that we are ignominiously living under.' [38] The Lisbon garrison joined him and the government unable to resist was dissolved. The king suspended the Constitution of 1820 and promised new legislation that would guarantee personal security, property and employment.[39]

RETURN TO BOM SUCESSO

On 17th June, the Vicar General of the convent of São Domingos in Lisbon wrote to the prioress, Mother Maria de Jesús Cunha informing her that his majesty, by decree dated 14th June had revoked the law of 24th October, 1822, thus restoring to the religious who had suffered under this law all their former property, goods and income. Consequently, 'Obeying as we should the royal decisions of the same august lord we command your reverence under formal precept and in holy obedience, in fulfilment of the said declaration, to proceed with your community to return as soon as possible to your convent; letting me know beforehand the day you choose so that I can give the means to the person accompanying you.'

Signed: Frei Caetano José Ramalho.[40]

A week later, on 25th June, the sisters returned to their home, a month after they had been expelled from it. The annals record, 'the miraculous statue of Our Lady of Bom Sucesso was borne in triumph through the streets of Lisbon to Belém where the inhabitants had assembled to welcome the nuns.' [41] There, the members of the Rosary Confraternity unyoked the horses from the carriages and they themselves drew the carriages the remainder of the way into the convent courtyard. To further welcome the sisters home, the Confraternity members had prepared a banquet in the lower parlour. During the sisters' absence, the Confraternity, with the king's permission, had transferred to the church of *Nossa Senhora da Ajuda* (Our Lady of Help) but it was now re-established in Bom Sucesso.

The convent was in a very bad state of repair because of 'the destruction perpetrated in our absence.' [42] The nuns had great difficulty in finding the new owners of valuables that had been sold off but succeeded in recovering them at a high cost. Order was restored, enclosure and other monastic observances were re-introduced and, in spite of the political turmoil in the country, the community settled down to a certain amount of peace.

In commemoration of their return to Bom Sucesso the community obtained permission to celebrate the feast of Our Lady of Good Success on 25th June, transferring it from the octave of the Assumption. It is always celebrated with great solemnity even to this day. The then Pope Leo XII granted a plenary indulgence to those who visited the Church on the feast-day.

KING D. JOÃO VI'S VISIT TO BOM SUCESSO

An amusing incident is recorded in the annals which throws light on life in the convent at this time. The king, D. João VI, in spite of political difficulties, always befriended the sisters of Bom Sucesso. In 1823, he had only three more years to live but, during that time he arranged to make a visit to the convent which, as a child, he had often visited with his mother, Queen Dona Maria I. On his arrival, the sisters, as usual, went to receive him at the door of the enclosure when a crazed sister who did not recognise him cried out 'You cannot be the king – my fine little Johnny could never have grown up as ugly as you are. I know who you are.' The king not understanding English asked the princess to translate for him but she avoided doing so. When the king stood up to go to visit the cloister his sword made some noise and this convinced the poor sister that he was the devil. She rushed off declaring that only the devil could be so ugly. The king pitied her and told the princess to give her some money, thinking that, because of her worn habit she must be in need.[43]

D.João VI was always held in high esteem by all in Bom Sucesso and his inability to prevent their expulsion did not derogate from the respect they had for this monarch who, during a very difficult period in Portuguese history, tried to guide his people with moderation. The memoir of 1823 attributes the return of the sisters to Bom Sucesso to his majesty, 'Our monastery was restored to us by King João VI whose piety and magnanimity prove him to have been the most religious of Portuguese monarchs.'[44]

The final paragraph of this memoir is addressed to the future daughters of Saint Dominic, 'when in future times you cast your eyes over these pages you will remember that those sisters of yours who suffered so much in a spirit of constancy given to them through the intercession of the most holy virgin of Bom Sucesso now no longer exist. However, they leave this memoir, even though poor, to serve as an example so that always fulfilling your religious obligations due to Almighty God, in order to become pleasing to the same Lord, you will respect your sovereigns and their immediate ministers on earth; so that, through the exact fulfilment of your duties, both religious and civil, you may attain the crown of eternal glory which God has promised to the chosen ones and which we wish to you.'[45]

8

The Foundation of the School

The community was now to begin a project that would, in time, make its imprint on the cultural life of Lisbon. In their 1823 appeal to the king, the Sisters had offered to establish a school but, now, financial difficulties due to government taxation of their landed property were obliging them to re-consider this option. However, unusual circumstances pointed the way forward.

From its foundation, as was customary in convents during the seventeenth and eighteenth centuries, girls of noble families spent some time in Bom Sucesso prior to their marriage. Each pupil was entrusted to one nun who would guide and instruct her in all that a young woman should know at this time. A music master was employed 'so that the arts should not be neglected.'[1] Ability to sing and play the piano was considered an essential accomplishment for a young woman. However, there was no organised school as such arranged for them and little group instruction given.

This situation was to change when, in 1829, the prioress, Sister Brigid Staunton, received an unusual request from the British vice-consul, Mr. Jeremiah Meagher. He and Mr. Thomas O'Keefe had been appointed guardians of a baby girl, the daughter of an Irishman, William Kennedy. His wife, Mrs. Russell Kennedy, had died at the birth of the baby, the 20th May 1828, and now Mr. Kennedy, an artist, aged only twenty-eight, was terminally ill with tuberculosis. On his death-bed, he implored Father B. O'Dea, O.P., of Corpo Santo (*Collegio do Rosario*) to ask the Bom Sucesso community to take and rear his baby daughter. Her mother, Mrs. Kennedy had been very friendly with these Sisters and, due to a family relationship, had shown great affection for Sisters Brigid and Teresa Staunton.[2] Father O'Dea not only approved of this request, but did all in his power to ensure that it was acceded to.

Permission was obtained from the Holy See and, on 8th December, 1829, the day of her father's death, the little girl was brought by her nurse Inácia to Bom Sucesso. Mariana Russell Kennedy was the first child boarder and, as she was later joined by other children, she is considered the first pupil of *O Colégio do Bom Sucesso*. In his will, William Kennedy decreed that, should Mariana die during her school days, 'all her fortune was to be disposed of in favour of the poor Irish residents in Lisbon.' [3]

With the authorisation of her superiors, Sister Teresa Staunton assumed responsibility for Mariana's education. The little girl enjoyed excellent tuition in the arts and languages. Her professor of music was the composer, Manuel Inocêncio Liberato dos Santos, tutor of the Infantas, Dona Maria da Assunção and Dona Ana de Jesús Maria. Years later, Mariana told her two daughters that she could not remember having begun to learn music, it was for her quite a natural accomplishment. When only eight years of age, she was dressed in a miniature Dominican habit and, sitting on the knees of one of the Sisters, she accompanied the sung Masses on the organ.

The Infanta Dona Isabel Maria was a friend of the Bom Successo community and through her visits to the Sisters came to know this little girl with an unusual upbringing. She lavished on her particular affection and would often send her coach to bring her to the palace. Mariana would spend an afternoon there, receiving from the princess gifts and other signs of affection. In later life many of these gifts were cherished souvenirs of the friendship that this little orphan had received from her royal friend.

Mariana had inherited her father's talent for painting and painted both in oils and watercolour. She even produced a very well executed stained glass window. Some of her many paintings were lovingly preserved by her family for many years afterwards. A painting of Sister Brigid Staunton in the Bom Sucesso archives is attributed to Mariana. In addition to her talent at music and painting, she became a linguist. 'She spoke fluently English, her own language (Irish), French, Portuguese, and Italian which she had learned because of her singing lessons. She read and translated Latin with facility....She was as good as she was beautiful and distinguished for good manners.' [4]

THE ADMISSION OF CHILD COMPANIONS FOR MARIANA

Meanwhile, so that Mariana might have companions, the Sisters decided to admit other children to be educated with her in the convent. Among her companions, as 'the daughter of the house,' the college's first pupil enjoyed a certain prestige in this small circle of peers. One of these was a little girl from Brazil whose parents were away in the city of San Salvador da Baía and who looked on Mariana as her sister.

A YOUNG VISITOR FROM BRAZIL

In this ambience of love and care the years passed happily for Mariana until in 1843, a young officer of the Marinha da Guerra Brasileira, Francisco Alberto Lopes dos Santos, Portuguese by birth, came to visit his family in Portugal. Before he left Brazil, the parents of the Brazilian girl in Bom Sucesso had asked him to visit their daughter in the convent. The latter requested that Mariana would meet this young man also. The two girls obtained the prioress's permission to entertain the young officer at the grille as the students lived within the enclosure. It was love at first sight, *Vé-la e amá-la foi obra dum instante* (I saw her and loved her instantaneously).[5] The young officer fell completely in love with Mariana and on 1st January, 1844, in the Church of Santa Maria de Belém, (Jerónimos) the parish Church of Bom Sucesso, the couple were married. The bridegroom was twenty-nine years old and the bride had not, as yet, celebrated her sixteenth birthday.

The young couple set off for Brazil and there, in the society of San Salvador da Baía, Mariana with her many talents began to shine. Their three children were born there, their son Adolfo, born in 1844, their daughters, Laura, born in March 1847 and Adelaide born in April, 1848. The family remained in Brazil only five years, returning definitively to Portugal in 1849.

Accompanying them were their black servants, formerly slaves whom Francisco Alberto had freed before their departure for Portugal.

The hazards of sea travel in the mid-nineteenth century are highlighted in the account of this family's journey from Brazil. The crossing from South America to Europe was delayed a number of times because the sailing ship was becalmed. The food and even the water for crew and passengers had to be rationed and it must have been particularly difficult for a couple with three young children.

A few days after their arrival, at the invitation of her godmother, *madrinha* (the name that Mariana always gave Sister Teresa Staunton) Bom Sucesso's former pupil with her little daughter, Laura, spent a week within the cloister of her *alma mater*. Later, the couple toured Europe, visiting, among other countries, England where Mariana met some distant relatives of her father.

THE FAMILY SETTLES IN LISBON

On completing their European tour, the family took up residence in Rua Nova de São Francisco de Paula, no.1, (later named Rua Ribeiro Sanches, no.5) where Mariana had been born. Surrounded by distinguished lovers of music they organised concerts for their many friends. Mariana who, in Brazil, had been a disciple of a famous Italian *diva* had a beautiful mezzo-soprano voice and articulated so well in Italian that every word was clearly heard. Some evenings, if the weather permitted, the neighbours of Travessa da Amoreira, sitting comfortably on chairs in front of their houses, enjoyed beautiful selections from operas and excellent chamber music.

Tragedy struck this happy family when, in 1852, Adolfo died, aged only eight years. Four years later, in 1856, when a severe epidemic of yellow fever struck Portugal, killing entire families, Mariana fell gravely ill. Due, according to her daughter, to the care given by her husband who never left her bedside, she recovered. The Bom Sucesso community was not spared either at this time, their numbers being reduced to seven due to the death from the epidemic of five sisters.

Later, Francisco Alberto acquired a glass factory in Rua dos Gaivotos and the family went to live beside the factory. They were now further away from Bom Sucesso but Mariana never failed to visit her beloved Sisters. In 1870, she fell ill again with a mild form of 'flu but, sadly, after only a short illness, she died on 18th March of that year, two months before her forty-second birthday. A few months later, her *madrinha,* Mother Teresa Staunton 'went to receive the reward of her virtues on August 24th 1870.'[6]

THE VISIT OF MARIANA'S DAUGHTER, LAURA

Many years later, in fact, almost a century, Laura, the surviving daughter of Bom Sucesso's first child pupil and Laura's son, Alfredo de Kennedy Falcão, were in contact again in 1940, with the Community of Irish Dominican Sisters. The then archivist, Mother Cecilia Murray, had a number of questions to put to them in order to complete the life story of Mariana Russell Kennedy. It is mainly from the correspondence between Mother Cecilia and Alfredo that many details of his grandmother's life in Bom Sucesso and later are recorded in the Convent archives. This correspondence between the convent annalist and Senhor Falcão was carried on during the Summer months of 1940 when Laura Kennedy Falcão was ninety-three years old but still endowed with a very clear memory of the significant events in her mother's unusual life.

About a year and a half later, on 30th December 1941, Laura died peacefully at her home in Mealhada. Her son wrote an account of his mother's last moments, revealing something of the spirituality which his grandmother must have imbibed at Bom Sucesso and which she passed on to her children, 'Moments before her death, she (Laura) called her servant who was devoted to her, pressed her hand and then, joining her own lovely little hands said, pray. My sister had just come into the room and the servant told her what had happened. They began to pray the Rosary, her breathing became irregular like the light which flickers on the candle before it fades; at the second mystery she turned her head to the left and passed away like a little bird.'[7]

MOST DIFFICULT YEARS FOR RELIGIOUS IN PORTUGAL

The years that Mariana Russell Kennedy spent in Bom Sucesso were some of the most difficult that the community had to endure in the convent's long history. Taxes imposed by the various so-called liberal governments were exorbitant and the introduction of a law prohibiting the reception into convents of new members placed a heavy burden on the remaining ageing sisters.

The 1800s were particularly difficult years in the history of Portugal. The conciliatory D. João VI had died in 1826 and his elder son and heir had already become Emperor of Brazil when, in 1822, that country achieved its independence from Portugal. Trying to reach a political compromise, D. Pedro, on his father death, renounced his right to the throne of Portugal in favour of his seven-year old daughter, Maria da Glória and arranged that his brother Miguel would act as regent during his daughter's minority. However, Miguel who had staged the conservative *coup d'état* of 1823 which had restored Bom Sucesso to its community now claimed the throne for himself. Pedro obtained support from both France and Britain and, after a bitter civil war lasting two years, victory went to Pedro on behalf of his daughter the young Queen Maria II. The English historian, David Birmingham summing up this tragic event in Portuguese history states, 'The civil war of 1832 to 1834 marked a brutal mid-point in the slowly developing revolution which carried Portugal from royal absolutism to constitutional democracy. The war bitterly pitted two brothers, Pedro and Miguel, against each other.'[8]

Portugal emerged from this war deeply in debt and, in order to deal with this problem, the liberal politicians adopted a radical agenda which targeted Crown lands and land belonging to Religious Orders. Most of the Crown lands which encompassed a quarter of Portugal's territory were confiscated by the State and their revenue appropriated or the land sold in order to reduce the national debt.

The second target of the government was land owned by Religious Orders. Since the Pombal reform of 1772, a virtual schism existed between Rome and Portugal in that the Marquês de Pombal had brought in legislation claiming the right of the Crown to nominate bishops for Portuguese dioceses. Bishops thus appointed would be practically exempt from links with the papacy. On the other hand, the Religious Orders being constituted on an international basis and directly subject to the Pope enjoyed freedom from the Pombal legislation. Now, however, the government by decree of 28th March 1834 proceeded to suppress them and acquire their property.[9]

Writing to D. Pedro, regent for his daughter, Queen Maria II, his minister, Joaquim António de Aguiar, boasts of this decree, 'Sire, today is extinguished the preconception which has lasted for centuries, that the existence of religious orders is indispensable to the Catholic religion and useful to the State. The dominant opinion now is that religion does not benefit in any way from them and that their preservation is not compatible with the civilisation and enlightenment of the century.'[10]

For this decree and the subsequent persecution it caused history has given Aguiar the cognomen *Matafrades* (Killer of Friars)[11]

Frei Raúl de Almeida Rolo, O.P., commenting on Aguiar's statement, describes this decree as 'the mercy blow for religious life already in agony.'[12] There followed a dissolution of the monasteries and confiscation of their property. Over three hundred religious houses of men were suppressed and their members driven out. Some of those who were priests were able to join the secular clergy but many others were reduced to penury. The elderly and invalids who had no families to whom they could look for help suffered most as the promised Government pensions did not materialise.

The pastoral consequences of the suppression of the Religious Orders was incalculable. In spite of the addition of some Order priests to their ranks, the number of secular clergy diminished also from 24,000 in 1820 to 10,000 in 1840. Since the seventeenth century, real evangelisation in Portugal, especially to remote, poorly populated areas was carried out mainly by periodic missions of itinerant groups of religious – Franciscans, Oratorians and Jesuits. Once the Orders were suppressed, people in rural districts had little spiritual guidance for years at a time. Worse still, according to Manuel Clemente, was the widened gap between intellectual formation and Catholic teaching and he quotes the writer Alexandre Herculano, 'Already in 1842, Alexandre Herculano had to beg bread for the expelled friars; and he begged it thus: "Bread for half of our intellectuals, of our virtuous men, of our priesthood." It was that half of our intellectuals, that great part of Portuguese Catholic intelligentsia, that was now missing.'[13]

The land cultivated by the monks for their own support and that of the peasants now began to be exploited by profiteering speculators. Thus the middleclass was enriched but the poor who depended on monasteries were worse off, both spiritually and materially.

Oliveira, the Church historian, is radical in his condemnation of the so-called liberal leaders, 'The State appropriated not only the religious houses but the personal patrimony with which the religious had entered and benefices to which were attached pious obligations the fulfilment of which was not taken care of. Mousinho da Silveira intended that with these national goods the external debt incurred by the civil war should be paid but the opinion to indemnify the heroes of the liberal cause prevailed.'[14] He concludes, 'Furnishings, domestic or agricultural utensils, precious objects, clothing, libraries...almost everything disappeared criminally.'[15]

A DIFFICULT SITUATION FOR WOMEN RELIGIOUS

The houses of women were allowed to remain but, as they were forbidden to admit any further candidates to religious life, it was expected that they too would, in time, cease to exist. Meanwhile, the women's convents were so heavily taxed that the communities were impoverished and were often unable to carry out necessary repairs to their buildings. Many of these communities, unable to continue their religious life, were suppressed and the remaining nuns were sent to other convents.

In the Bom Sucesso archives several documents concern government demands for the payment of extraordinary taxes in order to reduce the national debt. From 1829 to 1833, the community received a letter annually from the Ministry of Finance ordering either an exact account of its revenue and financial obligations or the payment of a large sum of money based on the value of the property. The opening formula is always, *Manda El Rey Nosso Senhor* – 'Our Lord the King commands' and the closing formula is rather cynical in view of the persecution current at the time, *Deus guarde V. M.ce.* – ' May God protect you.' In the 1829 letter the sisters are asked to give an account of the revenue they should have received in the previous year and not what they actually received. Thus, they would be taxed not on their actual income but on what should have been their income.

The 1830 document demands the payment of 100,000 *reis* for each of the four ecclesiastical years beginning on the Feast of Saint John the Baptist, June 1828 and ending on the same feast in 1832. Furthermore, 'the same August Lord ordains' that within thirty days from the date of this letter, 5th July, 1830, the sisters would pay the Treasury 200,000 *reis*, the amount demanded for the two years which ended in the previous June. If this payment is not made within the stated time, the Government will proceed to the confiscation of all the Community's income.[16]

All this tax was paid and in the following year, the letter is later in the year, 29th November, 1831, demanding only the 100,000 *reis* owed by the Convent for the year ending in June of that year. This must now be paid within twenty days and the letter concludes with a threat, 'The same August Lord hopes that it will not be necessary to make use of executive means for the exact fulfilment of this, his royal command.'[17]

The 1832 communication is dated 13th August and carries the same demand of 100,000 *reis* tax for the year ending the previous June. It must be paid within fifteen days and the same threat for its non-payment is imposed.[18] The last letter in this series is dated 28th January, 1833 and resembles the 1829 order – the prioress must again give an account of the income that should be received and the expenditure of the convent for the year ending on the Feast of Saint John the Baptist in June 1833.[19]

Describing the State's oppression of the Church at this time the ecclesiastical historian Padre Miguel de Oliveira writes, 'Liberalism did not wait for the definitive victory to start persecuting the Church. It was scarcely installed in Lisbon when D. Pedro's government began to give legal form to the most oppressive precepts under the appearance of reforms. Freemasonry secretly inspired it but the collaboration of the clergy was not lacking.'[20] This involvement of some of the clergy is testified to at this time, in the Community's surrender of its archives.

THE GOVERNMENT DEMANDS BOM SUCESSO'S ARCHIVES

By decree of the 31st July, 1833 the Commission for General Ecclesiastical Reform was instituted. It was composed of four priests and its president was Padre Marcos Pinto Soares Vaz Preto. On 23rd August, this Commission was dissolved and the Junta to examine the actual state and temporal improvement of the Regular Orders was re-established (it had been abolished by D. Miguel). The members of the Commission remained as members of the Junta and five more ecclesiastics were added to it.

This Government Department now demanded Bom Sucesso's archives of documents dating from its foundation in 1639, 'The Administrative Commission created by order of his imperial Majesty the Duke of Bragança, Regent in the name of the Queen. By edict of the examining Junta for the actual state and temporal improvement of the Regular Orders with responsibility for the General Ecclesiastical Reform dated 11ᵗʰ June of the current year informs the Superior of the convent of Bom Sucesso that the said Commission having been installed on 18ᵗʰ of the current month in the Convent of Nossa Senhora da Piedade e Esperança, is in session on Mondays and Fridays at 4p.m.; that you hand over without delay to this Commission the archive, title deeds and other documents belonging to the same convent, by your own procurators or whoever you appoint; besides, as from now, the same Superior may not undertake any transactions or contract with regard to the goods of the Convent which must only be undertaken by the same Commission in conformity with the royal decrees, any and every contrary transaction being its responsibility, which is communicated to you for your information.'

Lisbon, in the session of 18ᵗʰ July 1834 [21]

Sister Brigid Staunton was prioress and meekly handed over these documents. She was to discover that it was not at all easy to have them returned and in her distress at the loss of this precious documentation she appealed to the British Embassy in the hope that, through the ambassador's influence (Portugal being Britain's oldest ally) the documents might be restored to the Community. The vice-consul, Mr. Jeremiah Meagher who, as guardian of Mariana Russell Kennedy, had come to know the Bom Sucesso community, undertook to contact Padre Marcos of the Junta for Ecclesiastical Reform and was successful. The convent archives contain some charming letters from this gentleman who had a vested interest in Bom Sucesso because of his six-year old protégée but who also proved himself a genuine friend of the nuns.

HELP FROM BRITISH EMBASSY

The vice-consul informed the ambassador, Lord Howard Walden, of what had occurred and received assurance from him that he would protect the community. Mr. Meagher then composed a statement for Sister Brigid to sign and forward to the *Commissão*. This statement was to the effect that the convent was under the protection of the British ambassador and had a right to receive income from its landed property. This, finally, resulted in the return of the documents.

Later Mr. Meagher sent another letter to the prioress and enclosed a draft letter of thanks to be sent to Lord Howard. Mr. Meagher's final letter to Sister Brigid Staunton is quite brief but expresses his satisfaction at the successful outcome of the negotiations: 'Dear Miss Staunton, I have the pleasure to transmit the *aviso* (notice) from Padre Marcos to the President of the Commissão to deliver immediately your *cartório*. You see I have persevered and succeeded – I send it open to you to read – take a copy of it and then seal and send it by your *capelão* (chaplain). And now you will say I have been a good boy.

Yours sincerely

J. Meagher' [22]

QUEEN DONA MARIA II

In the Bom Sucesso archives a list of nineteen letters dating from the same time deals mainly with demands from government departments, local and national, for an inventory of goods and property belonging to the convent or information as to its foundation and the refusal of the nuns to give such information on the grounds that they were under British protection. The history of the convent's foundation made by the Countess of Atalaya and not by the king was extremely important and consequently, the documents concerning the foundation were invaluable in the defence of the Sisters' right of ownership. If the king had endowed the convent then, as crown property, it would have been confiscated by the Government.

Among these letters, number 6 is from the Queen, Dona Maria II ordering the archives of the Monastery of Bom Sucesso to be restored and the nuns to be allowed to administer their own property as formerly. It is dated 20th October 1834 when the Queen was only fifteen years old but was already the reigning monarch. On the death of her father D. Pedro in September 1834, she was declared to have reached her majority and she straightway abolished the Administration for Ecclesiastical Affairs. If this date and those of Mr. Meagher's letters are accurate, it must have taken about a year between the handing over of the documents and the decree to have them returned. Meanwhile, the community must have suffered great hardship as they were forbidden to administer their property.

This crisis of the documents was not the only occasion when the nuns appealed to Lord Howard Walden for help. In 1834 also, they had asked him to intervene when the Portuguese Government tried to oblige them to admit Portuguese nuns from some of the suppressed convents. The reason given is 'that such a mixture would cause much confusion.'[23] There were, at this time, seven Portuguese in the community of seventeen.The real reason was more likely the fear that by their admitting Portuguese religious the Government would gain control of the convent on account of the presence of its own nationals. This appeal was successful and the community remained mainly Irish or of Irish descent.

CONSTANT GOVERNMENT INTERFERENCE

The successful conclusion of the documents crisis did not prevent the Government from further intervention in the affairs of the community. From the 1830s to the 1890s there was constant interference on the part of one government department or another, usually demanding an account of the property together with its revenue and the circumstances of its foundation. Consequently, in order to ensure the protection of the British embassy in this period of such political turmoil in Portugal, the community and its property were formally registered as British in that embassy on 23rd November, 1835. However, members of the Portuguese royal family continued to befriend the Sisters of Bom Sucesso while the latter also developed a cordial relationship with the personnel of the British embassy. This culminated in the visit of the Prince of Wales, the future Edward VII in 1876 and later, when he was King of England.

In 1834, the community numbered seventeen the majority of whom were Irish or of Irish descent: the prioress – Brigid Staunton, sub-prioress – Honoria O'Flynn, Depositorian – Cecilia O'Neill (born in Portugal), Scrivener – Teresa Staunton, Mary da Cunha (Portuguese), Maria José Joyce, Gertrude Albuquerque (Portuguese), Catherine Butler, Dominic Butler, Margaret Dorran, Iria Quinlan, Isabel Brown.

Of the remaining five Sisters, four do not have their surnames recorded in the annals but, as their first names indicate, they are probably Portuguese, Ana Maria do Carmo, Isidoria, Ana Rita, Gertrudes, while the last named has a Portuguese surname, Teresa Silva. Sadly, by 1845, some of the prominent members had died – Cecilia O'Neill and Honoria O'Flynn in 1843 and Brigid Staunton in 1845. Two years later, the death occurred of Mother Mary of Jesus Cunha who had spent seventy years in the convent and had been prioress during the crisis of 1823.

A MOST DIFFICULT TIME FOR BOM SUCESSO

The period from 1835 to 1860 may be described as the most difficult time for Bom Sucesso in its long history. In 1835, 1841 and again in

1849, demands were made to furnish information concerning the foundation of the convent and its financial affairs. These demands were met with a refusal, the prioress claiming indemnity because the members were British subjects.

There were, however, occasions when the storm of anti-religious feeling abated as in 1839 when the Rosary Confraternity which had been suppressed in 1834 was again allowed to celebrate its special feasts and organise public processions. During the five years of its suppression, many members had died so that it was now impossible to celebrate the suffrages of fifty Masses for each deceased member. The Patriarch acceded to the Confraternity's request to reduce the number of Masses. Ten priests were engaged to say Mass on a given day for the deceased members. Forty Masses were said during the year and Mass at the Rosary altar was said every Saturday for the members.

In 1842, a new prioress was elected. Mother Teresa Staunton, a younger sister of Brigid and, at the time, *madrinha* (godmother) of Mariana Russell Kennedy. She would be instrumental in rejuvenating the community and would merit the title 'The Second Foundress' of Bom Sucesso. However, nearly twenty years would elapse before she would even glimpse the beginning of this restoration

In 1844, Cecilia, another member of the Staunton family came to the convent as a lady boarder. She joined the group of young women who were hoping to become members of the community if the law prohibiting religious profession were abolished. They were given habits to wear when they took part in the choral recitation of the Divine Office since, without their help, it was very difficult for a depleted community to maintain this daily celebration. Besides Cecilia Staunton, there were Mary and Ellen Davoren and Ellen Morris, niece of Mother Teresa Staunton. These women also helped with the teaching and, for a time, Ellen Morris was in charge of the boarders.

By the 1850s, the community, in spite of the number of the pupils in the school, was reduced to penury. We read the pathetic story of some Sisters making and selling artificial flowers or specialising in confectionery in order to make ends meet. Apart from the law against religious profession, the annals give another reason for the lack of religious coming from Ireland to Portugal. Since the Emancipation of Catholics in 1829, there was no need for Irish ladies to enter abroad as convents had sprung up in several parts of Ireland. Also, the treatment of religious in foreign countries was not calculated to encourage future aspirants to religious life to seek admittance where, at any moment, the authorities might appear and expel them.[24]

Some members of the community, among them Sister Ana Hayes, felt that the only solution to the crisis was to request the Dominican convents in Ireland to send out Sisters who were already professed. The two Irish Dominican priests resident in Portugal at the time, Dr. Russell and Fr. Wiseman agreed and the Patriarch of Lisbon, when consulted, said he would be willing to receive such Sisters into his diocese.

TRAGIC EVENTS IN THE 1850s

Meanwhile, two tragedies struck the community at this time, one personal to the nuns and pupils of Bom Sucesso, the other a tragedy shared by all the people of Lisbon. In 1854, Ellen Hay, niece of Sister Anne Hay, who had spent eight years as a boarder in Bom Sucesso went to visit England but on the homeward voyage the vessel was wrecked near Liverpool and nearly all the passengers were lost, including Ellen.[25]

The second tragedy affected not only the convent but the whole city of Lisbon – an outbreak in 1856-57 of cholera and yellow fever. The annals record that the people were panic-stricken, the danger of contagion making them desert even their own relatives.[26] However, there were also those who made heroic efforts to help the people during the epidemic. Among them were the two Irish Dominican priests, Dr. Russell and Fr. Wiseman who were conspicuous for their charity and devotion towards the plague-stricken, even helping to bury the dead.[27] The young king, D.Pedro V also gave proof of heroic self-sacrifice in visiting the hospitals to comfort the victims of this epidemic. He himself was to die of typhus at an early age in 1861.

Again, Bom Sucesso shared in the suffering of the people when five of its Sisters died from this outbreak, thus reducing the number in the community to seven. Added to their sense of loss was the fact that the place of burial of these Sisters had to be in a public cemetery, not in the Chapter Room of the Convent as was customary until this time.

During D. Pedro's reign (1853-1861) and that of his brother D.Luís (1861-1889), Portugal enjoyed a relative calm in political affairs. For the most part, two political parties, *Regenadores* and *Históricos* (later named *Progressistas*) alternated in power and, in general, there was a certain economic expansion with the consequent prosperity that favoured the ruling middle class.

APPEALS FOR SISTERS FROM IRELAND

The situation in the Bom Sucesso convent, on the contrary, had become critical in the aftermath of the yellow fever epidemic. The prioress, Mother Teresa Staunton, accordingly, wrote an appeal for professed Sisters to two Dominican Communities in Ireland, Saint Mary's Dominican Convent, Cabra, Dublin and the Dominican Convent of Siena, Drogheda, Co. Louth. Unfortunately, both communities felt unable to send anyone at that time.

However, Mother Teresa wrote to Cabra once again in February 1860. She explained her reason for her renewed appeal, 'I was roused to make another effort to save our house by the death of the youngest but one of my beloved sisters whom it pleased God to call to his divine Presence on the 12th of this month.' [28] She then reveals the intensity of her suffering with regard to the future of Bom Sucesso, '…my heart is ready to break to think that our magnificent convent nearly three hundred years old, dedicated to the love and service of the Living God, will after our deaths…pass into the hands of the Government and be converted into a manufactory as has been already the fate of some of the most splendid Churches in Portugal.' [29]

'The possibility of legal permission being given for religious professions to take place was remote because the present Government is most inveterate against convents.' [30]

Another reason for her making a second appeal to Cabra was that the Cardinal Patriarch of Lisbon, Bom Sucesso's ecclesiastical superior at the time had advised her to apply to friends in Ireland for personnel and she continued, 'Perhaps, if you have got an addition to your number since we last heard from you, you might for pity's sake spare one or two that would be capable to take the government of the school, as we are wretchedly off in the French and Music Department.' [31] She concluded the first section of the letter, 'I must now tell you that we have always continued saying the prayer to the Immaculate Conception that you sent me, and I have confidence that she will soften your hearts now to do something for us.' [32]

The second part of the letter is concerned with alternative propositions. She had heard that there were in Ireland well educated young women who wished to become religious but did not have sufficient means to enter a convent, 'If you would meet with any such, your Community could recommend them to come here, for we would receive them here with open arms, provided you knew them to be capable of teaching young ladies and the Portuguese are rather particular.'[33]

The other proposition was the possibility of young women from Portugal being trained in religious life in Ireland, '...if I sent them to Ireland, would you receive them into your convent to pass their novitiate and let them return immediately after being professed.'[34] From a later letter of Teresa Staunton, we learn that the refusal to this appeal arrived in Bom Sucesso the 7th March, 1860 and caused her to shed tears of bitter disappointment.[35]

APPEAL TO CARDINAL CULLEN, ARCHBISHOP OF DUBLIN

Nevertheless, this persevering woman made one final appeal, this time to Dr. Cullen, Archbishop of Dublin. After an introductory paragraph praising his achievements, typical of a nineteenth century laudatory address, Mother Teresa proceeds, 'This emboldens me to have recourse to your Grace.'[36] She gives a brief account of the foundation of Bom Sucesso and its present state, 'A hundred and forty-eight young ladies of most respectable families have dedicated their lives to God and professed within the walls. Out of that number there are only five remaining, poor old nuns, myself one of that number.'[37] She again states that the Cardinal Patriarch is urging us 'to use all diligence to try to get over a few Professed Sisters.'[38]

The specific reason for sending a letter to Dr. Cullen is because of his having three Dominican convents within his jurisdiction, 'By this packet I have written to the three Convents in your Diocese. If any of them volunteers to come I trust you will give your consent.'[39] On 27th April, 1860, Dr. Cullen forwarded to Mother de Ricci Maher the Staunton letter with the following brief note, 'Dear Mrs. Maher, Be so good as to read the enclosed and see what you can do for the good nuns of Lisbon. Yours sincerely, Dr. P. Cullen'[40]

CABRA'S FIRST MISSION ABROAD

The Bom Sucesso annals record that when the Staunton letter was shown to Father Thomas McNamara, C.M., chaplain to Cabra Convent, he remarked that nuns who would refuse such a request would not deserve to have the *De Profundis* said for them after death.[41] The Cabra Community consented to send four sisters to Lisbon in August, 1860. This was their first foreign mission and it initiated Cabra's great missionary movement of the later nineteenth century: New Orleans, October, 1860; Cape Town, South Africa, 1863; Adelaide, South

Australia, 1868. Between 1860 and 1870, of the ninety-four professed Sisters in Cabra forty-nine went to foreign missions.

Meanwhile, more letters were sent between Cabra, Lisbon and Dr. Cullen. Early in June 1860, Mother Teresa wrote to Cabra, expressing her joy at the positive result of all her efforts, 'In my last communication I informed you that your favour of the 7th March caused me to shed tears of bitter disappointment; now, thank God, the case is reversed, the tears of sorrow have been turned into joy by your unexpected letter.' [42] She then explains that Cabra's consent to send Sisters to Lisbon was truly an answer to prayer, 'We had devotion of the month of May in our Church and the principal favour begged each day of Our Blessed Lady was the preservation of our house for I resolved that if nothing good turned out this month not to think any more about it for it appeared to be the Divine Will that Bom Sucesso should become extinct....When lo and behold, on the 29th May, I received your letter.' [43]

REPLIES TO QUESTIONS PUT BY CABRA'S PRIORESS

The remainder of this letter is devoted to answering the Cabra prioress's questions on practical issues. These throw light on the daily life of these elderly religious. The first issue was that of jurisdiction – the community was under the jurisdiction of the Cardinal Patriarch of Lisbon for about twenty-seven years. During the crisis of the 1830s, it was thought wiser to be under the Patriarch's jurisdiction rather than that of the Master of the Dominican Order. However, the community always entertained the hope of returning to the Order's jurisdiction. 'Where community prayer is concerned, the Divine Office is still kept up regularly. You are aware that there is not a sufficient number of nuns to keep up the choir, so I was obliged to take four young girls for that purpose. In almost all the convents of Portugal, the choir is kept up by that means. Some of the convents are already reduced to one or two nuns, so that in a short time there will be but few religious.' [44]

The next issue to be dealt with is the Bom Sucesso income, 'We have between lands and houses about five hundred pounds a year but of which we have to pay very high taxes for in this country convents are not exempt from them.' [45] Mother Teresa then gives something of the local colour of Belém in the nineteenth century. It was a popular seaside resort and the building beside the convent grounds was, in the nineteenth century, a hotel. The community benefited from the popularity of the area as a seaside resort because some of the houses on their estate were rented by holidaymakers. This was not altogether a lucrative enterprise as this letter explains, 'We have also to expend a large sum on the houses for they are very old and generally are only let during the bathing season.'[46] Nevertheless, she adds, 'I can tell you with all sincerity we want for nothing.'[47]

The greatest need of Bom Sucesso at this time was in the boarding school. Because of the age of the Sisters, they were no longer able to run a school. However, 'I have not the least doubt that if we had sufficient subjects we would have a flourishing school in no time.'[48] There are other educational needs which could be met by a more active community. 'In the Summer months, we would also have a dayschool for young ladies for in the bathing season there is a great concourse of persons in our neighbourhood.'[49]

A further advantage that Bom Sucesso had at this time is now mentioned: 'We also possess the advantage of sea-bathing which no other convent in the country has for the sweet water of the Tagus washes the walls of our garden.'[50] The reference here is to an indoor pool which was filled with salt water from the Tagus. This pool continued to be used well into the twentieth century.

Dispensations are then dealt with: 'If you should join us, I will also get a dispensation for the Divine Office for, of course, we could not have separate choirs.'[51] As to the fasts of the Order, 'we were a long time ago obliged to get a dispensation for we could not keep up to it.'[52]

Finally, the question of the difficulty of learning the Portuguese language requires reassurance for those intending to come to Lisbon. 'Do not be alarmed about the Portuguese language, it is not at all difficult to learn particularly for anyone who knows French.'[53]

In her letter of thanks to Dr. Cullen in June of 1860, Teresa Staunton gives Bom Sucesso's daily timetable at this time:

5.30 a.m.	Rising
6.00 a.m.	Choir – Office of Our Lady, Prime, the Rosary, Half-hour Mental Prayer, Mass
8.30 a.m.	Breakfast
1.00 p.m.	Dinner
3.00 p.m.	Vespers
5.00 p.m.	Matins
8.00 p.m.	Tea
10.00 p.m.	Bed [54]

This was a rather rigorous horarium for an elderly community but the recitation of the Divine Office was faithfully maintained.

FURTHER REQUESTS TO DR. CULLEN

The remainder of this letter further reveals the courage and determination of this ageing but dynamic woman. She requests Dr. Cullen to obtain from Rome permission to re-open the novitiate in Bom Sucesso. Her reason for this is that three Irish women have waited for fourteen years in order to become religious in Bom Sucesso but 'never were they (the Government) more inveterate against religion than they are at present.' [55]

For surmounting the prohibition concerning profession, she has also an idea as to how to circumvent the State's law, '…it could be done quite privately and at the end of the novitiate if he (the Pope) did not give leave to profess them here, they could go to a convent of the Order in England or Ireland to make final vows.' [56]

At the end of this letter, Mother Teresa makes a rather amusing request of Dr. Cullen, 'Will Your Grace pardon me for asking you to forward the enclosed (her letter to Mother de Ricci Maher). I have not a second Irish postage stamp, I must send to my friends for a few, as I am told letters do not go safe without being stamped. Is it true?' Another amusing aspect of this letter is the familiarity with which the writer closes it. Whereas, in her first appeal to Dr. Cullen, a few months previously, she had signed, 'I remain Your Lordship's most humble servant,' in her June letter she signed, 'Believe me your affectionate sister in Christ.' [57]

WARNING FROM DR. CULLEN

Another letter from Dr. Cullen to Mother de Ricci Maher dated the 26th June, 1860 reveals the circumspection with which this first journey of Cabra missionaries to Lisbon was to be undertaken. He wrote, 'I have also got permission for the sisters to go to that city on a visit for the improvement of their health. No one is to know in Lisbon that they have any other object but to change air, and to learn, if they like, the Portuguese language.' [58]

9

A New Venture

In the Cloister of Bom Sucesso

A scented rose and silence as I watch the swallows kiss
And touch the ancie nt marble – I, too, am part of this.
Kind light and bougainvillea and an evening calm
And I think what prayers have circled all these stones
                    -the softly fingered Rosary, the holy psalm
What lilting canticle, what blessing song
What rites of adoration moved these hours along
                    (*Maria Mackey, O.P., June 1999*)

REASONS FOR DR. CULLEN'S WARNING

When Dr. Cullen warned Mother de Ricci Maher that the real reason for these four women setting off on their mission was not to be made known in Lisbon, he had very good reason for doing so. For four years, 1857-1861, the so-called 'question of the Sisters of Charity' was in the forefront of public debate in the Portuguese capital. 'The conflict was caused by the arrival in Portugal of French religious of the Congregation of Saint Vincent de Paul....Progressive elements deemed that the return of the sisters and especially their engagement in education was the beginning of a plan for regaining power by conservative forces.'[1]

A large rally took place in Lisbon and 'The Popular Association for promoting the Education of the Female Sex' was founded. The historian, Alexandre Herculano undertook the intellectual direction of this movement and even wrote its manifesto. In this document the writer denounced the admission of foreign teachers as incompatible with national sovereignty. This principle could be equally well applied to the Irish sisters who were about to arrive from Dublin. The issue of the five French Sisters was only resolved when, in 1861, the French government sent a warship up the Tagus to rescue the sisters and bring them back to their own country. Meanwhile, the first missionaries from Dublin were already happily installed in Bom Sucesso and working at developing the school there.

THE FIRST SISTERS FROM CABRA

The first four sisters to leave the Cabra convent, Dublin were Thomas Aquinas Tarrant, Mary Bernadine Bodkin, Scholastica Guitar and Antoninus Evans. Sister Thomas Aquinas, originally, Charlotte Tarrant, was born in Dublin in 1818. She entered the Dominican Convent, Cabra on 25th March, 1847, was professed on 27th October, 1848 and was to die in Lisbon on 1st June, 1903. Sister Bernadine, originally, Margaret Bodkin, was the daughter of John Bodkin Esquire of Arnagh, County Galway and was born there in 1816. She entered the Dominican convent Cabra in 1840, was professed on 29th April 1852, and died in Lisbon in 1866.[2] Two of her sisters, Anna Bodkin and Lady Harriet Daly lived in Dun Laoire (formerly Kingstown). The latter was instrumental in bringing a group of Dominican Sisters from Cabra to found a convent and school there in 1847. She provided the house known as Echo Lodge with its extensive grounds and paid yearly for its upkeep.[3] Lady Harriet certainly appears to have been a wealthy lady and from 1847 until her death she gave the nuns in Kingstown £100 every year to support the community and at her death the community received £2,000, the sum for which her life was insured.[4]

The third member of the group was Sister Scholastica, originally, Maria Guitar, born in India in 1831. She was a pupil of the Immaculata Boarding School Cabra, Dublin from 1845 to 1848.[5] She entered Dominican Convent, Cabra on 1st March, 1849, was professed on 23rd September, 1850 and died in Lisbon on 8th July, 1905. She had an older sister, Teresa Guitar who also entered in Cabra, on 25th March, 1847 but died ten years later on 19th September, 1857.[6] Finally, the fourth member of the group was Sister Antoninus, originally, Mary Joseph Evans, who was born in Dublin in 1839. She entered Cabra on 8th August, 1858, was professed on 26th March, 1860[7] and died in Lisbon on 12th January, 1904. She was the youngest of the group, being only twenty-one years old at the time of their departure from Ireland and in the account of their voyage to Lisbon is referred to as the child. They were accompanied on their journey by Father Thomas McNamara, C.M. and we are fortunate in having an account of their travels which one of the four sent back to the Cabra community.

Sister Bernadine Bodkin lived only six years in Lisbon but her three companions lived there some forty years, each dying in the early years of the twentieth century. All three held the office of prioress a number of times during there long lives. When they arrived the remaining members of the Bom Sucesso community were Mothers Teresa Staunton and Dominic Butler; Sisters Iria Quinlan, Eliza Browne and Isidoria, a Portuguese Sister.

In her letter of gratitude to Dr. Cullen, Mother Teresa wrote, 'We are all delighted with our new Sisters, they are everything we could wish for and I do hope and trust through the mercy of God that we shall be always as we are at present happy and united; we have but one will.' She had yet another request to make of Dublin's archbishop – to obtain from Rome dispensation from the Divine Office for the whole community. 'The position of matters in this country does not warrant the Patriarch to apply for it but we have his consent if Your Grace can accomplish it.'[8] This request shows Teresa Staunton's gift of empathy in her willingness to sacrifice the community celebration of the Church's official prayer in order to help the newcomers. She further explains her approach, 'If we obliged those that came to say the long office, the object for which they came would be frustrated, the school duties take up their whole time and I think uniformity in the observances of the house renders the dispensation indispensable.'[9] Nevertheless, the annals state that the members of the original Bom Sucesso community continued to say also the Divine Office and when only one sister of the group remained, she recited it daily until the community recitation of the Office was restored in 1881.

RE-ORGANISATION OF THE SCHOOL

The new arrivals took over the running of the school in October 1860, changing its organisation from being principally a system of tutorials to graded class teaching. In a short while the school began to flourish as Teresa Staunton had predicted. On 9th April, 1861, the Cabra community generously sent out four more Sisters: Petronilla, originally Maria O'Reilly from Cavan. Born in 1823, she was received as a Dominican on 9th July 1841 and professed on 5th October, 1842. She died in Lisbon in 1899. Mother Imelda Timmons had been a pupil of the Immaculata Boarding School, Cabra. She entered the Cabra convent, was professed in 1853 and died in Lisbon in 1914. Sister Veronica Sheridan was professed in Cabra convent in 1852 and died in Lisbon in 1911. Sister Thecla Murtagh was professed in Cabra in 1858 and died in Lisbon in 1909. This group of Sisters was accompanied to Liverpool by Father M. Gleeson, C.M. On 22ⁿᵈ April, 1862, three more sisters left Cabra for Lisbon: Columba Matthews, professed in Cabra in 1858, she died in Lisbon in 1909; de Paul Coghlan professed in Cabra in 1862, she died in Lisbon in 1916; Margaret Murphy from Carlow, professed in Cabra in 1847, she died in Lisbon in 1903.[10] Thus, the Cabra sisters ensured that Bom Sucesso would not only exist into the twentieth century but would be a flourishing and apostolic community at the dawn of that century. The community now numbered sixteen.

In 1861, permission was obtained from the Holy See to open a school for the poor children of Belém. As these pupils would not be boarders, their classroom was outside the cloister and only two sisters received permission to go outside the enclosure to conduct this school. Immelda Timmons had been trained in the education of deaf children in the Cabra College for the training of teachers of the Deaf and she undertook this work also with some of the poor children who were deaf.

TERESA STAUNTON'S OTHER PROJECTS

Very soon, the Sisters from Cabra assumed responsibility, not only for the running of the schools, but also for offices within the community. In 1862, Mother Thomas Aquinas Tarrant was elected prioress, thus freeing Teresa Staunton from the responsibility she had carried for so many difficult years. However, she would live to see some more of her projects become a reality. One of these was to have Bom Sucesso returned to the jurisdiction of the Dominican Order. In 1863, a preliminary step was taken when Père Jandel, the Master of the Order, visited the community and approved of the educational work that the sisters were engaged in. Though it would not be until 1907 when the community was formally transferred from the jurisdiction of the Patriarch to that of the Dominican Order, the approval of the Master for the apostolic work of the sisters was a hopeful sign of the fulfilment of this ideal.

Another project dear to the heart of Mother Staunton was the re-opening of the novitiate in Bom Sucesso. In 1865, this took place with the arrival of one postulant, a past-pupil of the Dominican Convent of Siena, Drogheda, Co. Louth, Ireland. She was followed later in the same year by two more women. With the entrance of more candidates for the religious life, the novitiate was full in a very short time and now the question of their profession had to be addressed. The law of 1834 forbidding religious profession to take place in Portugal was still in force. Some of the Sisters felt that, as they were registered as British subjects, the law did not apply to them. However, it was thought more prudent to keep the law and arrangements were made for the first five novices to travel with their mistress of novices to Zafra near Badajoz in Spain, in order to make profession in the convent of Saint Catherine of Siena there. The prioress of that convent, Madre Maria Aurora, received the profession of these five Sisters in the name of the Bom Sucesso prioress. This arrangement proved to be both costly and inconvenient. Consequently, in 1869, the next group made profession secretly in Bom Sucesso.

THE DEATH OF MOTHER TERESA STAUNTON

In August, 1870, the community was saddened by the death of Mother Teresa Staunton. A stone tablet over her grave in the small cemetery pays a simple, concise tribute to this great woman,

'To the memory of our beloved Mother Teresa Staunton who went to receive the reward of her virtues on August 24th 1870. She entered Bom Sucesso the 3rd March 1804, made her profession 25th August 1805. She was a prudent prioress during many years of dangers and difficulties, and may be considered as a second Foundress, for, after unwearied exertions, she succeeded in getting Sisters from Saint Mary's Dominican Convent, Cabra, Dublin, at a time when the community of Bom Sucesso was almost extinct.'

In the same small cemetery are buried Dominic Butler and Iria Quinlan. Thus, three of the five Dominican sisters who welcomed the Cabra sisters are united even in death.

GOVERNMENT INTERFERENCE AND HELP FROM BRITISH EMBASSY

During these years, the government tried to interfere in the affairs of the Bom Sucesso community but with the advice and support of the British Embassy the sisters succeeded in maintaining their independence. During the lifetime of Teresa Staunton, in 1857, the government had issued a decree regarding religious women's foundations in which a demand was made for a detailed account of each convent, its other buildings and their material state; the evaluation of the whole property; the dates of title deeds and even a description of moveable assets, especially precious objects whether sacred or not.

This demand was issued by the Secretariat of State for Ecclesiastical

Affairs on 21st July, 1857 but not until the 28th December of the same year did the Vicar General of the Patriarchate forward it with a covering letter, indicating all the detailed information to be given. The then Prioress, Teresa Staunton, had replied that, since the decree of the extinction of Religious Orders, the Community had been subject to the Cardinal Patriarch in spiritual matters only and that, while they respected the orders of His Majesty, they were always exempt and considered British subjects as in 1835, when an inventory was taken of other convents. Hence, the forms were being returned as not applicable.[11]

In the 1870's, the government made a number of attempts to send an inspector to Bom Sucesso in order to assess the suitability of the convent's accommodation for pupils and also to evaluate the standard of education there. The community considered this an intrusion on the part of the government and, on advice, refused admission. This may seem strange to us today when school inspections are accepted as part of the educational system. However, a document in the archives dated 16th April, 1875, and written by Fr. T. J. Smyth, O.P., of Corpo Santo clarifies the community's position at the time.

On the morning of 15th April, Fr. Smyth received a letter informing him that, with the approval of the Patriarch, the inspector, Senhor Ghira, had been commissioned by the government to examine the progress being made by the pupils of Bom Sucesso, the Salesians and the Oblates. The following day, the prioress of Bom Sucesso received a letter informing her of this inspection.

Fr. Smyth consulted the British consul and the advice was 'that the Official deputed by the Government ought to be refused admittance into the Convent and that the nuns should claim their privilege as British Subjects.'[12] However, if the government persisted on the grounds that they had the authority of the Patriarch, the nuns should reply that they were subject to the Patriarch in spiritual matters only but that their house was their own and its 'privacy is secured by the treaty between Great Britain and Portugal.'[13]

The civil authorities were obliged to accept this refusal and, instead, sent a list of questions concerning the number of pupils and the subjects taught. This is fortunate for us because the answers to these questions throw light on the high standard of education in Bom Sucesso during the late 19th century. In the *Mappa Estatística* for the academic year 1876-1877, seventy pupils were registered – thirty in the primary section and forty in the secondary and their ages ranged from seven years to twenty.

The subjects taught and the number of students taking each were as follows:

Portuguese	40
French	70
Art	15
English	70
German	11
Italian	30
Piano	64
Harp	11
Singing	14
Sewing	70
Embroidery of every kind	70

To the question, *Names of the Teachers,* the answer was 'All the Irish Religious are engaged in the different branches of education which include all the subjects.' [14] In another similar document of the 1870s, to the question of rewards and punishments the answer was: Rewards – books of history or storybooks in the different languages being studied by the pupils; Punishments – being obliged to study during recreation or to stand in a prominent place. For the more serious offences the pupil would be obliged to wear her dress inside out.[15]

Another example of government interference at this time concerned the convent's landed property. Again in 1875, the civil authorities communicated their intention of disposing of a plot of land belonging to Bom Sucesso. In December of that year, the prioress, Sister Scholastica Guitar, wrote to Lord Lytton, the British ambassador in Portugal, appealing for his help where this issue was concerned. After outlining the many occasions when the community had enjoyed the protection of the Embassy she goes on to explain their present dilemma, 'In direct opposition to this long exemption from foreign intervention an order was lately directed to the Prioress of Bom Sucesso to appoint valuators in reference to a small plot of ground held by the nuns, the result of sale to be converted into Portuguese funds over which the Portuguese Government, it is feared, will claim control. Now the Prioress and Community of Bom Sucesso see in this interference a direct violation of their rights.' [16]

Lord Lytton contacted the minister for Finance and all proceedings were stopped.[17]

The result of this appeal became public knowledge as it was

reported in the daily newspaper *Diário de Notícias*, dated 18th February, 1876 where it stated that the English minister had asked the government to suspend the order to proceed to freedom from entail of the Bom Sucesso property. In its edition of the 25th February, 1876, the same paper reported that the necessary order had been given at the request of the British minister. [18]

VISIT OF THE PRINCE OF WALES

The following year, the Prince of Wales, the future Edward VII, on a State visit to Portugal, included in his itinerary a visit to Bom Sucesso. The annals record, 'His Highness was received at the enclosure door by Mother Prioress and community and conducted through the cloister to the Reception room where his Highness was entertained to some vocal and instrumental items. The performers were warmly applauded and his Highness declared he had never heard a more pleasing rendering of "Kathleen Mavourneen" than in Bom Sucesso; the vocalist had accompanied herself on the harp.'[19]

Prince Edward invited the pupils to visit his yacht but, because they too lived inside the enclosure, they could not accept the invitation.

The vocalist and harpist on the occasion of the royal visit was Sister Augustine of the Incarnation Begge, a past pupil of the Dominican Convent, Taylor's Hill, Galway, who had made profession in Bom Sucesso in 1869. She was a gifted musician and composer but, in the late 1870s she began to seek a transfer from Bom Sucesso to Taylor's Hill. In her letter to the newly elected provincial, Fr. Towers, she explains the efforts she has made to verify the genuineness of her seeking this transfer, 'I am happy to tell you that I have left nothing undone to test my own motives regarding this step. It has been in my mind for the last three years and only this time last year when the labours of school were over, did I venture to lay my doubts and convictions before Fr. Carbery' (the former provincial).[20] She lists other steps she has taken to ensure that her decision is in line with the Will of God and concludes, 'After all this I think I am right in confiding the rest to Providence who never abandons those who trust in Him as I now experience.' [21]

LITURGICAL RENEWAL

Sister Augustine Begge was not the first to seek a transfer from a Dominican convent to Taylor's Hill. During the early nineteenth century, the renewal of the Church's liturgy undertaken by the Benedictine monks of Solesmes in France began to have a widespread influence and this liturgical movement inspired the Dominican community of Falls Road in Belfast to study Latin with a view to praying the Divine Office.[22] However, the bishop of Down and Connor did not approve of this and contacted the Mother house, Cabra. Consequently, some sisters decided to seek a transfer from Belfast to the Dominican Convent in Galway.

It was only natural that a gifted musician such as Augustine Begge should be attracted to a community where the liturgical Hours were solemnly chanted. In her letter to Sister Joseph Moran, prioress of Taylor's Hill, she speaks of the suffering which her coming departure from Bom Sucesso entails, 'the separation is no less painful to me than when first entering religion. My heart and affections were long centred in Bom Sucesso and I owe it much, very much indeed. But God in His all-wise providence has destined this trial for me in satisfaction, I hope, for my infidelity in His service and for other ends known to Him alone.'[23]

RETURN TO THE JURISDICTION OF DOMINICAN ORDER

This sister's departure from Bom Sucesso seems to have precipitated the putting into effect of the Community's long held desire to restore the communal recitation of the Prayer of the Church/Divine Office and to return to the jurisdiction of the Dominican Order. Consequently, only two months after Augustine Begge's return to Galway, the Irish Provincial, Father Towers accompanied by his *socius*, Father Tom Burke sailed to Lisbon in order to hold visitation in Bom Sucesso in accordance with the decree of the Master of the Order. This was the first visitation made by an Irish Provincial since before 1833. The result was that, with the full approval of the Papal Nuncio, the Patriarch of Lisbon and the Master of the Dominican Order 'The Convent of Bom Sucesso henceforth will form part of the Irish Province, to be externally governed by the Provincial as Vicar *pro temp.*'[24]

A month later, on Thursday, December 9th, Father Towers presided in Galway at what was described as 'an Extraordinary Conventual Chapter.'[25] At this Chapter he proposed that those wishing to become members of the Bom Sucesso Community should be received and professed in Galway prior to setting off for Lisbon. The majority of the Galway sisters voted in favour and subsequently, three sisters were professed there. They set sail for Lisbon in July 1884. Like their predecessors they too had their adventures when they had to go into quarantine in Lisbon because of an outbreak of cholera in France.

RESTORATION OF THE DIVINE OFFICE

Early in 1881, the term of office of the Bom Sucesso prioress was ending and the Community informed the Provincial that they wished to elect as prioress a member of the Galway Community. This would facilitate their training in the choral recitation of the Divine Office which they were anxious to adopt. Accordingly, Father Towers gave them the names of three sisters of Taylor' Hill and on 27th March 1881, Sister Jordan Connolly, aged twenty-seven, was elected prioress of Bom Sucesso.

On May 27th 1881, Sister Jordan accompanied by the Provincial and his socius Father Tom Burke set off for Dublin and 'in accordance with an arrangement that would serve to break the journey and give mutual pleasure, she spent a few days in Drogheda where the nuns showed her every kindness.'[26] She changed into secular dress in Dublin and, accompanied by her sister-in-law, set off for Lisbon where she spent three years guiding the Sisters in the choral recitation of the Prayer of the Church and also perfecting her French.

The restoration of the official Prayer of the Church was a special joy to the only remaining member of the community prior to the Cabra Sisters' arrival. She was Sister Eliza Browne who 'when asked her name would say 'My father was Browne of Athenry and my mother an Eyre of Eyrescourt.'[27] She had entered Bom Sucesso at an early age and when, in 1823, the community was being forced to transfer to Rey Salvador, Sister Eliza was too ill to be move. The date of the Sisters' departure had to be postponed on her account. 'On the 23rd Sister Eliza Browne was carried down and placed in a carriage. Evidently, the drive to Rey Salvador had no bad results for Sister Eliza recovered her health completely and was able to hand on all the traditions to the members of the present Community.'[28] When the other sisters of the earlier Community had died, she continued to say the Divine Office alone for about ten years but she happily lived to see the it fully restored in 1881. She died in 1894, thus closing another great chapter in Bom Sucesso's history.

ANOTHER CRISIS FOR BOM SUCESSO

The end of the nineteenth century, like its early decades, would be characterised by further government interference. In April 1883, a most sinister crisis arose for Bom Sucesso when the Government issued a *Contra-fé,* that is, a summons to convert all the Bom Sucesso property into government stock. Dr. Patrick Bernard Russell, O.P., of Corpo Santo was alarmed at the wording of this document and decided to take immediate steps to prevent the disentailment of the Bom Sucesso property. He wrote to the prioress, Sister Jordan Connolly, 'My dear Mother Prioress, I am sorry to tell you that the citation contained in the *Contra-fé* is a formal and undisguised summons to subject all your house and land property to the law obliging all corporations to convert their similar properties into Government stock. A close examination of the wording leaves no doubt on that point. It therefore, becomes necessary not to lose a moment in meeting this attempt.'

He undertakes to go on the following Monday to the British ambassador, Sir Charles Wyke in order 'to put the case clearly and forcibly before him. I must give him an analysis of the Countess of Atalaya's will.' The prioress must send 'by our servant Germano that copy from which I yesterday read the substance to you. I will make a clear analysis of it and turn it to the immediate source of the ambassador's action.' [29]

In a further letter Dr. Russell explains that he had visited the ambassador's secretary twice on the Sunday and had given him both the *Contra-fé* and his own analysis of the Countess's will. Consequently, Sir Charles Wyke wrote 'a remonstrance' to the minister for Foreign Affairs with which he included Fr. Russell's analysis of the Will. 'Moreover, I took a step beyond him but away from him and with one almost as powerful with the government, the Viscount Chancelleiros.' Dr. Russell's hope was that the latter 'would induce the government to respect not some but all your rights passive and active.' [30]

A third letter from Fr. Russell, dated the 17th April informs the prioress that Viscount Chancelleiros spoke to the Prime Minister, Senhor Fontes 'about the citation to sell your property. Fontes had not heard a word about it but he would give orders to suspend all proceedings to your annoyance.' [31] Dr. Russell assures the prioress where this matter is concerned and gives her further reason for confidence because 'the Viscount desires me to tell you not to be uneasy and should any other citation appear, simply say the matter is placed in the hands of the Ambassador and lies between him and his Majesty's ministers.' [32] Another matter with regard to the selling of some property was also referred to the Viscount and received another re-assuring response, 'I spoke to him about your wish to sell these properties…he promises that, when you are ready, he will so manage that you will sell without any embarrassment.' [33]

On April 28th, Dr. Russell received the following letter from Mr. Charles Duff of the British Embassy, 'My dear Dr. Russell, I am authorized by Sir Charles Wyke to communicate to you the following notice received yesterday:

Ministério dos Negócios Estrangeiros

Direcção Política,

Lisboa, 24 d´Abril de 1883

Most Illustrious and Excellent Sir,

In reply to the note that you addressed to me on 9th of the current month, I have the honour of communicating to you that, though still dependent on a higher resolution, the question raised with respect to the disentailment, nevertheless, appropriate orders have been sent to the competent authority to suspend the making of an inventory and other stipulations tending to effect the disentailment of goods belonging to the Convent of Bom Sucesso to which your Excellency's note refers.

Signed, A. de Serpa [34]

Copy (translation from Portuguese)

This note further signed by Sir Charles Wyke was passed on to Mother Jordan on 28th April. It had taken almost a month to have this very serious matter resolved and one can imagine how much anxiety these Sisters endured during that time.

Fr. Patrick Bernard Russell, O.P.

Patrick Russell, the Dominican priest who was instrumental in saving Bom Sucesso at this time, had lived in Portugal for many years before this crisis. He was born in Cork in 1811 and, at the age of seventeen, set off for Portugal in order to enter the Irish Dominican novitiate and to study for the priesthood. He was ordained in 1835 and remained in Lisbon in order to teach philosophy and later theology to the Irish students. He continued to do so until the Irish Dominican college closed and the students were moved to Tallaght outside Dublin where the studium was opened in 1856. This became possible due to the enactment by the British Parliament of the Catholic Emancipation Act of 1829.

When the greater part of the college was sold in 1854, Dr. Russell

154

opened a school for the education of boys at Corpo Santo and later another in Caparica. During the plague of yellow fever in 1856, he was indefatigable in attending to the sick and dying. Ten years later, in 1866, he gave every assistance to Mother Teresa Saldanha in her founding of the Dominican Congregation of Portuguese Sisters. In 1887, for his outstanding apostolic work in Portugal, he was decorated by the King with the title, *Comendador da Real Ordem Militar de Nosso Senhor Jesús Cristo.*

Dr. Russell was not only a most apostolic priest but he was, also, a highly cultured man and was often consulted by the King concerning the choice of works of art. Most importantly, he was a man of prayer, 'He saw God in every thing beautiful and it was inspiring to hear him at night in the choir, when he thought that he was alone, pouring out his soul to God in prayer before the Blessed Sacrament.' [35] He caught an illness during a sick-call and died on 17th November, 1901, at the age of ninety.

10

The Third Centenary

In the Cloister of Bom Sucesso (*continued*)

Dawn vision, dreams and ecstasies
A sacred line
Ah, surely there's some reaching out
from their great souls to mine?
I shall watch again in sunlight
Search the whole
for signs of those who prayed here
And wove the strands of history
in my soul

(Maria Mackey, O.P., June 1999)

ANTI-CLERICALISM IN TWENTIETH CENTURY PORTUGAL

The Bom Sucesso annals open the chapter on the twentieth century with a reference to an anti-clerical movement at the dawn of the century. The then English minister, Sir Hugh Mc Donnell intervened to protect the communities of Corpo Santo and Bom Sucesso. King Edward VII himself expressed the wish that they would not be interfered with. The king of Portugal, D. Carlos replied that 'as long as he reigned no harm would come to them.'[1] Tragically, before the first decade of the century had passed, he himself together with his son, the heir to the throne, D. Luís Filipe, would fall a victim to the crime of regicide.

Meanwhile, the Bom Sucesso sisters decided to re-open their novitiate which had been closed for many years. They applied to the Dominican Convent of Siena, Drogheda in Co. Louth, Ireland and two sisters, Mary Teresa Condon, mistress of novices and Mary Michael, sub-mistress, arrived in Lisbon during February 1901. A number of candidates entered and the novitiate continued to flourish for a number of years.

Visit of King Edward VII of England

At this time, Bom Sucesso was in the public eye both in Portugal and England because King Edward VII had expressed a wish to visit the community during his State visit to Portugal. Through the British ambassador, the sisters had replied with a welcoming letter. On the appointed day, 6th April, 1903, officials and friends gathered in the courtyard of the Convent, among them, Sir Martin Gosselin, the British ambassador, and the Fathers of Corpo Santo. Punctually at 10 a.m., 'His Majesty arrived in a carriage drawn by four white Arabian horses richly caparisoned, preceded by two out-riders on steeds of the same breed.' [2] Accompanying the King were the Honourable Mr. Ponsonby, Sir Francis Laking and the Lord-in-Waiting, Count Tarouca.

When the King alighted from his carriage, the British minister presented the Fathers of Corpo Santo and then his Majesty approached the enclosure door where the sisters and their pupils stood on either side. *God Save the King* was sung to the music of the harp and, at its conclusion, the King expressed a wish to visit the Choir and Church. Escorted by the senior sisters and preceded by two children strewing flowers he went from the Church to the community room where the children again sang while the guests took their places and His Majesty a throne especially arranged for the occasion.

When all were seated, a little child dressed in white walked from the end of the room through the two rows of guests to the throne where she presented a bouquet of flowers and a greeting to the King. The ribbon of the bouquet had the arms of the royal Houses of Portugal and England, one of the last occasions when the Portuguese royal emblem would be used.

Father Paul O'Sullivan, Rector of Corpo Santo gave an address of welcome and King Edward replied, 'I thank you most warmly for your kind words. It is a great pleasure for me to come and see you, my subjects. I am delighted to see that everything is in so flourishing a state.' [3]

His Majesty and guests had some light refreshments, special wine of one hundred years' vintage being supplied by Count Burnay. The annals continue, 'Chatting for a considerable time to those around him, his Majesty told them how well he felt in the glorious sunshine. The visit was quite an intimate affair, the King paternally making enquiries about the sisters. When leaving the enclosure the Mother Prioress said, "We are praying for Your Majesty"; "Many thanks, Mother", replied the King in a deeply touching tone.'[4] King Edward had a special regard for the Prioress, Sister Scholastica Guitar and considered her among the outstanding ladies he had met in Portugal. The annals conclude with a little episode at the entrance where the King's detective, Mr. Melville from Kerry had remained. The sister portress not knowing what his rôle was invited him to go up to the Reception Room to which he replied, 'Ah, no Sister, no necessity, no one will touch His Majesty here.'

BOM SUCESSO RETURNS TO JURISDICTION OF DOMINICAN ORDER

Another significant event for the Bom Sucesso community occurred in 1907 when, on 28th November, the rescript came from Rome informing the Sisters that the transfer of their jurisdiction from the Cardinal Patriarch of Lisbon to the Master of the Dominican Order was confirmed. The then Master, Père Hyacinth Cormier (now Blessed) sent a petition to the Sacred Congregation of Bishops and Regulars stating, 'the Dominican nuns of the second Order of Bom Sucesso in Lisbon humbly ask that they be restored to the jurisdiction of the Dominican Order now that the violent persecutions which troubled the kingdom of Portugal have ceased.'[5]

A short history of the foundation in 1639 is then given, including the formal acceptance by the Order of Preachers at the General Chapter of 1644. Dealing with the religious problems in Portugal during the nineteenth century, the document mentions the expulsion of the sisters from their convent in 1823 and their subsequent return a month later. It continues, 'Only in 1833, for the first time, does the intervention of the Patriarch of Lisbon in the affairs of the Dominican monastery (occur), on the occasion of the election of the prioress and later for Receptions and Professions.'[6] However, for some time, the political and religious conditions in the kingdom of Portugal have changed, improved so much as to render the life of the Dominican nuns and the Irish Fathers secure and tranquil especially through the protection that England in Portugal affords its British   subjects. And it is for this (reason) that the Dominican nuns have made and make lively and repeated requests to return to the jurisdiction of the Order.'[7]

In Père Cormier's 'humble opinion' the monastery of Bom Sucesso has always remained in full vigour under the jurisdiction of the Order since the right does not cease if taken by violence because it was suspended following the violent expulsion of religious.

'No canonical act exists to prove the legal transfer of jurisdiction consented to by the Master General of the Preachers and accepted by the Patriarch of Lisbon. For the rest, in the present question there is the consent of the parties. The sisters ardently wish to return to the jurisdiction of the Order, which is proved especially by the enclosed letter written by the sisters themselves to the Cardinal Patriarch of Lisbon. The Cardinal Patriarch is equally favourable as is attested by the reply which he sent to the sisters (Allegato A). Moreover, he has shown his desire to fully entrust the care of the monastery to the Dominican Fathers because of the difficulty of finding among the clergy persons suitable for this kind of ministry. Finally, the Master and his Council have considered the sisters' requests and are in favour of taking the monastery under the jurisdiction of the Order. I include the Act of deliberation voted by the Council (Allegato B).'[8]

Some months later, on 29th November, 1907, the rescript signed by Cardinal Ferrata, Prefect of the *Sacra Congregatio Episcoporum et Regularium,* was issued and, a week later, it was joyfully received by the sisters of Bom Sucesso.

Blessed Hyacinth Cormier continued his interest in and friendship for the Bom Sucesso community. On 30th December, 1907, he wrote his good wishes for the New Year of 1908, 'A happy year on earth and especially happy years in eternity.' In this letter the Master of the Dominican Order shows his appreciation of the cloistered vocation 'without frontiers, embracing all nations, crossing seas, reaching the most distant shores.... Oh prayers of our Sisters which ceaselessly mount to heaven, fall as beneficial rain on all our houses, on all those living in them, on all the works to which they are dedicated.'[9]

KING D. CARLOS OF PORTUGAL

Few outside the political arena could have foreseen the tragedy that was about to take place in Lisbon at the beginning of February, 1908. The King of Portugal, D. Carlos (1863-1908), the son of the former king D. Luís and Dona Maria Pia, daughter of Victor Emmanuel, came to the throne of Portugal on the death of his father in 1889. He had married Dona Amélia of Orléans, the daughter of Louis Philippe, Count of Paris. The historian, José Hermano Saraiva sums up the political position adopted by him at the beginning of his reign: 'D. Carlos, intelligent, aware of the climate of social innovation of the time in which he lived was for many a reason for hope. As monarch, he always tried to remain within the constitutional limits laid down by the Charter and, though he might be tempted to give to royal power a more dynamic emphasis, he never accepted to enter by the way of disrespecting the norms which limited the king's power.' [10]

According to another historian, he was intelligent but haughty and far from enjoying the popularity that his father had enjoyed.[11] Very early in his reign, a crisis was caused by an ultimatum from Great Britain obliging Portugal to surrender its vast African territory between Angola in West Africa and Mozambique in East Africa, the territory, today, of Zambia and Zimbabwe. This ultimatum provoked a national wave of indignation against Great Britain and the pro-British king of Portugal. He was accused of not having paid sufficient attention to overseas territories, thus compromising national interests. Protests took place in many parts of the country and on 31st January, 1891, the first Republican revolt took place in Oporto. Though this revolt was crushed, it revealed the existence of a real threat to the monarchy.

The European economic crisis of 1890-1891 had repercussions in Portugal and successive governments failed to tackle its financial problems until, in 1892, a coalition headed by the economist, José Dias Ferreira, an independent, succeeded in dealing with the major financial issues, thus creating political calm. Until 1906, two parties alternated in government – the *Regeneradores* whose leader was Hintze Ribeiro and the *Progressistas* led by José Luciano de Castro. 'The Constitutional Monarchy had succeeded in overcoming the profound crisis – the penultimate of its existence – and in moving forward.' [12]

During this period, Portuguese territories were under threat from the major European powers. In 1904, Germany considered the possibility of occupying all Portuguese colonies. Aware of this threat the government and the diplomatic service tried to control the situation. 'The king himself, D. Carlos was a good ambassador in this cause, frequently visiting European courts and receiving in Portugal the heads of State from England, Germany, France and Spain.' [13] However, the principal reason for Portugal's retaining sovereignty over Angola and Mozambique was, according to Oliveira Marques, due to rivalry between the great Powers and anxiety to maintain European equilibrium.[14]

The maintenance of public order was an important issue, at this time, as it was often threatened by anarchical movements. In May 1906, the prime minister, Hintze Ribeiro, resigned because he and his government had wanted to postpone parliamentary sessions on account of their being disrupted. The King, however, did not think it opportune as he was unwilling to use repressive tactics unless absolutely necessary for public safety and there were still other ways of securing this. João Franco, leader of the *Partido Regenerador-Liberal,* was asked to form a government. His political programme was considered tolerant and liberal.

According to Saraiva, behind the reforms of the new government was the political thinking of D.Carlos. The Crown's speech at the opening of Parliament on 29th September, 1906, was 'a genuine proclamation of a political project innovative in many respects.'[15] Among other projects, the King announced a more efficient administration, ministerial responsibility for putting into effect acts of government, electoral reform which would extend the right to vote to the working class and which guaranteed freedom of association.

Where education was concerned, the King announced the re-organisation of central services, autonomy, both pedagogical and financial for the universities, the opportunity to study abroad for better students and for teachers, both primary and secondary, in order to acquire modern pedagogical techniques. This was the first time that the King appeared before Parliament to propose a concrete plan of political reform.

POLITICAL UNREST

During the following year, 1907, the government with the collaboration of the *Partido Regenerador* enacted legislation in fulfilment of the King's programme. However, the Republican party, through protests inside and outside parliament, intensified its anti-monarchical activity. When the question of finance for the royal family arose, some parliamentarians of the Opposition denounced it as a crime and there were tumultuous scenes in the chamber.

Parliamentary agitation continued and the King was obliged to grant to João Franco what he had refused to Hintze Ribeiro, government without parliament – a dictatorship. This was condemned everywhere and the King by suspending in this way the Constitution was accused of renouncing, *de facto*, his rights and of signing a formal act of abdication.

The Revolution was prepared by groups of citizens who undertook the collection of arms and the manufacture of bombs. At the beginning, the troops and police remained loyal to the Government, foiling the revolution planned to take place on 28th January, 1908. Consequently, the Government resolved to intensify its repression and prepared a decree authorising the expulsion from the country or deportation to the colonies of anyone convicted of crimes against the security of the State.

The King who was in his country residence of Vila Viçosa signed the decree on 31st January, 1908. The following day, accompanied by the Queen and his elder son, D. Luís Filipe, the heir to the throne, he returned to Lisbon and disembarked at Terreiro do Paço/Praça do Comércio.

THE ASSASSINATION OF THE KING AND HIS SON

It was a Saturday afternoon and crowds had gathered in Praça do Comércio. The Duke of Oporto, the King's brother and the King's younger son, D. Manuel who was in Lisbon because of his studies were waiting for the royal family's arrival. Due to a minor rail accident, the royal party was an hour late. An air of foreboding pervaded the scene and when the royal couple together with their elder son arrived no signs of welcome, the usual *vivas* were given.

The royal couple and their two sons took their places in an open carriage without an escort and drove along the western side of the colonnaded square. As they were turning into Rua do Arsenal, a man jumped up on the back of the carriage and shot the King, killing him instantly. A second assassin approached and had his foot on the step of the landau when the Crown prince already wounded shot him.

The Queen also showed great presence of mind and courage, trying to protect her sons by brandishing a bouquet of flowers which had been presented to her a short while before. Summing up the attack one account states, 'Many other shots were fired at the royal carriage, one wounding the young prince and twelve penetrating the woodwork of the vehicle. The royal party was literally between two fires and had to drive through a perfect fusillade of bullets. The regicides were distributed into two ambuscades, facing each other on opposite sides of the road and posted under the arches at the point of junction of Black Horse Square, Rua do Arsenal and Gold Street.'[16]

Panic seized the crowd and in the midst of the turmoil the royal carriage drove into the Arsenal da Marinha. At the Queen's request, the Marquis de Pombal went to the nearby Church of Corpo Santo and the Portuguese Dominican, Fr. Fructuoso, preceptor to the princes came to give absolution. He then sent for the Holy Oils and the Irish Dominican, Fr. Dyson came to anoint the victims.

REACTION IN BOM SUCESSO

In Bom Sucesso, the community was shocked and plunged in grief at this double tragedy. The sisters owed so much to the patronage of successive members of the Bragança dynasty for nearly three hundred years and the protection by the late king together with the special friendship which existed between the sisters and Queen Dona Amélia. 'All hearts went out to her majesty in her hour of agony. The British residents signed a letter of condolence. Then the letter couched in most touching language was sent to Bom Sucesso and the sisters signed their names. A similar letter was sent to the King D. Manuel II' [17], the late king's younger son who had survived the ambush.

D. Carlos had, like his predecessors, been an honorary member of the Holy Rosary Confraternity. Consequently, at the request of its members, a solemn Requiem Mass was celebrated for him in the Convent Church on 5th March, 1908. 'A magnificent catafalque surmounted by a crown veiled in crepe occupied the centre of the Church. Representatives of the Young King and Queen Dona Amélia, Court officials, members of public bodies and numerous friends assisted. The *Libera me* was chanted.' [18] On 19th March, 1908, King D. Manuel II, the thirty-fourth and last king of Portugal, signed his name as honorary member of the Royal Confraternity of Our Lady of the Rosary, Bom Sucesso.

A FURTHER WAVE OF ANTICLERICALISM

A further wave of anti-clericalism became evident in Lisbon. The Irish Cardinal Logue visited the Portuguese capital in September, 1909 and was not given the public reception traditionally accorded to cardinals and which he had received earlier in Madrid. Accompanied by Dr. Brown, Bishop of Cloyne and Dr. O'Neill, Bishop of Dromore, he visited Bom Sucesso where he said Mass in the Church and gave a special blessing to those present. As a souvenir of the visit to the nuns, the Prioress presented his Eminence with a copy of the writings of the late King D. Carlos.

On the feast of Saint Michael, the Cardinal's patron, a High Mass was celebrated in the Church of Corpo Santo and the Cardinal presided at it. About a month later, a bomb was placed in the same church but was discovered and diffused by one of the priests. From his confessional, he noticed a man bending over some object and, alerted to the possible danger, he called another member of the community. To their horror, they found that it was a bomb already ignited and containing sufficient dynamite to blow up the church and surrounding buildings. When the Bom Sucesso community heard of the narrow escape of their Dominican brothers, they sang a solemn *Te Deum* in thanksgiving.

Consequences of the Regicide

On the day following the regicide, the politicians seized the reins of government. 'The prevailing idea was naturally to close party ranks behind the young man who had just ascended the throne, an inexperienced, timid young man whom every party hoped to dominate.'[19]

On the republican side the consequences of the regicide were very serious. The deed had been done by members of the *Carbonária*, a secret republican society not accepted by the directory of the main Republican party which viewed with alarm the use of violence and especially the political use of sectors of the population that, in their eyes, were a mob. However, the regicide did not cause for the Republican party the grave consequences that it feared. It led the government to a position of great tolerance, possibly out of fear.

The consequence for the *Carbonária* was propitious in that it ceased to be a small clandestine movement of terrorism and became the great popular instrument of the Revolution. The number of its members increased dramatically so that, by the Autumn of 1909, it had reached thirty-four thousand scattered all over the country and, within Lisbon alone, between eight and ten thousand.

Revolution

The Revolution was planned for the 4th October 1910 when three simultaneous attacks would be made: on the Palace of Necessidades where the King would be arrested; on the army headquarters; and on the Carmo barracks where the commando of the Municipal Guard was stationed. The attack on the palace was checked and the revolutionaries did not reach the other two targets. By early morning of the 4th October, everything seemed lost as most of the army units remained loyal to the King. Consequently, many rebels dispersed. Machado Santos, a member of the high command of the *Carbonária*, however, with some soldiers and armed civilians remained and, during the morning, carbonários from all over the city arrived to join them. 'The Rotunda was, only in appearance, an isolated nucleus of resistance; in fact, it was the commando of an invisible but very active army which dominated the popular districts and which, placed near the barracks loyal to the Government, impeded the movements of the troops by hurling bombs on any forces that would venture out into the city's streets.' [20]

The navy's revolt made critical the situation of the forces loyal to the monarchy. During the afternoon, two warships bombarded the royal palace and the King was obliged to escape to his palace at Mafra. The D. Carlos, the navy's strongest ship was overcome, thus putting the Tagus estuary under the control of the revolutionaries.

By daybreak on 5th October, the troops were only in control of the barracks but dared not go outside. The Government gave orders for regiments in nearby towns to converge on Lisbon and there was fear that the conflict would escalate. At that point, the German plenipotentiary decided to ask for an amnesty of one hour to allow German citizens board their warships. As his car made its way to the Rotunda to obtain this armistice, the people in the nearby buildings thought this concerned the Government's surrender and, suddenly, crowds filled the Avenida da Liberdade proclaiming victory for the revolution. The soldiers posted in the Rossio joined the people in the streets and, shortly after, the Republican flag was hoisted over the army headquarters.

The leaders of the Republican party went to the city hall where, according to the original plan, a proclamation was made. A supplement to the *Diário do Governo* for that day announced, 'Today, 5th October, 1910, at 11a.m. the Republic of Portugal was proclaimed in the noble hall of the palaces of the city of Lisbon after the movement of the national revolution had ended.' [21]

The King in Mafra learned by telegraph that the Republic had been proclaimed in Lisbon. On advice, he with the two queens, Dona Maria Pia and Dona Amélia went to Ericeira where the royal yacht lay at anchor. Convinced that the revolutionary movement was confined to Lisbon he intended going to Oporto but the captain persuaded him to sail to Gibraltar, 'the first stage of an exile from which there was no return.' [22]

BOM SUCESSO'S LAST PUBLIC ROSARY PROCESSION

The annals of Bom Sucesso recording the events of this memorable week in the history of Portugal begin with a description of the Holy Rosary Confraternity's annual procession which took place on the Sunday prior to the Revolution. 'On a beautiful October day, the first Sunday of the month, the Confraternity of the Rosary assembled in full force to honour Our Lady of the Rosary.' [23] High Mass was celebrated at which Canon Álvaro dos Santos, chaplain to the Royal family preached. At 3p.m., the procession left the church and, in the traditional Portuguese custom, the Confraternity members carried a large number of statues – Saint Michael, Saint Sebastian, Saint Rose of Lima, Saint Catherine de Ricci, Saint Thomas, Saint Dominic and Our Lady of the Rosary. 'When Our Lady's statue appeared all knelt down and the soldiers, as usual, presented arms, The brilliant procession was accompanied by a guard of honour from the infantry with its band. Crowds of spectators lined the streets through which it passed.' [24] On the return of the procession to the church, the celebrant gave the people a final blessing with the relic of the true cross. The annalist concludes, 'Did any of the participants or spectators realise that this procession which had taken place for one hundred and fifty-five years had left the pátio for the last time or that, within forty-eight hours, the city would be in the throes of the greatest revolution the country had ever experienced.' [25]

During the night of the 4th October, some sisters heard firing in the distance and, in the morning, news reached them that the Revolution had broken out. The booming of cannon continued during the early morning of the following day but, as all communication was cut off, they did not know what the outcome would be. Finally, later on the 5th., news came of victory for the revolutionaries and the departure of the king.

CRISIS IN BOM SUCESSO

A provisional government was formed prior to the elaboration of a new constitution. Among its decrees were included the separation of Church and State, the law concerning family and divorce and the expulsion of all religious from Portugal.

The Bom Sucesso sisters fearing the convent would be attacked by rioting mobs contacted the British embassy. Sir Francis Villiers, the English minister, sent word through his secretary, Mr. Hugh Gaisford, that there was no cause for alarm but, at his request, the Provisional Government agreed to give protection. In the midst of the anxiety caused by the volatile situation, an amusing incident occurred. After profound silence one evening, thirty soldiers arrived for the purpose of protecting the convent but the prioress thinking that she was going to be arrested said good-bye to her sisters before she met the lieutenant in charge. To her surprise, she was greeted with deference and, immediately, the whole community was engaged in furnishing the building adjoining the convent with everything necessary for the soldiers' accommodation.

Alarming reports continued to be circulated and, to increase the community's fears, the Brazilian ambassador sent his secretary to take away the Brazilian pupils from the boarding school. Two Brazilian sisters, on being asked also to go, decided to stay with their community. Mother Cecilia Murray who was a young member of the community at this time describes the panic which set in. 'The [Brazilian] secretary's visit aroused our suspicions that there was truth in the rumour that our expulsion was more than probable. General consternation. Mother Prioress assembled the community and informed us that there was little hope of our being exempt from the decree.'[26]

The main question was where should the community go. Some sisters began packing the sacred vessels for divine worship and other objects of value. Parcels labelled, 'Care of British Legation' lined the cloister. However, one senior sister had a different approach to this difficult situation. To those packing the convent's possessions she said, 'You are losing your time, dear sisters, packing up. Our Lady will never let us leave Bom Sucesso. Have confidence. I shall keep on at the Rosary.'[27]

RE-ASSURANCE FROM BRITISH EMBASSY

Word of these preparations and the sisters' fears reached the British embassy and the secretary, Mr. Gaisford, came to reassure the community. Moreover, he contacted the Brazilian minister and later wrote to the prioress stating that he had made enquiries at the Brazilian embassy and learned that its secretary only went to the convent on behalf of the anxious guardian of a Brazilian pupil.

FR. PAUL O'SULLIVAN'S ROLE IN THE CRISIS

The persistent rumours of Bom Sucesso's closure were allayed when Fr. Paul O'Sullivan, Prior of Corpo Santo, accompanied by Mr. Gaisford came with an assurance from the minister of Foreign Affairs that the community could remain on two conditions: 1) that the nuns would not wear their religious habit (to prove that they were allowed stay, not because they were religious but because they were British subjects); and 2) that no Portuguese subject would be received as a postulant to religious life. The annalist concludes, 'The situation for us was pathetic in the extreme – to see the native religious driven out of their own country whilst we as "foreigners" were allowed to remain.'[28]

Fr. Paul O'Sullivan, O.P. of Corpo Santo, who played an important role in securing that both Bom Sucesso and Corpo Santo should remain in Portugal, gives his personal account of the events which ended in good success for both communities. 'A most radical anti-Catholic

Republic was declared and a violent attack was, at once, launched against the Church.... Though the firing had ceased, the wildest excitement still prevailed. No priest dared be seen in the streets. In fact, the poor nuns were being dragged from their convents and taken in open cars to the Arsenal, to the number of 265. They were hooted and insulted as they passed by the infuriated mobs...'[29]

Fr. Paul went to the British embassy and asked the ambassador, Sir Francis Villiers, for a letter for the minister of Foreign Affairs, Bernardino Machado, demanding a guarantee of safety for persons and property of Corpo Santo and Bom Sucesso *in statu quo ante*. Accompanied by the British consul he then went to meet the minister for Foreign Affairs. 'Dr. Bernardino Machado, Foreign Minister received us with a show of cordiality, as coming on the part of the British Minister but would not commit himself in any way until the arrival of Senhor Afonso Costa who was the leader, the strong man of the Republican Party and acting, at the time, as Minister of Justice.'

On Senhor Costa's arrival, Fr. Paul left the consul talking to the Minister for Foreign Affairs and went to sit beside the Justice Minister, tapping him on the shoulder. 'On my touching him on the shoulder, Afonso Costa glared at me.' The Irish Dominican told him why he had come. 'What! He shouted. You foreigners demand to be left in your convents when we are, as you see, expelling our own Portuguese religious.' 'Yes, I do, I replied, because, first of all, let me tell you that we are personal friends of the King.' 'The King, he said, What do I care for the King!' Fr. Paul explained that he was referring not to the King of Portugal but to the King of Great Britain and, as proof of this friendship, he could consult the Portuguese newspapers of 1907 which had reported the late King Edward VII's visit to Bom Sucesso.

Finally, Afonso Costa agreed to all Fr. Paul's demands. When they both joined the British consul and the Minister for Foreign Affairs, the latter objected to all the concessions made to the Irish communities in Lisbon but Senhor Costa replied, 'What I have said, I have said and it will remain so.' The consul then asked for a written confirmation of the concessions and, on the following day, 'a document signed by all the Republican ministers, guaranteeing the safety of the persons and property of Corpo Santo and Bom Sucesso *in statu quo ante* was received by Sir Francis Villiers.' [30]

REJOICING IN BOM SUCESSO

When news of Fr. Paul's success reached Bom Sucesso, there was great rejoicing and Mother Pius O'Carroll wrote to thank him and invited him to the convent so that the community could thank him personally.

PÈRE CORMIER'S SUPPORT

During these difficult days, the saintly Master of the Dominican Order, Blessed Hyacynth Cormier gave the Bom Sucesso community comfort and support. On 18th October 1910, he wrote to re-assure them on a few points, 'I confine myself to saying that: 1) it is not within your power to leave your cloister; it is a question of your vows and you represent the rights of the Church. 2) The wearing of the habit is desirable but it is not the essence of the cloistered life. We must serve the Church under all forms especially now….As for the other conditions, it is to be hoped that they will be mitigated with time. For the rest: *sufficit diei malitia sua*. Keep yourselves informed of current events out of duty….Send me your news. I have told the Holy Father that you have kept up, he is happy about this and sends you his blessing. Adieu, Do not forget us in your prayers,' Fr. Hyacinth Cormier, O.P. M.G.

A few days later, on 21st October, Père Cormier wrote again, 'I wrote directly to Bom Sucesso, I hope you received my letter. I understand your anxiety in the beginning of the trouble but, now, that is all over. Live then in peace, replace by your spirit of prayer the expelled communities, redouble your zeal that you may merit the continued protection of God. Thank the Fathers for all they have done for you. The enclosed letter is for the English minister who has been so kind and solicitous for your welfare and who protected your community.'

Throughout his years as Master of the Dominican Order, Blessed Hyacinth continued to support and inspire the Bom Sucesso community with his letters. In 1916, after he had retired as Master, he wrote from San Clemente in reply to the community's letter of gratitude, 'If I have been able to do anything for you, I have been well rewarded by your filial docility, your faithful affection and your prayers. Continue these for me so that I may use my time well and have a good death. Adieu, I bless you and will always be happy to receive news of you.'[31]

THANKSGIVING FOR PRESERVATION

The convent annalist recalls the sisters' acts of thanksgiving for their preservation. These were the typical acts traditional in Portuguese culture

– processions with the statue of Our Lady of Bom Sucesso. 'During the last week of October, a procession round the cloister took place daily in thanksgiving for the preservation of the community. The statue of Our Lady of Bom Sucesso was carried in triumph, as it was due to her intercession that the nuns were not expelled. From this time on, for about a year, the sisters wore secular dress and, thus, in the history of the convent, 1911 is known as the year of mourning. (November 1910-November1911),'[32]

The school which had been closed for about a month re-opened and when it became known that the sisters had permission to stay, not only did the Bom Sucesso pupils return but many more girls from the schools of the suppressed convents applied for admission. In a short while, the school was filled to its capacity of one hundred and six. As religious instruction was forbidden in every other college of education, it was a consolation to the sisters that they could, at least, form their pupils in the Christian religion and help keep the light of faith alive in some families. Unfortunately, the school for the poor of the district, being a day-school, had to remain closed because of the risk of government interference.

ANOTHER CRISIS RESOLVED

Some months later, with the promulgation of the law separating Church and State[33] another crisis arose for Bom Sucesso and Corpo Santo as the government withdrew what had already been conceded. In the midst of this crisis, Sir Francis Villiers was recalled to London in June 1911 and Mr. Hugh Gaisford was left in charge of embassy matters in Lisbon. Negotiations continued and the British Foreign Minister in London was constantly informed of the proceedings. He demanded a definite statement from the Portuguese government and when this was not delivered, he sent the following note to Mr. Gaisford, 'Tell the Provisional Government of Portugal that we shall not recognise the Republic unless they guarantee the safety of the persons and property of the two British houses of Corpo Santo and Bom Sucesso.' The guarantee was given.[34]

The new British ambassador, Sir Arthur Hardinge, and Mr. Gaisford paid a visit to Bom Sucesso on 1st November, 1911. When asked if the Sisters could wear the Dominican habit, the ambassador replied that he knew of no law which would prevent a lady from dressing as she pleased in her own house. Some of the Sisters went away immediately and came back wearing their habits.[35]

DIFFICULT YEARS FOR PORTUGAL

The years following the 1910 revolution were critical for Portugal. Prior to the fall of the King, the Republican party had only one objective – to overthrow the monarchy; but, as soon as this was achieved, the lack of a concrete programme of government became evident. There were party conflicts and personal oppositions. 'The leader of the Democratic party, Afonso Costa, was gifted with vigour and a capacity for action which placed him above the general political personnel of the new regime.'[36] In 1913, as president of the government, he temporarily succeeded in controlling anarchy in the administration and in balancing the budget. However, while he became more popular with the people, opposition from the other parties increased.

At the outbreak of the First World War, the different parties were divided as to whether Portugal should support Germany or the allies. The problem was solved in 1916 when a large number of German merchant ships surprised by the outbreak of war took refuge in the Tagus as a port of a neutral country. At England's demand, Portugal seized these ships. Consequently, Germany declared war on Portugal and two divisions of Portuguese soldiers were sent to France early in 1917. Other forces were sent to Angola and Moçambique which had been invaded by Germany. Tragically, some five thousand were killed but this gave Portugal a right to be included among the conquerors and to obtain recognition for its African colonies. The inter-party agreement established by the war did not last very long when another revolution led to the dictatorship of Sidónio Pais. His presidency ended with his assassination towards the end of 1918. The period from 1920 to 1926 was one of great political agitation but in 1926 a military dictatorship was set up and lasted until 1933.

BOM SUCESSO DURING THOSE YEARS

Of this period, the Bom Sucesso annals have a more positive account. President Sidónio Pais had allowed religious instruction to be given in the parishes. Religious could live in small communities of four and, in the face of much opposition, he re-established relations with the Holy See. When the Nuncio, Monsignor Locatelli arrived, the president had already been assassinated but he was received by the new president.

In the post-war period, the epidemic of broncho-pneumonia which spread all over Europe also claimed the lives of many in Portugal.

The prioress of Bom Sucesso, Mother Pius O'Carroll had a picture of the Crucified Christ placed at the enclosure entrance and on every door in the convent. Special prayers were said and processions took place until the epidemic ceased. For a term, the school was closed but no member of the community and no pupil, even while at home, caught the illness. 'The community owed its immunity to Jesus Crucified.' [37]

During the period of political agitation from 1920 to 1926, Bom Sucesso enjoyed a certain peace and security and the community succeeded in celebrating two centenaries within the cloister. In 1921, the seventh centenary of Saint Dominic's death was celebrated in the traditional way with High Mass and Exposition of the Blessed Sacrament. The procession, however, had to be confined to the cloister.

The First Centenary of the Sisters' Return to Bom Sucesso

In 1923, the first centenary of the sisters' return to Bom Sucesso after their expulsion a month before was also solemnly celebrated. The Master of the Dominican Order, Fr. Lewis Theissling, sent, on this happy occasion, a letter of congratulations together with 'the special blessing of Saint Dominic for yourselves, for the children of your schools, for your benefactors and all the faithful who frequent the Church of Bom Sucesso.'

The 1923 celebration had as its highlight a solemn procession in which nuns and pupils took part. It began in the Upper Choir and pride of place was given to the statue of Our Lady of Bom Sucesso carried by four children, two Portuguese, one Irish and one Peruvian. The participants on leaving the Upper Choir proceeded to the veranda and down into the cloister to the Lower Choir where the Magnificat was sung. 'A canticle in honour of Our Lady of Bom Sucesso specially composed for the occasion ended the celebrations which lasted three days.' [38]

At this time, the community requested the Sacred Congregation of Rites to have the invocation to Our Lady of Bom Sucesso included in the litany of Loreto. However, the Congregation's reply was that the Holy Father did not wish 'a multiplication of further invocations in the litany.' Consequently, the answer was *non expedire* but permission was given to include the invocation provided the litany was said by the Sisters in their private oratory, not in the Church.

Fr. Finbar Ryan's first Visitation of Bom Sucesso

In 1923 also, Fr. Finbar Ryan, the Irish provincial, came on behalf of the Master of the Dominican Order to hold visitation in the convent. When he discovered that the novitiate had been closed since 1915, he decided, on his return to Ireland, to make every effort to encourage young women from Ireland to enter in Bom Sucesso. He was eminently successful because in October of the following year four postulants from Ireland arrived. The Dominican sisters of Eccles Street also undertook to foster vocations not only for their own convent but also for Bom Sucesso.

In May, 1926, at the General Chapter of the Dominican Order held in Ocana, the Spaniard, Fr. Bonaventure G. Paredes was chosen Saint Dominic's successor as Master of the Order. Replying to the community's letter of congratulations he wrote, 'In our common vocation your mission of teachers and educators, of angels of light and of sanctity, is a beautiful one. It is blessed by God. It is appreciated by him who has become your father by the will of the Order. Your pious sentiments and fervent prayers are a consolation to me and another reason for me to trust in God for the accomplishment of the arduous duties of my office.' In 1929, Fr. Paredes resigned the office of Master of the Order and returned to Spain where, during the Spanish civil war, he was martyred.

Political Agitation in Portugal

The Bom Sucesso annals of 1920 to 1926 give no indication of the political agitation in Portugal during those years and of the military revolt being prepared in the early months of 1926. A document was circulated in the army barracks, demanding a national ministry outside all parties but within republican institutions in order to stabilise public administration – in reality, an interim dictatorship.

After months of political agitation, General Carmona, by decree of 26th November, was nominated interim president of the Republic. Attempts at revolt were suppressed and more than six hundred people were deported to the Azores, Guinea, Cape Verde and Angola. Other political figures went into voluntary exile in Spain, France and Brazil. All this only consolidated the dictatorship.

With the suppression of opposition a period of political calm set in and the government used this peace in order to bring about internal reforms. On 24th February 1928, the election of a president was declared but the only candidate was General Carmona who was duly elected. On 27th April 1928, the portfolio of Minister for Finance was given to a Coimbra professor, António Oliveira Salazar. He would remain in government until 1968.

The revolutionary movement of May 1926 now began to undergo a profound change in the style of government and political thinking. There was a return to moral standards and the value of the Christian Faith. On 1st August, 1928, the first budget without a deficit was published. On 30th June, 1930, a non-party organisation called the União Nacional was founded. It was made up of 'Portuguese disposed, through an understanding of their major civic duties, to work for the saving and aggrandisement of Portugal.'[39] There was considerable resistance to the idea of a one-party government and many of those already deported to the islands of Madeira, Azores and Cape Verde organised revolts. Protests were held at the universities and in August 1931, a military revolt showed that even within the army officers were unwilling to accept the new development in government.

On 28th May 1932, the text of the project for the Constitution approved by the National Council was presented by the Minister for Finance, Dr. Salazar. On the same day, he received from the Ministers of War and the Marine the insignia of the Grand Cross of *Torre e Espada* and a message of gratitude signed by four thousand officers. The project was not accepted by many in government and consequently, the whole Cabinet resigned on 25th June 1932.

The President of the Republic convoked the National Political Council and on 28th June 1932, the new leader of the government was announced – Dr. Salazar.

The projected Constitution was put to a plebiscite on 19th March 1933. 'The official publication of the result of this scrutiny made on 11th April 1933, formally marks the beginning of the new fundamental statute and represents the beginning of the period of the New State.'[40]

BOM SUCESSO 1924-1939

During those years of turmoil in political circles, Bom Sucesso enjoyed relative security. In its tranquil setting the four novices who had entered in 1924 made their profession. They were Sisters Thomas Kennedy, Catherine Walsh, Finbar O'Driscoll and Imelda Warner. The Papal Nuncio, Monsignor Nicotra who took a special interest in the community, from time to time visiting the convent, now presided at the profession of the four novices.

Other frequent visitors were the British ambassador, Sir Launcelot and Lady Carnegie who, on one such occasion, presented the community with autographed portraits of King George V and Queen Mary. Sir Launcelot added 'a few words to the usual formula in presenting such a gift, to the effect that the English embassy would always be ready to protect the convent should need arise, and that he and Lady Carnegie fully appreciated the cordial welcome they received on the many occasions they had visited Bom Sucesso.' [41] On their retirement from diplomatic service, having spent fourteen years in Lisbon, they came to say goodbye to the community who had often benefited from their friendship.

In 1930, the principal of the school, Sister Catherine Walsh, undertook to prepare pupils for the Lyceum examinations. Consequently, the sisters had to undergo an examination in order to qualify as teachers. At this time, the visitor, Fr. Louis Nolan, decreed that the midnight recitation of the Divine Office should be discontinued during the school year. On account of the onerous work of teaching it was to be celebrated only during holiday time. The number of pupils began to decrease as religious communities returning to Portugal after their expulsion in 1910, were re-opening schools and colleges.

The 1930s were memorable in Bom Sucesso for the number of centenaries celebrated. In 1933, the sixth centenary of the death of Blessed Imelda was significant for the pupils as they were members of the Imeldist Confraternity, an association for children the focus of which was devotion to the Eucharist. In honour of their patroness, Blessed Imelda, they performed a play entitled *Imelda* in the presence of the Papal Nuncio, Monsignor Beda Cardinale, parents of the pupils, the British vice-consul and past-pupils. With the Nuncio's permission the little Imeldists from Corpo Santo were able to enter the enclosure and join the Bom Sucesso Imeldists.

In 1934, another centenary was celebrated – the seventh centenary of the canonisation of Saint Dominic. A solemn Triduum with Exposition of the Blessed Sacrament was held and concluded with High Mass, *Te Deum* and Solemn Benediction. In 1937, the twentieth anniversary of the apparitions at Fátima commemorated this great spiritual event in the history of Portugal. Dr. Finbar Ryan, now archbishop of Gabula in the Caribbean, who had written one of the first English accounts of the Fátima apparitions, visited Portugal on this occasion.

During the years of the Spanish Civil War, Portugal was in danger of being invaded by Spanish revolutionaries. 'The community had many an anxious hour, hearing how the Spanish nuns were treated…convents burnt, priests killed among others our ex-Master General.'[42] In the face of this threat, the Cardinal Patriarch of Lisbon and the Hierarchy of Portugal promised that, if Portugal were spared the ravages of war, they would go on pilgrimage to Fátima. Consequently, on 13th May 1938, this promise was fulfilled and the Cardinal Patriarch consecrated Portugal to Our Lady, thanking her for having protected the country and its people.

THE TERCENTENARY OF BOM SUCESSO

The final centenary to be celebrated in the decade of the 1930s was a very important one for Bom Sucesso. It was the tercentenary of the foundation of the convent on 12th November, 1639. The community began its commemoration of this great event with an act of charity – the making of clothes for three hundred poor children ranging in age from one year to seven.

A concert was organised for the 6th June, 1939. A stage surrounded by ferns and other greenery was erected in the garden. Seating accommodation together with tables for refreshments was arranged for four hundred guests when, suddenly, the sky darkened and a thunderstorm broke out saturating everything with torrential rain.

Meanwhile, about three hundred past-pupils had assembled in the Church to recite the Rosary. The Papal Nuncio, Monsignor Ciriaci, presided and read a discourse in Portuguese. Later, he gave the Papal blessing especially requested for this great occasion.

At 4 p.m., the Nuncio accompanied by his secretary, Monsignor César, Monsignor Cullen of the English College, Monsignor Nogueira of Belém, Fr. Holmes, vice-president of the English College and the priests of Corpo Santo followed by past-pupils entered the enclosure. Though the storm had passed, it was impossible to hold the garden party and outdoor entertainment. Consequently, the pupils' concert was held in a large classroom and later, the Nuncio and his suite had tea in the atrium while the other guests went to the recreation room.

The highlight of the tercentenary celebrations was the solemn *triduum* commemorating the actual date of the foundation of the convent on 12th November 1639. This *triduum* began on 11th November with High Mass celebrated by the Corpo Santo Dominicans, Fr. Joseph Dowdall, O.P., with Frs Enda Mc Veigh, O.P., and Fr. Gerard Gardiner, O.P., deacon and sub-deacon, respectively. At 5p.m., a procession of the sisters and pupils went round the cloister, the statue of Our Lady of Bom Sucesso being carried by four Children of Mary. The nuns and pupils alternated in singing hymns and antiphons. On their reaching the entrance, the past-pupils joined the procession and the prioress handed over the statue to them to carry it back to its shrine in the church. There, a Holy Hour was held during which the fifteen mysteries of the Rosary were recited with intervals of hymn singing in honour of the Sacred Heart, Our Lady and in conclusion, *Salve Portugal*. Monsignor Nogueira of Belém presided at the Holy Hour and at Benediction. The sisters sang the *Te Deum* in thanksgiving for all the graces bestowed on the monastery since 1639. A similar celebration took place on 12th and Dr. Finbar Ryan was celebrant of the morning Mass.[43]

On 13th November, the Bishop of Portalegre, Dom Domingos Fructuoso,O.P., celebrated 10 a.m. Mass in the presence of past-pupils who, at 11 a.m., met in the upper parlour where the new association of past-pupils of Bom Sucesso was inaugurated. Dom Fructuoso presided at the meeting and 'delivered a very practical lecture on the duties of Christian mothers.'[44]

At 2 p.m., the final Holy Hour of the *triduum* took place and again the *Te Deum* was sung in thanksgiving. After Benediction, the past-pupils formed in procession while four senior members carried the statue of Our Lady of Bom Sucesso to the enclosure entrance where the nuns and present pupils were waiting. The prioress received the statue and the nuns with the pupils went in procession round the cloister to the choir where the statue was placed on the altar. Thus ended the solemn triduum of the tercentenary.

The final celebration was held on the feast of Saint Albert the Great, on 15th November,1939 and recalls the pomp and ceremony attached to such celebrations even in the early twentieth century. Archbishops, bishops, monsignori and the fathers of Corpo Santo assembled in the patio to await the arrival of the Cardinal Patriarch, Dom. Cerejeira. On his arrival, the choir, made up of students from the English College, sang *Ecce Sacerdos* as the procession entered the church. It went first to the altar of the Sacred Heart where the Blessed Sacrament had been placed and then proceeded to the High Altar.

The Cardinal Patriarch took his place on a special throne at which the assistants were Canons Carneiro de Mesquita, Damascene Fiadeiro, Sequeira Mora and Manuel Vieira. Pontifical High Mass was sung, the celebrant being Dr. Finbar Ryan with Fr. Whitty deacon and Fr. E. Crowley sub-deacon. The Master of ceremonies was Dr. Crowley with Fr. E. Robertson assistant. The Master of ceremonies for the Cardinal was Monsignor Honorato Monteiro.

In the sanctuary were His Grace, the Archbishop of Mitylene, Dr. Senna Oliveira, the bishop of Portalegre, Dom Fructuoso, Monsignor Nogueira of Belém, Monsignor Cullen, president of the English College and the Fathers of Corpo Santo – Paul O'Sullivan, Dominic Clarkson, Joseph Dowdall, Enda Mc Veigh and Gerard Gardiner. V. Rev. Fr. Martins, O.P. represented the Portuguese Dominicans. 'In the place of honour, beside the Cardinal's throne, the English ambassador, Sir Walford Selby, assisted at the Mass.'[45]

Dom Domingos Fructuoso preached on the theme, God is our Father, and referred to Albert the Great together with his famous student, Thomas Aquinas. At the end of Mass, the *Te Deum* was sung during Exposition of the Blessed Sacrament and Benediction followed. To conclude the ceremony the choir sang *Laudate Dominum, omnes gentes.*

Afterwards, lunch for the many dignitaries was served in the Upper Parlour where Fr. Paul O'Sullivan read an address on behalf of the prioress and community who were not present as it was outside the enclosure. After lunch, the Cardinal and the other guests entered the enclosure where the prioress conducted him to a classroom for the pupils' concert. At its conclusion, Cardinal Cerejeira addressed those present, 'This is a triple feast – for the Church in Portugal, for the nuns of Bom Sucesso, for the past-pupils who do the nuns so much credit and the present pupils preparing to do their part on leaving school.'[46] All the guests then went to the garden where photographs were taken and people conversed informally until the Cardinal gave a final blessing to the Community and the pupils. He and all the other guests then left the enclosure.

Two months prior to this celebration, the Second World War had begun but no reference is made, at this time, to it in the annals. However, in her concluding observation the annalist indicates that she and her community were aware of the horror of this catastrophe. She writes, 'What will the next hundred years bring? Judging by the present state of the world, the future looks dark and threatening. If great suffering, even persecution, come in the next hundred years, Our Lady of Bom Sucesso will protect the venerable monastery till the last inmate departs for the better land.'[47]

11

The 1940s

During the years of the Second World War, the atmosphere of peace and tranquillity within Bom Sucesso is in marked contrast to the global state of affairs. The annals have little to record except the celebration of important feast-days and concerts given by the pupils on special occasions or at the visit of famous guests. In January 1940, the sisters' fingerprints were taken with a view to their receiving identity cards and, as the year progressed, the war began to have its effect on the community. In May, it was decided to have a 'Holy Hour daily until the War ends.'[1] On June 1st, the annalist records, 'News continues alarming – sisters' anxiety increasing as to the safety of relatives in England.'[2] Two of the community had brothers in the British armed forces. Sister Hyacinth White's brother was in the Royal Navy while Sister Philomena Sisk's brother was serving in the British Army. Both were at Dunkirk when the retreating soldiers were evacuated by the Royal Navy.

In 1940, Portugal celebrated the eighth centenary of its foundation and the tercentenary of its liberation from Spanish domination. In honour of this historical event, on 27th June, High Mass was celebrated in Jerónimos at which all the bishops of Portugal, the President of the Republic, General Carmona, Dr. Salazar, government ministers and the diplomatic corps attended. The Duke of Kent, representing King George VI of England was in a place of honour in recognition of the traditional alliance between Portugal and England.

Visit of the Duke of Kent

On 29th June, the Duke of Kent accompanied by the British ambassador, Sir Walford Selby and Lady Selby, following the tradition established by former royal visitors, paid a visit to Bom Sucesso. He was greeted at the enclosure door by the prioress and community while the pupils sang *God Save the King*. The prioress conducted the Duke through the cloister to the Upper Choir and the Community Room where one of his attendants placed on a table a magnificent bouquet of flowers. 'His Royal Highness said, "I brought these flowers for you, Mother."' [3] He was offered a glass of wine and after some conversation the prioress brought him to see the refectory. On his leaving the cloister, the pupils again sang *God Save the King*. The annalist concludes, 'His Royal Highness appeared very sad. No wonder, his country undergoing a crisis unheard of in the history of England.' [4]

Tercentenary of Portuguese Independence

December 1st being the actual date of Independence from Spain in 1640, Portugal had further celebrations. The National Exhibition, held on land opposite the convent, had opened on 23rd June and did not close until 1st December, 1940. The customary celebrations of fireworks and salvos fired from warships on the Tagus took place. 'Finally, at 2 a.m., the vast concourse dispersed and then the great silence told us all was over and we nuns could at last rest in peace after six months of nocturnal noises of every description.' [5]

During the *Estado Novo* years, persecution of Religious Orders ceased and the Church enjoyed a time of peace when it could recover from the years of repression. However, the country was not free of natural calamities. On 15th February, 1941, after some weeks of intense cold, a severe cyclone occurred uprooting trees and causing considerable damage. Hundreds of people were killed, other severely injured and many were left homeless. In Bom Sucesso, the convent bell was so damaged that it had to be replaced. On 3rd March, the new bell was blessed and christened Gabriel Thomas Michael Joseph.[6] On 25th November, 1941, an earthquake occurred. Fortunately, no lives were lost in Lisbon and very little damage was caused.

Many people, principally priests and religious, having left Rome because of Italy's involvement in the war, were often detained in Lisbon, awaiting departure elsewhere, mainly to Ireland or Brazil, and Bom Sucesso was often called upon to give hospitality. The entry for annals of Saint Stephen's Day 1941, recording the visit of two Augustinians, Fathers Harnett and Ryan, states, 'Since the outbreak of the war in 1939, the community never had so many clerical visitors – priests and students from Rome, one priest, Fr. Ellison, from Switzerland and Br. Allen, Superior of the Christian Brothers from America.' [7]

One historic visit occurred on 10th March, 1941, when the Irish Minister to Spain, Mr Aiken, and the Irish Minister of Defence, Mr. Noonan, were received by the Community. This is the first official visit of a member of the Irish Government recorded in the Bom Sucesso annals though Irish independence from Britain had been established in 1922. In March of the following year, 1942, Mr. O'Donovan, as the first Irish Charge d'Affaires to Portugal, opened the Irish legation in Lisbon. Shortly after their arrival, Mrs. O'Donovan and their children visited the Community. Later, on 23rd April, as first Irish minister in Lisbon, Mr. O'Donovan paid an official visit. Thus began the cordial relationship which exists between the Community and the successive members of the Irish Embassy in Lisbon.

FR. LOUIS NOLAN, VICAR OF BOM SUCESSO

During the war years, as Portugal was neutral, the prioress of Bom Sucesso was called upon by its vicar, Father Louis Nolan, O.P., to act as intermediary on his behalf in matters referring to religious in Italy, England and Malta. In a letter dated 24th May 1940, he asks her to send regularly financial aid to a community of Dominican sisters in Rome whose mother-house was in London. Later, Bom Sucesso would be reimbursed from London. In the same letter he requests that his correspondence between Rome and Malta might be directed via Bom Sucesso.

In a letter from Malta dated 5th February 1942, the prioress is asked to obtain from Rome permission 'a) for Father Dominic Lewis to make the Lectorate examination this year...b) for permission for Brother Denis Lewis to receive the Major Orders in due time.' In a later letter dated 5th September of the same year, Father Nolan requests Bom Sucesso's prioress to contact the Dominican Prioress General in London to have three of her prioresses appointed for the third time in their mission: Mother Gregory Coffey at Umzumbi, Natal, Mother Antoninus Cullinane, Umtwalumi – both in Marianhill vicariate, South Africa and Mother Lewis Kostial at Lennoxton in the vicariate of Durban. His reason is that they 'could not without detriment to the work be changed at the present time.' [8] This correspondence throws light on one Dominican's method of communication during war time and reveals the positive rôle that Bom Sucesso played in this.

In the account of a century of ministry by the Dominican Sisters of Newcastle, Natal, South Africa, the writers pay tribute to Mother

Gabriel in the help she gave their sisters in Rome during the war years: 'With the entry of Italy on the German side all direct communication with England came to an end. Father Nolan, as vicar of the Irish Dominican Sisters of Bom Sucesso in Lisbon, asked the Prioress, Mother Gabriel to be in contact, receiving cheques from Mother Rose (in England) and forwarding them to Villa Rosa (in Rome). Soon Mother Rose was refused to send money even to neutral Portugal but Mother Gabriel continued to send cheques to Villa Rosa from time to time even though it is very likely that Bom Sucesso's own resources were stretched to the limit.'[9] And fellow Dominicans were not the only ones helped, the annalist writes of Mother Gabriel, '...She has been a kind friend to many religious in Rome during the war, helping them most generously and kindly in their correspondence with the communities and families.' [10]

Bom Sucesso's Mina de Água/Well

While the community was able, in the 1940s, to continue without government interference both religious life and the education of their pupils, the sisters had to confront other difficulties with civil authorities. In 1940, the Câmara Municipal de Lisboa took possession of land on the Ajuda hillside which had, at one time, been the property of the Countess of Atalaya through her first husband. On her death, this land became the property of his heirs. However, the Bom Sucesso Community retained the use of a well or *mina de água,* situated in one section of this land. This was the main source of the water supply to the convent and it had two springs which, in the summer season supplied nine cubic metres of water daily and more in the winter.

The sisters were not officially informed of the confiscation of the land containing this invaluable asset. Consequently, when they became aware that the pipes carrying the water to the convent's tank had been cut, the prioress wrote to the president of the Câmara explaining their right, on an historical basis to the water, 'Since the 3rd August, 1639, the Convent, in virtue of a public deed of that date, granted by the Countess of Atalaya, Dona Iria de Brito, took possession of the same Convent's lands including a mine of excellent water with which, since then, the Convent is supplied.' [11] The water ceased flowing on 25th July, 1940, began to flow again from March to October, 1941 and from April to June 1942. 'Since then, we are without water from the mine.'[12]

Another document in the archives gives the history of this land and its well or *mina.* 'The mine is situated on the Ajuda hillside on land which belonged to the Countess of Atalaya, Dona Iria de Brito, foundress of the Convent of Bom Sucesso to whom it had been given as an inheritance by the Count of Feira, her first husband. At the death of the Countess, the land passed to the Duke de Cadaval, direct heir of the Count of Feira. However, the Religious of the said Convent retained the mine, the water from which was piped directly to the Convent through land belonging to the Religious.'[13]

The writer (probably the convent's lawyer) goes on to show that when some of this land south of the well was sold by the community, a legal agreement was drawn up whereby the buyer was 'obliged to preserve this piping exactly as it is, neither diverting the water nor doing work that may be prejudicial to the plumbing and when the piping needs to be repaired this will be undertaken and paid for by the sellers.' [14]

The author of this unsigned document continues an account of the repairs done by the Convent to the piping system. In 1909, iron pipes substituted the old plumbing and these extended from Vila Correia to the convent's tank. In order to carry out this work, the Religious had to ask the Câmara's permission. However, for the City Council this was not sufficient proof of ownership. Unfortunately, the *mina* or well was not officially registered though it was argued that the three hundred years of supplying water to the convent together with the fact that the piping went directly there were *authentic documents* of the community's ownership. However, these proofs of possession were not accepted by the Câmara and thus, on a legal technicality, there was little hope of the Community's obtaining justice.

This valuable document goes on to state how the sisters learned of the expropriation: 'On 18th April 1941, the Religious became alarmed on seeing in the *Diário de Notícias* (a daily paper) the plan of urbanisation of the Ajuda hillside where the mine is situated. Having gathered information they discovered that the municipal council had expropriated the Cadaval estate with a view to selling it in lots to residents.' [15]

The problem dragged on for many years and various lawyers undertook the case. When Dr. Pinto Coelho died, Dr. Abel de Andrade acted for the Community and then, in 1952, an English solicitor, Mr. Guy Wainewright whose daughters were at school in Bom Sucesso took over the case. His first letter to the Prioress in which he says that he has been studying the issue with his Portuguese colleague is dated 18th November, 1952.

In a second letter dated 26th November, 1952, he explains that it is a question of how the expropriation was effected and whether the Câmara did all that it was legally required to do. The issue now is compensation for the loss of the water as there is no hope of recovering the mine. However, he warns, 'I am afraid that it may be found that there is no legal basis for a claim on your behalf and that we shall have to stress the moral rather than the strictly legal standpoint.'[16]

Correspondence and interviews between Mr. Wainewright, his colleagues and the members of the Câmara continued during the early months of 1953 and the on 23rd June, 1953, he sent the Câmara's reply disclaiming obligation where the expropriation of the well and the land was concerned. Always anxious to give some positive information he continued, 'I noticed, however, that in the *Diário do Governo* of the 9th June, is published a list of *estabelecimentos de beneficiência, instrução* etc. which have a right to have up to 50% of their water consumption paid for by the State, and in this list your convent is included.'[17] His final letter to the prioress concerning this matter is dated 29th June 1953, and in it he refuses any payment of fees, 'I have no charges to make in this matter.... I am very pleased to be able to render you this little service and am only sorry that we have achieved nothing for you.'[18]

Today, apart from residences on most of the land, a beautiful park stretches from the Bom Sucesso windmills on the brow of the hill down the Ajuda hillside and a restaurant with the name *Queda das Águas* (Waterfall) is reminiscent of the Bom Sucesso *mina de água* expropriated some sixty years ago. In July, 1965, the Association for the Restoration of Windmills in Portugal invited members of the Community to attend the ceremony of inauguration of the restored Bom Sucesso windmills. Two sisters, Imelda Warner and Aedris Coates accepted the invitation and enjoyed cakes made from Bom Sucesso recipes.

THE DARING JOURNEY OF TWO IRISH GIRLS

The Community's novitiate had been closed for many years. Consequently, one of the most important events in the Bom Sucesso history of the 1940s was the arrival in March 1944 of two Irish girls who wished to enter this ancient monastery. They were Philomena Talty and Margaret O'Faherty, later Sisters Agnes and Teresa respectively. Sister Agnes describes their hazardous journey from Ireland, 'Sister Teresa Faherty from the Aran Island and myself set out on 11th March from Dublin to Foynes, Co. Limerick....Our leaving Ireland during the war had to be a secret. So, on our arrival in Foynes, we put up in a hotel, not knowing when exactly we were destined to leave for Lisbon. Days passed with always the same answer, "You will be told later".... On the evening of the 17th March, Saint Patrick's Day, a man appeared at the hotel and told us not to go out anymore and not to give information to anyone; sometime and some day soon a car would come to take us to the plane.... Then, late on the evening of the 18th March, the car arrived. We got to the plane in Foynes.... It was a small sea-plane with no lights and black curtains and seats available for four passengers, placed around a wooden table. There was one other lady and two young children with us on the plane.... Eventually, at 2 a.m. we landed at the beautiful Tagus river.'[19]

The lady who had befriended the two girls on the plane explained to the driver of their taxi where they needed to go and Sister Agnes continues her story when they arrived at the gate of the convent. 'After much ringing of the bell, two quaint, kind old ladies appeared. They spoke Portuguese to us and brought us into the parlour where we saw the grille. Then, with the appearance of two sisters in the Dominican habit we knew we were at home.'[20]

The annals take up the story, 'Mother Prioress and Mother Thomas received them at the grate (grille), made them take a glass of wine and sent them to rest in the chaplain's house.'[21] The following day, a past pupil took them on a tour of Lisbon and at 4.30 in the afternoon, the whole community assembled at the entrance to the enclosure to welcome the two new postulants. They received the Dominican habit on 24th September, 1944 at the conclusion of the Community retreat.

1944 was a year of hope in many other ways as the tide of war had turned in favour of the Allies. On 5th June, there was general rejoicing because Rome was declared an open city as the Allied forces took possession of it. The entry in the annals for that day reads, 'Great rejoicing! Rome is saved – All the prayers over the world have been heard for the preservation of the Holy City.'[22] And on 8th May, 1945, 'Great rejoicings, the War is over. Crowds passing during the night, singing and shouting.'[23] Prior to this, on 15th April of the same year, the annalist records the appointment of the Community's new vicar, Father Garde who would be instrumental in changing the canonical status of this ancient monastery. 'At last, news from the Master Genera! His Paternity has appointed V. Rev. Fr. Garde to be our vicar.'[24]

Relationship with the British embassy continued even after the establishment of the Irish legation. On 18th October, 1945, the British ambassador, Sir Owen O'Malley visited the community and again on 28th December, accompanied by Lady O'Malley. The third secretary had his two daughters at the school at this time.

ESTABLISHMENT OF IRISH LEGATION IN LISBON

On 26th October, Mr. Cremin, the new *charge d'affaires* from Ireland, and Mrs. Cremin paid their first visit to the community. At the distribution of prizes on 16th December, Mrs. Cremin presented the awards while Mr. Cremin and family were in the audience. Early in the New Year, 9th January, 1946, Mrs. Cremin brought her brother-in-law, Fr. Cremin from Maynooth to visit the sisters.

A flavour of the centrality of Bom Sucesso to Irish visitors is given in 1946 when the annals record the excitement created by the football match between Ireland and Portugal. The Portuguese won but, when the crestfallen Irish team visited the community on 18th June, the sisters cheered them up by telling them to go and defeat Spain. The next entry concerning the team is recorded on 27th June, 'The Irish team departed today. They defeated the Spaniards.' [25]

Just before the decade of the 1940s ended, Ireland's gift to the shrine of Our Lady of Fatima would be presented and again this enclosed community had a share in the presentation in that the beautiful monstrance was brought to Bom Sucesso prior to its going to Fatima. 'Fr. Mc Veigh accompanied the Gunnings and Conroys who brought the magnificent monstrance to show the nuns. Mother Prioress opened the door of the Upper Grate and the monstrance was passed in for all to examine the masterpiece – the Irish have reason to be proud of the gift to Our Lady of Fatima's shrine.' [26]

HISTORICAL EVENTS IN PORTUGAL

1950 was a Holy Year and probably because of pilgrimages to Rome, it was less eventful in Portugal. In 1951, two historical events connected the community with public life. On 18th April, the President of the Republic, General Carmona died. All the schools sent their pupils to the House of Parliament where the President was lying in state. The funeral took place from Jerónimos. 'Bells tolled all the evening until the cortege arrived at Jerónimos.' [27]

The second historical event was the death in France of the last Queen of Portugal, Dona Amélia whose body was brought back to

Portugal to lie beside that of her assassinated husband. On 29th November, 1951, the annalist records, 'The funeral cortège was magnificent; in memory of the terrible tragedy which took place at Blackhorse Square in 1908, the cortège passed there and then wended its way to Saint Vincent's. The streets were lined with soldiers and various schools also were represented, our pupils among the number.' [28]

DIFFICULTIES IN BOM SUCESSO

The 1950s would prove to be yet another momentous decade in the colourful history of Bom Sucesso. In July 1949, Fr. Thomas Garde, O.P., as vicar to the community, made visitation in the name of the Master of the Order. Personnel-wise, Bom Sucesso was in a healthy position and the boarding school was flourishing. However, in view of the great upsurge in religious vocations occurring in Ireland at this time, the future of Bom Sucesso, where the question of new candidates was concerned, was not at all promising. In the aftermath of the Second World War, many girls preferred missionary congregations to a specifically cloistered convent.

An early indication that the sisters were finding it physically difficult to combine liturgical observance with the onerous task of teaching is in the prioress's decision to dispense the community from midnight office for the feast of Saint Dominic, 4th August, 1952. At the same time there was the issue of extending their ministry to include not only the boarding school but also to accept day pupils especially from the growing residential area in the neighbourhood.

These two issues concern much of the correspondence between Fr. Garde, the then vicar of the Master of the Dominican Order to Bom Sucesso, and Mother Gabriel, its prioress during the early years of the decade. In September of 1952, he writes from England on his way to Rome, 'A practical point that calls for immediate attention is the day school. Apparently, Mother Catherine (the Mistress of Schools) has answered all the objections. So, I think you can put it to the vote of the Council.' However, he puts in the proviso, 'if the sisters can combine this truly apostolic work with the life of observance, it will bring a blessing.' [29]

In his December letter of the same year Fr. Garde brings up the second important issue – that of vocations. Writing from Saint Saviour's, Dublin, he states, 'When in Rome I discussed some of your problems with the Master General. His Paternity (Fr. Suarez) has a personal interest in Bom Sucesso. The big problem is the question of vocations.

It is most urgent. A solution must be found – and quickly.' [30]

In the vicar's January letter, 1953, the same two issues are paramount. A final decision with regard to the opening of the day school had not been taken. A further complication – the possibility of the Portuguese Dominican sisters opening a school in the neighbourhood – had seemingly caused some hesitation on the part of the Bom Sucesso community. Fr. Garde writes, 'it all depends now on the need for such a school in your immediate neighbourhood. If the school which the Dominican Sisters intend to open fills the need, then there is no reason for you to open another one. The matter should be carefully examined. It is possible that there may be still a need.' [31]

Finally, in March 1953, the vicar's approval for the day school arrived, 'Yes, go ahead with the alterations in view of the day school. If the sisters from Ramalhão do not come, the need will be all the greater. I will inform the Master General that you are going on with the project.' [32]

OPENING OF THE DAY SCHOOL

On October 6th 1953, the day school opened with just twenty-five pupils. Inserted in the annals of that date is a cutting from a daily newspaper dated July 1953 in which this historical occasion is announced, 'The College of Nossa Senhora do Bom Sucesso, Lisbon's oldest college for the education of girls, since it has existed for over a century, had only a boarding school. This prevented many children whose parents did not wish to be parted from them, from attending the school. In response to numerous requests mainly from residents of the Ajuda, Belém and Algés, the Board of the College the members of which are Irish Dominican Sisters decided to create for the coming school year a day school which, while functioning in the same building, will be separate from the boarding school. The College of Nossa Senhora do Bom Sucesso whice enjoys a well-established tradition and in which religious education is given, instruction is undertaken by teachers of recognised professional competence.' [33]

IMPORTANT VISITORS TO BOM SUCESSO

1953 was also memorable for the important visitors to the community. On 9th March, continuing the traditional privilege accorded members of the British royal family and their ambassadors in Lisbon, the British ambassador, Sir Nigel Ronald accompanied by Frs. Dowdall, O'Sullivan, Clarkson and Mrs. Cape (wife of the secretary to the embassy) entered the enclosure. Later in the year, the boarders who lived within the enclosure were allowed out – a free day granted by the British ambassador in honour of the Coronation of Elizabeth II of England.

On September 12th of the same year, the Cardinal Patriarch's permission was obtained to allow the President of Ireland, Eamon de Valera, and his suite to visit the cloister. The community was on retreat but 'emerged from the desert for three-quarters of an hour', and at the enclosure door they greeted the President. The Irish *charge d'affaires*, Count O'Kelly introduced the guests who included the President's wife, Bean de Valera and son, Dr. de Valera who assisted his father as his sight was failing. 'On being shown the Irish flag in the cloister he said, "I can only see the orange."' [34] The prioress presented Mr. de Valera with a framed picture of Our Lady of Bom Sucesso and Mrs. de Valera with a hand-made table centre. Later in the month, Count O'Kelly brought the Irish Minister for Finance, Mr. Seán Mac Entee and Mrs. Mac Entee to visit the community and they also were able to enter the enclosure.

CHANGES FOR THE BOARDERS

Before the year's end, another historical change took place. The pupils of the College, being boarders living within the cloister attended daily Mass in the Upper Choir and came down to the Lower Choir only to receive Communion. On 12th November, 1953, Feast of all Dominican saints and the anniversary of the Convent's foundation, 'the pupils assisted at Mass in the Church for the first time since the boarding school was opened in 1860. In the future they will also go to the Church for confessions and for lectures during the annual retreat.' The Church also served the local area especially on Sundays and so the annals explain, 'On Sundays, on account of the large congregation, the pupils will assist at Mass in the Upper Choir.' [35]

During the Salazar period, the Portuguese Youth movement was entitled *Mocidade Portuguesa* and it was customary for girls' schools to dress cradles and make clothes for poor families. An exhibition of these cradles with embroidered linen was usually held about the 8th December each year. The first mention of the Bom Sucesso pupils taking part in this charitable activity is recorded on 12th December, 1953, 'At their celebration in honour of Our Lady, the pupils presented a cradle with clothes for the poor children to the *Mocidade.*' [36]

THE MARIAN YEAR

1954, a Marian year, opened with a spell of intensely cold weather and the annalist's entry for the 2nd February reads, 'After Vespers, on leaving the Choir, an unusual sight met our gaze. Snow fell thickly in the cloister garden and continued for some hours. It was a lovely sight and the children were enchanted as the majority had never seen snow, not to speak of a snow-storm.' [37]

A NEW MEMBER FOR THE COMMUNITY

On 12th March, 1954, an Irish girl, Margaret Lally, entered. The community welcomed her at the enclosure door and brought her to the novitiate. On 15th September, at the close of the community retreat, she was received and given the name, Sister Frances. It was 'the first reception for eight years.' [38] Writing of her novitiate Sister Frances states that besides specifically spiritual disciplines, cultural studies were also engaged in: 'Sister Thomas who was novice mistress got permission for me to have classes with some of the sisters. Sister Gabriel taught me embroidery and took me watering the plants early in the morning. Sister Joseph taught me to play the piano and harmonium. A past pupil gave me lessons in oil painting and a primary school teacher lessons in Portuguese.' [39]

Awareness of people in need was also inculcated: 'Every Saturday, Sister Thomas made an enormous slab of toffee and she and I wrapped the sweets she had cut. She sold them to the children and sent the money to Dr. Finbar Ryan for the Missions.' [40] Frances concludes her account of her novitiate, 'These few years were some of the happiest years of my life.' [41]

Apart from this important event and the recording of visits from a few illustrious people such as the Papal Nuncio on 17th May and the tragic death in a car accident on 30th June of Father Suarez, Master of the Order, the annals give the impression of a tranquil lifestyle full of active service of the People of God; for example, on 24th June, the First Communion of a large number of pupils and the Confirmation of fifty boarders and day-pupils.

DR. FINBAR RYAN INTERVENES IN BOM SUCESSO'S DIFFICULTIES

Meanwhile, unknown to the majority of the members of the community, negotiations were under way which would considerably affect this tranquil lifestyle. In November, Dr. Finbar Ryan accompanied by Mr.

Ward arrived. The latter brought a beautiful crown for the statue of Our Lady in Coimbra and on the feast of all Irish saints the two visitors set off for Coimbra in order to present the crown. Back in Bom Sucesso, His Grace preached on the saints of the Dominican Order on 7th November and on 13th 'a stirring sermon on lively Faith, firm Hope and ardent Charity as bequeathed to us by Our Holy Father Saint Dominic.' [42] In these two sermons, it would seem that their long time friend was attempting to prepare the community for the changes about to take place.

On 20th December, Father Garde wrote from Dublin, prefacing the letter with the following words typed in red, '*Confidential, for yourself and Council*: Archbishop Ryan spoke to me about a possible way of saving Bom Sucesso from eventual extinction.' His solution was some kind of help from the Cabra Congregation.' [43] The Cabra Congregation had come into existence on 11th April, 1928, when the majority of Dominican convents in Ireland amalgamated. Two convents remained independent, the Convent of Jesus and Mary, Taylor's Hill, Galway (founded 1644) and the Convent of Saint Catherine of Siena, Drogheda (founded 1722). As Cabra (founded 1717) [44] was the oldest foundation from which the other houses directly or indirectly had been established the new Congregation received its name from it.

Fr. Garde explained to Mother Gabriel that he and Archbishop Ryan had already discussed the matter with the General Council of the Cabra Congregation and warned her of any resolution to join this Congregation, 'the decision is a momentous one. It should be made clear to the members of your Council and *later* to the Community that it will in time lead to Cabra absorbing Bom Sucesso which will *then* lose its present status of direct dependence on the Order (jurisdiction) as well as solemn vows. In other words, at that stage Bom Sucesso will begin to follow the Cabra Constitutions.' [45]

However, Fr. Garde assures the prioress that the Holy See's permission will be sought at every stage. He is aware that the prospect of such a radical change in the status of the sisters is alarming for them but to continue as they are can only lead to 'the gradual extinction of Bom Sucesso and all it stands for.' [46] A very important issue is to ensure that future candidates should be fully qualified to teach and he considers this crucial, 'This is a very important, almost an essential aspect of the whole problem since Bom Sucesso depends on its schools for its very existence.' [47] He did not, it would seem, envisage that the sisters could obtain permission to attend the University of Lisbon or other third level colleges in Portugal.

Some twenty-five years earlier, Finbar Ryan, as Irish provincial, had played an important role in encouraging the Dominican communities in Ireland to amalgamate and this project of uniting Bom Sucesso with them must have been very dear to him. On 12th November, 1954, from Lisbon, he wrote to Mother Benignus Meenan, Prioress General of the Cabra Congregation, 'I spoke to the council of Bom Sucesso on the lines you suggested, without letting them know that I had been speaking also to you' and he continued, 'the situation of the community is perilous indeed and it is not easy to see how its continuance can be safeguarded.'[48]

In his December letter to her, he wrote, 'I discussed the Lisbon possibility with Fr. Garde to whom even a possibility gave enormous comfort: for his anxiety regarding Bom Sucesso is so much the greater because he has…to see its grave position. He authorised me to speak with you and your council (if you think well of it) in his name. He knows (for I told him) that already, in an informal way, I had spoken to the Bom Sucesso council.'[49]

Early in 1955, matters began to move very quickly. Fr. Garde's January letter is in acknowledgment of Mother Gabriel's with the result of her council's vote on the issue – 6 in favour, 1 against. 'In view of this so far favourable reception, we have decided to go out to Lisbon so as to arrive there while His Grace is in Lisbon.'[50] After detailing their travel plan to be confirmed later [he was to travel with two Cabra sisters], he asks Mother Gabriel to obtain the Patriarch's permission for the Cabra Sisters to stay within the enclosure. The community must also be given some information to explain the visit of these two sisters, 'Please tell the community that the Cabra Congregation is considering the question of giving Bom Sucesso some help, without going into details. Later, His Grace – helped by me if necessary – can then put the whole project (with all its implications) before the community.'[51]

DOMINICAN SISTERS FROM IRELAND

The Bom Sucesso annals now take up the story to record the visit of Mothers Benignus Meenan and Reginald Lyons accompanied by Dr. Finbar Ryan and Fr. Garde, 'At 4p.m., V. Rev. Fr. Garde, Mother Prioress General and Mother M. Reginald arrived and went to the Lower Grate to see the Sisters. After tea, V. Rev. Fr. Garde conducted the Mothers to the *Portaria* (enclosure entrance) where M. Prioress and community had assembled to welcome the guests. Then, an

Professions 1925: left to right, Srs Reginald Hayden, Imelda Warner, Catherine Walsh, Raymond Farrelly, (prioress), Thomas Kennedy, and Finbar O'Driscoll.

Students in Art Room 1920s.

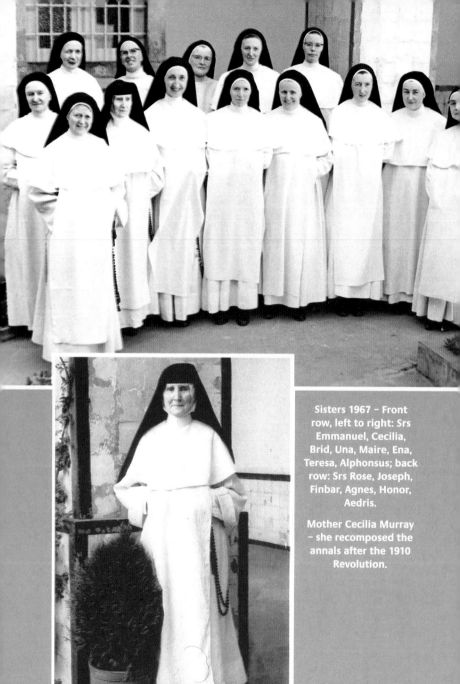

Sisters 1967 – Front row, left to right: Srs Emmanuel, Cecilia, Brid, Una, Maire, Ena, Teresa, Alphonsus; back row: Srs Rose, Joseph, Finbar, Agnes, Honor, Aedris.

Mother Cecilia Murray – she recomposed the annals after the 1910 Revolution.

Sisters 1973 – Left to right: Srs Aderis Coates, Feighín, Michelle Forde, Agnes Talty, Hyacinth White, Catherine Walsh, Joseph Dorr, Margaret Purcell, Una Dempsey, Medical Mission sister, Maire Corbett, Catherine Connolly.

Sisters 1979 – Left to right: Srs Colm McCool, Rose Niall, Agnes Talty, Thomas Kennedy, Antoninus O'Rourke, Joan O'Shanahan.

Sisters 1956 – visit of Master of the Order, Michael (later Cardinal) Browne.

Visit of Cardinal Cerejeira 1970, 3rd Centenary of Bom Sucesso church. Left to right: Srs Hyacinth White, Agnes Talty, Emmanuel Davis, Imelda Warner, Honor McCabe, Una Dempsey.

1979 Meeting of Cabra Congregation in Bom Sucesso – General Council and Vicars of Regions: Left to right: Srs Aedris Coates (Portugal), Breda Hourigan (Ireland), Simeon Tarpey (Councillor), Marian O'Sullivan (South Africa), Vivienne O'Beirne (Councillor), Veronica McShane (Louisiana), Jordana Roche (Prioress General), Aine Killen (Argentina), Aquinas McCarthy (Councillor), Joan O'Donovan (Councillor).

Srs Deirdre O'Neill and Emmanuel Davis with Cristina Maria de Seixas Gonçalo on her First Communion day 1971.

Belfry

Upper parlour
after grille
was removed
– early 1950s

Tercentenary of Bom Sucesso church 1670-1970. The Patriarch of Lisbon,
Cardinal Cerejeira gives blessing at the end of Mass;
on his right is Fr Pedro, parish priest of Jeronimos, while on his left is Fr
Terence McLoughlin OP of Corpo Santo

Choir

Golden Jubilee 1986
– Sr Philomena Sisk

Golden Jubilee 1995 – Srs Teresa Faherty and Agnes Talty

Former members of St Anne's Community 1983-2002: Srs Anne Patricia Morgan, Teresa Wade, Honor McCabe, Agnes Talty, Aedris Coates.

Four Sisters: Srs Nuala McKinstry, Bernadette Pakenham, Michael Forde, Alicia Mooney

President of Ireland, Mary Robinson with husband Nick,
Sr Teresa Wade and others.

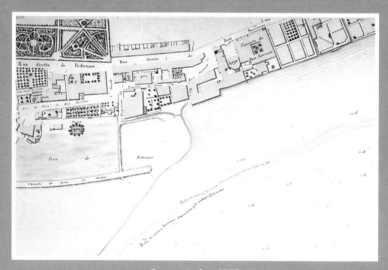

Convent plan 1857

Cloister and Cloister garth

**Azulejo plaque to
Blessed Sacrament**

Refectory

Crucifix in refectory

Azulejo – refectory

Upper choir ceiling and detail (below)

Srs Aedris and Agnes in choir

Clockwise from top left:
infant school,
primary school,
recital,
morning break Alges

St Dominic's International School

Lectio divina in Zambujal

informal procession through the cloister and a short visit to the Lower Choir. The members of the community who were past-pupils of Eccles Street (one of the Dominican schools in Dublin), were particularly happy to meet their former teachers.' [52]

The stress on the confidential nature of the discussion prevented the annalist from revealing details of this meeting. The visiting sisters remained in Bom Sucesso until 31st January but included an overnight visit to Fátima. The annalist concludes, 'Mother Prioress General and Mother M. Reginald seemed very pleased with their stay in our monastery and we felt quite at ease with our Sisters from Cabra.' [53]

On 28th January, 1955, Fr. Garde wrote to Mother Gabriel, stressing the need for silence on the part of the Bom Sucesso sisters regarding the issue of amalgamation, 'On no account should they discuss the question with people outside the community – not even with the Fathers of Corpo Santo, much less should they write to anyone.' [54] The reason for this was that the negotiations were only at the preliminary stages, 'We await the official decision of the Cabra Congregation. Then, the Order and the Holy See will have to be consulted. Any imprudence or indiscretion at this stage might have very serious consequences.' [55]

Early in April, Fr. Garde wrote to say that there was unanimous acceptance of Bom Sucesso by the Cabra General Council. However, nothing further could be done until the Master of the Order and the Sacred Congregation of Religious had given their consent. [56] He was also concerned that Sister Frances, the novice, who had not as yet made First Profession, would be fully aware of the change in status of Bom Sucesso. The prioress explained the situation to her and promised that, if she wished to transfer from Bom Sucesso, care would be taken to ensure that she would join a community of her own choice. Sister Frances replied that she would stay in the Bom Sucesso community. [57]

ELECTION OF FR. MICHAEL BROWNE AS MASTER OF THE DOMINICAN ORDER

Meanwhile, a new Master of the Dominican Order was elected, an Irishman, Fr. Michael Browne, O.P. The annalist expresses the considerable joy which this election caused among Irish Dominicans, 'Great rejoicing everywhere. The result of election was so unexpected as Dr. Browne, being Master of the Sacred Palace, none of us thought he could be elected – Such an honour for the Order and for Ireland.' [58]

In May, Fr. Garde wrote again to inform the prioress of Bom Sucesso concerning his discussions in Rome, 'The Master General understands the situation. In his opinion, it seems to be the only way to save Bom Sucesso from extinction.' [59] Concerning the Sacred Congregation of Religious he writes, 'I had an interview with the Secretary of the Sacred Congregation of Religious and with the Prefect, His Eminence Cardinal Valeri. I found both most favourably disposed.' [60]

RESCRIPT FROM ROME

Months passed before news came from Rome and the first was a telegram to Fr. Garde from the Master of the Order, 'Rescript Nuns Granted.' [61] A few days later, Fr. Garde was able to let Mother Gabriel know that copies of the Rescript had come and that he was forwarding one to her together with a document entitled *Executio* to be sent to the Patriarch of Lisbon.

In another letter later in the month of August, Fr. Garde gives suggestions where practical details are concerned. 'As soon as the Cardinal Patriarch has given the *Executio* you could proceed to make the necessary alterations –taking down the grilles for instance. I think some kind of light grille or division between the choir and public Church would be desirable. The Sisters should proceed to write letters mentioned in the rescript (to be eventually kept in the archives).' [62] In the same letter, Rosary Sunday, 2nd October, is suggested as the day for the Solemn Inauguration.

SOLEMN INAUGURATION

Prior to this date, on 29th September, Fr. Garde arrived, accompanied by Mothers Colm Cille Flynn and Alberta Grant. The first two sisters from the Cabra Congregation to be assigned to Bom Sucesso, Mother Imelda Joseph Mc Evoy and Sister Bríd Trant, also arrived. Fr. Garde wished to obtain a habit from Corpo Santo and brought Sister Bríd to accompany him and see some part of Lisbon. There was further delay as the document from the Patriarch had not been received so that again Fr. Garde had to set off to obtain this and the permission for all the Cabra Sisters to enter the enclosure. He was successful and all were welcomed into the cloister.

On 2nd October, 1955, High Mass was celebrated, Fr. Garde being celebrant with Frs. D. Clarkson and J. Collins, deacon and sub-deacon respectively. 'During the Mass, the curtains of the Choir grating were drawn back for the first time in three hundred years.' [63] The annalist continues her detailed description of yet another historic occasion in the long life of the Bom Sucesso convent, '11.30. The Sisters assembled in the cloister wearing their cloaks. The procession led by crossbearer and acolytes proceeded to the *Portaria*. On opening the door, the delegate of the Cardinal Patriarch, Rev. Fr. Rosa Pereira, V.Rev. Fr.T. Garde, Provincial and Vicar of this monastery, Rev. Fr. Dominic Clarkson, O.P. and Rev. Fr. J. Collins, O.P., stood at the entrance. The chantress then entoned the responsory *Cives*. The procession wended its way to the Chapter Room.... At the head of the Chapter Room, the delegate, V. Rev. Fr. Garde and Rev. Fr. Clarkson being seated, Rev. Fr. J. Collins read the rescript. At its conclusion the Delegate gave a summary of its contents in Portuguese and added a few words of his own. Then, the Sisters made the *venia*. V. Rev. Fr.Garde read a most touching and paternal letter from the Master General. He spoke himself most eloquently and referred to the change in our status as manifestly the Will of God. Referred to all that Dr. Finbar Ryan had done for the community, his interest extending over a period of forty years. Also to the late V.Rev. Fr. Louis Nolan's fatherly interest in the welfare of Bom Sucesso. At the conclusion of this most impressive and historic ceremony, the *Te Deum* was chanted, the Delegate and Fathers and Sisters singing alternate verses. A new era for Bom Sucesso has begun.' [64]

Letters of Support

Mother Benignus Meenan (possibly due to ill-health) did not attend the ceremony of amalgamation on Rosary Sunday but wrote to the prioress on that day, 'Mother Reginald and I are with you in spirit today.... I hope you feel happy – you feel lonely, I am sure, how could it be otherwise? But surely today's action has our Holy Father's (St. Dominic) approval. He will petition our Divine Master that Bom Sucesso may live and flourish for many more centuries and that it may nurture many and great saints as it has done in the past – nearly three hundred and fifty years....God has asked a big sacrifice from you all and you are giving it to Him gladly. He will not be outdone in generosity.'[65]

In his letter of the 27th September, 1955, the Master of the Order, Fr. Michael Browne gave words of encouragement to the Bom Sucesso Sisters as, once again, the community was leaving the Master's jurisdiction, 'I have followed everything closely with Father Provincial (Fr. Garde) during these recent months since my election. I feel sure that the best has been done and that God's blessing will be on it.... I feel sorry indeed that you are leaving my jurisdiction, but, uniting with Cabra, you don't cease to be my children from every spiritual point of view.' He then praises the Cabra Congregation for its educational work and also because 'Cabra in its Constitutions has preserved the great elements of the Dominican tradition regarding choral life and monastic observance. It embodies, without a doubt, a Dominican ideal for the salvation of souls inspired and vitalised by a life guided to contemplation by choral life and conventual observance.' He then deals with the advantages accruing to the school which amalgamation brings while, at the same time, it solves the problem of vocations to the community. He concludes with the promise of continued interest and support, 'My interest in Bom Sucesso and its welfare will continue as before when it was under the jurisdiction of the Master General, exercised mainly by his vicar. Any help that the Order can ever give will be given to this dear community and to each one of its members.' [66]

In October, 1956, true to his promise of his continuing interest in Bom Sucesso, Fr. Michael Browne not only visited the community but said Mass in the Church, 'Never in the annals of Bom Sucesso had a Master General said Mass in our Church – Memorable day! The eve of Rosary Sunday will always be remembered by the community and it is to be hoped the blessing of Our Holy Father's representative will bring many blessings to the community.' [67]

In his farewell letter, as vicar to Bom Sucesso, Fr. Garde wrote shortly after amalgamation, 'This is just a line to ask how you are and how everything is going. Although I have no longer directly charge of you, I will never forget Bom Sucesso. How could I after such repeated kindness over all these years. You may count on an habitual remembrance in my prayers – and any little help I may be able to give.' [68]

VARIOUS CHANGES

As the year drew to a close various changes in the convent and school were recorded. On 1st November, for the first time in the history of the school, the boarders were allowed to go out to see a film in the cinema nearby and on 12th of the same month the grille was removed in the pupils' reception room. On the 20th, the annalist observed, 'the children are delighted with all the changes except one, the older pupils have *saudades* (nostalgia) for the Upper Choir where they heard Mass and recited the Rosary for years.' [69] Yet another change took place on 21st November, 'The workmen began to tear down the walls in the *Portaria* (entrance). A parlour will replace the large hall.' [70] In December, the Sisters changed their headdress to conform to the one worn by the Cabra Sisters.

During 1956, changes continued to take place. Some were reasons for joy as when all the sisters for 'the first time in the history of Bom Sucesso went to the entrance door to the patio' [71] to welcome Mother Benignus and Mother Jordan, accompanied by Fr. Garde on his way to Trinidad. Others were painful as symbolic of the old order changing. Such was the removal of the heavy grille between the choir and the Church. The entry in the annals of 17th July, 1956, reads, 'Memorable day for Bom Sucesso! The nail-garnished grate in Lower Choir has been removed. It had been there since the building of the Church, nearly three hundred years.' [72] To an historian, it would have been a reminder of the evils of the Inquisition since it was erected by Manuel Cerqueira de Campos, member of the Holy Office and its *bicos* or spikes on the outside were a formidable sight to people visiting the Church. However, to those sisters who had lived their religious lives behind it, it was symbolic of their separation from the secular world. A further entry in the annals on 31st July, reveals something of the drastic nature of the change, 'The new grate has been put up – less austere. Sisters now receive Holy Communion (four) kneeling together. This arrangement is a great help to the priest' [73] since, previously, each sister individually received Communion through a very narrow opening in the former grille. The annalist's silence concerning the Community's acceptance of this change conceals the regret, even the pain of those who had been accustomed to the privacy of receiving Communion through a very small aperture and, today, this part of the former grille is preserved as one of the convent's precious heirlooms.

THE CHURCH AND *O ESTADO NOVO* IN THE 1950S

The 1950s marked a change also in the relationship between the Catholic Church and the Salazar regime. Throughout Portuguese history, the Christian Faith had played an important role as the majority of the people were Catholic. The Church having been materially weakened by the confiscation of its property in 1911 tried to reorganise and renew its structures. This process of renewal, begun as early as the last decade of monarchical rule, was helped by the efforts of *Estado Novo* to re-christianise public life. The increase in Catholic Action through various lay organisations and the phenomenon of Fatima are also considered aspects of this process of renewal.[74]

Though Salazar had been a prominent member of the Catholic Centre Party prior to his entering government, he held that he was Head of Government, not as representative of Catholicism, but 'by legal nomination of the President of the Republic.'[75] Church and State would remain separate. Catholicism was accepted as part of Portuguese tradition and culture but was not a State religion, 'The State would be secular but its secularity would not prevent it from recognising Catholicism and the Church as important factors in the stabilisation of society and missionary work as an important factor in colonisation.'[76]

In education, the regime protected the public school system which had formerly been hostile to the Church. The government was prepared to allow a Christian perspective to animate all pedagogical activity but it did not subsidise Catholic schools. On the occasion of the twenty-fifth anniversary of the publication of Pius XI's encyclical on Christian Education, the State was publicly criticised for its failure and injustice in its system of education.[77]

While in the first phase of the regime, from 1926 to the signing of the Concordat in 1940, relations between Church and State had been characterised by open collaboration, increasing tensions and problems in this relationship both within the country and with the Vatican, in the 1950s, led to open dissidence on the part of some members of the Hierarchy. These tensions increased as the Church was inspired by the Vatican II Council and the political philosophy of Salazarism failed to adapt to a new era. Change in every sphere of human activity within Western civilisation would characterise the sixties and any system or organisation that failed to update was destined to disappear. This would be the fate of Salazarism in its continued refusal to allow freedom of the press and freedom of association together with its reliance on the secret police to maintain order.

12

Vatican II and Later

The participants in the historic events of amalgamation could not have foreseen that the changes were but a forerunner of those which were soon to take place within the universal Church itself. On 9th October, 1958, Pope Pius XII died and nineteen days later, Cardinal Angelo Roncalli was elected Pope, taking the name of John XXIII. He was nearly seventy-seven years old but he assumed his papal responsibilities with extraordinary energy and immediately set about a renewal of the Church. On 25th January, 1959, at the Benedictine monastery of Saint Paul, he announced the holding of an ecumenical Council and on 25th December of the same year his Apostolic letter, *Humanae Salutis*, was promulgated in which the Pope announced that the Second Ecumenical Vatican Council was to take place in 1962. Then, on 2nd February, 1962, his Motu Proprio, *Consilium* set the exact date for the opening of the Council – 11th October, 1962. Bom Sucesso recorded the Pope's coronation and recalled his visit to Fatima two years before, 'Some of the sisters listened in to the ceremonies and nearly all heard the Holy Father giving the blessing after the coronation…. The pupils also heard the Holy Father's voice for the first time from Rome. Some of them were present in Fatima when His Holiness led a pilgrimage there.' [1]

FATHER PAUL O'SULLIVAN

Another important entry in the annals of 1959, is the death in Corpo Santo on 21st November of Fr. Paul O'Sullivan, O.P. He had lived in Portugal for sixty-four years and had played an active role in securing that the Religious of Corpo Santo and Bom Sucesso would remain in Portugal when the Religious Orders were expelled in 1910. He worked tirelessly for the Catholic Faith during these years of persecution, publishing booklets which are still available today. The annalist who knew him personally wrote of him, 'Director of the Terti-

199

aries and Rosary Confraternity, his zeal knew no bounds.... He succeeded in infusing faith and zeal into many lukewarm souls.' [2] Another document in the archives states that from the moment he arrived in Portugal in 1895 'he literally fell in love with the people and the country. He was attracted by the good manners and courtesy of the Portuguese and often declared that they surpassed other races in these respects. Whatever failings he noticed were always explained away as a result of the political upheavals that for many years had disturbed the equilibrium of Portuguese life.... He referred with deep feeling to the people's outstanding devotion to the Blessed Sacrament and to the Blessed Virgin Mary. Portugal was indeed for him the "Land of Holy Mary."' [3] Father Paul had lived to see the restoration of the Catholic Church in the country of his adoption during the years of the *Estado Novo*.

It is difficult to understand Salazarism without reference to Catholicism since Salazar found his main ideological inspiration in it. However, Church and State were separate, the name of God was not in the Constitution and Catholic schools were not subsidised by the State. Though the Head of State was not necessarily a Catholic, there was publicly a certain relationship between the Government and the Catholic Church.

THE CHURCH AND THE *ESTADO NOVO*

This relationship between the Salazar regime and the institutional Church was evident in May 1959 when, on the 13th, following the ceremonies in Fatima, the statue of Our Lady of Fatima was brought to Lisbon for the inauguration of the monument to *Cristo Rei,* overlooking the Tagus. It is also an example of popular piety when, in the absence of priests, due to persecution, people had expressed their faith through their devotion to statues.

On arrival at Lisbon, the statue was taken to the Church of Our Lady of Fatima and on the night of the 16th it was solemnly brought across the river. The annalist describes the celebration: 'On its arrival, bonfires, fireworks, all sorts of illumination greeted the statue.' [4]

The following day, after High Mass the statue was brought to the base of the monument and at 5 p.m., the solemn inauguration of the *Cristo Rei* took place. Church and State were well represented at the inauguration of this monument promised, in 1939, by the Cardinal Patriarch if Portugal would be preserved from the calamity of the Second World War. The President of the Republic, the Prime Minister, Dr. Salazar and members of the Government were all present at this ceremony. This was somewhat ironic since the feast of Christ as King had been introduced by the Church in order to counter the evils of the totalitarian regimes of Communism and fascism.

According to Padre Roque de Almeida, the Church in Portugal was rejuvenated at this time: 'Although the secular Republic had succeeded in interrupting diplomatic relations between Portugal and the Holy See (1910-1919), separating the Church from the State, expelling bishops from their dioceses, confiscating Church property...persecuting and banishing religious...it did not succeed, however, in suppressing popular fervour.' [5] This writer considers that the Concordat of the 7th May, 1940 only confirmed an established fact, giving it a juridical foundation and clarity in the political sphere. While it is never good for the Church to be too closely linked with the organs of government, this period of peace made it possible for the Church to re-establish its religious institutions in Portugal. Seminaries could now be legally reopened and facilities for catechesis e-established. Missionary expansion in Portuguese overseas territories occurred. Not all the clergy, however, were satisfied with the government and had the courage to express their opinion. They would suffer the consequences as did the bishop of Oporto.

The Bishops and Salazar

By the 1950s, many committed Catholics were not happy with government policies especially in education. In 1954, on the occasion of the twenty-fifth anniversary of Pius XI's encyclical on education, *Divini Illius Magistri*, Professor Guilherme Braga da Costa, speaking at the Geography Society meeting, publicly criticised the Government's failure and injustice in the educational system of Portugal. His speech was unanimously approved by the bishops.

In April 1957, the Bishop of Oporto, D. António Ferreira Gomes was invited by Catholic Action to address the first Week of Portuguese Rural Studies being held at Fátima. He complained of 'the unmerited misery of the rural world – a situation that violates equity among the members of the national community.' [6] He stressed the need for the education of rural people and emphasised the contribution of the seminaries in this sphere. He criticised the State's monopoly of education and stated that education in Portugal, instead of being a necessity, had become a luxury.

At the time of the presidential election in 1958, the same bishop sent an open letter to Dr. Salazar expressing his apprehension concerning the religious and political situation: 'The cause of the Church is constantly losing ground in the soul of the people, of the worker and of youth.' [7] He asked if the State would object to the free instruction of the Church's social teaching and the development by Catholics of their own civic and political formation.

In response, Salazar did not receive the bishop to discuss these matters, as had been requested, but obliged him to leave his diocese and go into exile. The other bishops showed their solidarity with the bishop of Oporto. Early in 1959, they wrote a collective pastoral letter stating that 'the hierarchy would betray the divine authority with which it is invested placing itself at the service of that for which it did not receive it and would also be culpable of negligence and weakness if it did not further preach prudently but firmly Catholic doctrine in all exigencies, in the life of the individual, the family, society , politics and culture.' [8] These interventions had considerable influence among Catholics and some groups of lay people began to show their dissatisfaction with the regime.

CRISIS IN GOVERNMENT

In 1958 also, a crisis arose when a more liberal group within the National Union itself was anxious to modernise administrative methods and reform government attitudes not only in relation to the internal affairs of the country but to overseas territories and foreign affairs in general. This group was willing to collaborate with the Government but believed that Salazar should be replaced by a younger leader such as Marcelo Caetano. The President of the Republic seemed to be of the same opinion and when the presidential election was being held in 1958, Creveiro Lopes was passed over by the Central Commission of the *União Nacional* and Admiral Américo Tomás was chosen as the government's candidate.

The Centre-Left and the Extreme-Left Opposition Parties chose an agreed candidate, Humberto Delgado, director-general of Civil Aviation. He was the more popular candidate and expected to win the election. In spite of this however, the result of the voting gave less than 25% to Delgado and Tomás was declared President. **Neverthe**less, it was generally held that Delgado had actually won the election. Once the elections were over, repression intensified and Delgado was obliged to leave Portugal for Brazil. He was later found assassinated on the frontier between Spain and Portugal as he was returning to his country.

Internationally also, the regime's political thinking was outmoded. In the aftermath of World War II, global opinion had turned against nationalism, extremes of which had caused great suffering to many peoples. The United Nations' Charter signed by fifty countries in California in 1945, proclaimed, in article 55, 'universal respect for and observance of human rights and fundamental freedoms for all without distinction as to race, sex, language or religion.' This meant that the great colonial powers had to reconsider the right to self-government of their overseas possessions.

The British Labour Government of Clement Attlee granted independence to India in 1947 and to Pakistan in 1948 though both remained within the British Commonwealth. Gradually, all the former colonies of Britain, France, the Netherlands and Belgium gained autonomy so that, by 1963, most colonial peoples had obtained some degree of sovereignty. Portugal continued to hold its colonies in spite of warfare beginning in Angola (1961), Portuguese Guinea (1963) and Mozambique (1964). In December 1962, India annexed by force the Portuguese territory of Goa, Damão and Diu, thus severing the centuries-old link between Portugal and the subcontinent.

The Government's determination to retain the colonies isolated Portugal from other States especially within the United Nations. Nevertheless, Portugal was able to join NATO at that organisation's inception in 1949 and in 1955, was admitted to the United Nations by an agreement between the Soviet Union and the Western Powers as to the number of Communist and non-Communist members.

In May 1964, the Catholic chaplains of NATO attending a conference in Estoril asked if they might say Mass in the Church of Bom Sucesso. Concelebrated Mass had not, as yet, been established. Consequently, during the three days of the conference, all the six altars of the Church were occupied by the priests saying individual Masses. About fifteen Masses were said daily there.

BOM SUCESSO AND PORTUGUESE MISSIONS

At this time, Bom Sucesso had a part to play in Portugal's missionary work as the Portuguese Dominican Sisters asked for a member of the Community to spend some time with their missionary Sisters in Moçambique. Sister Feighin who had been assigned to Bom Sucesso in 1956 was appointed to this mission. She set off on 20th October, 1960. Over a number of years also, members of the Medical Missionaries of Mary, Ireland, stayed in Bom Sucesso while studying in Lisbon in preparation for their mission in Angola. When war broke out in Biafra in 1968, Bom Sucesso became a house of hospitality for Irish missionaries who were obliged to leave the war zone. In July of that year, two Bom Sucesso sisters, Máire Corbett and Úna Dempsey and one Medical Missionary, Eithne Walsh, studying in Lisbon and living in Bom Sucesso went to São Tomé to help with the airlift of food for the people of Biafra.

THE DOMINICAN FAMILY IN PORTUGAL

However, for the daily Mass and other liturgies, the community was fortunate in that the Irish Dominican priests of Corpo Santo were chaplains and confessors both to the Sisters and the pupils of the schools. Thus, the Dominican family spirit was already fostered and this also extended to the wider Dominican Order in Portugal – the Portuguese Dominican Sisters, the Spanish Dominican Sisters of the Holy Rosary and the Portuguese Dominican priests. Over the years, many Bom Sucesso Sisters attended the annual Summer Theology Course conducted by the Portuguese Dominican priests in Fátima while the community was always invited to the celebrations of the Sisters' Congregations. Retreats and holidays were often spent at the Monastery of Pius XII in Fátima or the convent of the Dominican Sisters in Castelo Branco where they were always given a cordial welcome. The Dominican family is now well established in Portugal with all the benefits for the small group of Irish Dominicans in Lisbon.

During the fifties and sixties, some share in the traditional life of the Portuguese people was also given to the Bom Sucesso Community in that the annual Mass for the fishermen who set out for the cod fisheries in Newfoundland and Greenland was celebrated in the Church of Bom Sucesso. The Mass for the main fishing fleet was customarily celebrated in Jerónimos and afterwards, the sea was solemnly blessed. The smaller fleet had its Mass in Bom Sucesso and inset in the January annals of 1960 is a newspaper cutting (without a date) giving an account of the Mass celebrated that year, at which, in his homily, Rev. Sá Rosa asked the help of Our Lady of Bom Sucesso for a good result for the forthcoming cod fishing enterprise as, the previous year, it had not been successful. In 1968, to commemorate the fiftieth anniversary of the apparitions of Our Lady at Fatima, the Sisters were asked to translate into English a booklet on the story of Fatima and in May of that year, several Sisters were at the ceremonies in Fatima which were celebrated by Pope Paul VI and attended by Sister Lúcia.

YEARS OF VITALITY AND GROWTH

The 1960s were years of great vitality in both the convent and the school of Bom Sucesso. In 1963, a modern building for the Junior school was opened and, in 1964, as boarding-schools were becoming outmoded, the historic boarding-school closed but, in September of the same year, a new venture was undertaken – the establishment of a junior school for foreign children whose first language was English. Thus, Saint Dominic's International School was opened on 12th September, 1964.

During the sixties, many sisters were assigned from Ireland to Bom Sucesso and they enthusiastically undertook the study of the Portuguese language and culture. In 1963/64, four sisters attended the University of Lisbon's afternoon course on Portuguese for foreign students and enjoyed lectures not only on the language but the history, geography and art of Portugal. A valuable interchange of cultures also took place within the school: while the sisters taught English literature to them, the senior pupils advised the sisters what works of Portuguese literature they should read.

The original members of the community also began to enjoy the benefits which union with the Cabra Congregation had brought. They were now able to go on pilgrimage to Fátima and Calaruega, Saint Dominic's birthplace or spend their holidays in a Dominican convent in Castelo Branco or Fatima or again attend the Dominican Theology Course there. Their ministry was also extended beyond the convent in that some became catechists in the parish of Belém while Sister Antoninus developed a special ministry to *os ciganos*, nomadic people.

In the mid-sixties also, the secondary school expanded to include 1st to 7th years. The 1st-2nd year cycle was remodelled and, for the first time, the examinations at the end of this cycle were held in the school. Formerly, pupils had to go to the local lyceum for all exams at the end of each of the three cycles – 2nd, 5th and 7th. Having the 2nd year exams in familiar surroundings was a great advantage to the younger pupils. Students of the 5th and 7th years continued to have both written and orals in the lyceum and sisters accompanied them there.

As part of the educational and cultural programme in Portugal at that time, Bom Sucesso pupils were taken on school tours abroad. In London in 1970, they were given an excellent opportunity to practise English. In April 1974, while on a school tour to Austria, sisters met Ursulines in Innsbruck who described what they had endured during the Hitler regime and, when asked how Austria had not succumbed to Communism, they replied, 'The politicians have one answer, we have another.' Very soon, Catholics in Portugal would recall Austria's Rosary processions in its efforts to retain freedom of religion.

THE FINAL YEARS OF THE ESTADO NOVO

Meanwhile, the regime struggled to contain political protests. In order to satisfy public opinion, many public works were undertaken throughout the country, industrialisation was developed and wages increased. At the same time, repression intensified. 'The ivory tower in which Salazar was shut up had hardened according as the President of the Council was ageing and losing contact with lower levels of administration and the public in general.' [9]

Progressive Catholics were in conflict with the regime which they judged prejudicial to the Church, alienating many from it and preventing it from updating. From March 1959 to May 1962, there were some attempts at a *coup d'état* ending with the University students' revolt which was put down with severely repressive measures against both professors and students.

Salazar emerged seemingly victorious from these years of unrest and a final period of stability for the regime began. 'Repression characterised the end of Salazarism as in the golden years of its establishment and implanting.' [10] In September 1968, António Oliveira Salazar became terminally ill and the President of the Republic asked Marcelo Caetano to take over the reins of government.

THE SPRINGTIME OF HOPE

The new head of the Government was a prestigious figure, an historian, professor of law and formerly rector of the University of Lisbon. His political career had been made within the regime but he was liberal in his political thinking and a believer in a Western-style democracy. He was opposed to violence and valued persuasive tactics where political action was concerned. 'He knew well that powerful forces – the army, the navy, the police, wealthy capitalism, higher bureaucracy, a part of the Church's hierarchy – were watching him closely, granting him support only if they were sure that stability and their interests would be maintained at all costs.' [11]

Leaders of the Opposition and others, including the bishop of Oporto, were allowed to return from exile. The secret police lost some of its power and censorship was lessened. However, political parties were not permitted to be organised and this was unacceptable in 1968. According to the historian, Hermano Saraiva, 'The end of the regime was fast approaching by the very fact of the lapse of time and the ageing of ideas.' [12]

By 1970, the springtime of hope which had dawned with the accession to power of Marcelo Caetano was beginning to fade. Repression returned and leaders of the Opposition again went into exile. The army which had enjoyed a relative independence in the era of the Estado Novo would now become responsible for putting an end to this period of Portuguese history.

BOM SUCESSO IN THE 1970S

Meanwhile, Bom Sucesso celebrated yet another centenary – the tercentenary of its church. On 12th July, 1970, the anniversary of the first Mass celebrated in the church in 1670, the Cardinal Patriarch of Lisbon, His Eminence D. Manuel Cerejeira concelebrated with Canon Gonçalves Pedro, parish priest of Santa Maria de Belém, four Dominicans from Corpo Santo, Fathers Tom Cleary, Prior, Dominic Clarkson, Hilary Griffin and Terence Mc Loughlin as well as and one of the priests from the English College. Frei Tomás Videira, O.P., preached the homily in which he recalled the history of the convent and emphasised the influence it had had on the religious and cultural life of Portugal. The Cardinal Patriarch spoke some words of praise for the work being carried on in the schools. Lunch followed and was attended by the Cardinal and other invited guests.

During the early seventies, the private schools began to form associations with a view to obtaining financial support form public funds for their work in education. Meetings were held in different parts of the country which two Sisters from Bom Sucesso attended. The Government responded with the promise of financial help for the private schools. However, changes in the political life of the country were about to take place.

In February 1974, General Spínola who, as Governor of Portuguese Guinea (1968-1973), had created local assemblies of all ethnic groups in his jurisdiction now published his work, *Portugal e o Futuro*. In this book, he openly criticised the Government's policy, both internal and external. Consequently, on 14th March, he was dismissed from his post as Deputy-Chief of Staff of the Armed Forces [*vice-chef do Estado Maior General das Forças Armadas*].

The Chief of Staff, General Costa Gomes, who had also expressed the opinion that it was impossible to retain the colonies as they were, was also dismissed.

THE FLOWER REVOLUTION OF 1974

On 16th March 1974, a column of the army left Caldas da Raínha and marched on Lisbon but was intercepted before it reached the capital. A more complete military operation was in preparation and early on the morning of the 25th April, 1974, the Revolution occurred.

In Bom Sucesso, the sisters learned of the Revolution when the driver of the school bus arrived before 7.30 a.m., Mass and explained that no buses could travel that day. After community Mass, the two principals of the Junior and Senior schools went to the school entrance to advise any pupils who might arrive to return home. An ominous silence hung over the street which, at 8 o'clock in the morning, was usually bustling with activity. A few people huddled in groups in the doorways of the old, dilapidated buildings on the opposite side of the street. Then, as the sisters waited, an armoured vehicle slowly moved into the street. The soldiers on the tank were each wearing a red carnation. The Flower Revolution had come to Rua Bartolomeu Dias.

The people huddled in the doorways furtively waved to the soldiers as they moved on through the street. Later in the day, news came that the government had surrendered and had handed over power to General Spínola. Marcelo Caetano, Américo Tomás and other government ministers were deported to Madeira and afterwards, went to Brazil.

The government was assumed by a Junta of seven members – two members each of the army, the navy, the air force and one other person. It had the title, *Junta de Salvação Nacional*. In May, a provisional government was formed and General Spínola was chosen as first President of the new Republic. The Revolution had begun simply with the army's revolt against the maintenance of the colonies but soon ideologies were introduced when political parties were made legal. Several parties were founded but the three principal parties were the Communist, the Socialist and the Partido Popular Democrático.

The first provisional government was led by a civilian and lawyer, Adelino da Palma Carlos who was a moderate democrat and a mason. He included among his ministers Communists, Socialists, Democrats and members of the Monarchical Party. The inclusion of people with such divergent political views prevented the government from fulfilling its functions and in July, 1974, Palma Carlos resigned, being replaced by General Vasco Gonçalves, a Communist. Between July 1974 and August 1975, there were four provisional governments, each presided over by General Gonçalves and each tending more and more towards Communism.

In September, 1974, General Spínola was obliged to resign as President of the Republic and was replaced by General Costa Gomes. In March 1975, some members of the Centre-Right staged a *coup d'état* but it failed and many people were imprisoned or forced into exile, including General Spínola. The *Junta de Salvação Nacional* was replaced by the larger Revolutionary Council which intended to remain in power for six years.

The Threat of Communism

On 25th April 1975, the promised elections took place – the first free elections in fifty years. 90% of the people exercised their franchise and the result was a clear victory for the non-Communist parties – the Socialists, Popular Democrats, Democratic Socialists and Popular Monarchists. On the basis of this result the victorious parties tried to convince the Revolutionary Council to allow them to govern but the parties of the extreme left opposed this. There followed many months of great agitation throughout the country when an intense anti-communist reaction caused the offices of the Communist party to be attacked in several towns. In July 1975, the fifth provisional government was formed with the support of the Communist party as Socialists and Democrats had withdrawn from government.

The economic state of the country deteriorated considerably and pressure from Western Powers increased so that President Costa Gomes was obliged to dismiss the Communist head of government and he appointed Admiral Pinheiro de Azevedo who formed government with Socialists and Democrats. This government began the slow process of stabilisation. The parties of the left tried to take over in November 1975 but failed, due principally to General Ramalho Eanes. In the June presidential elections of 1976, he was the candidate chosen by the Socialists and Democrats and was elected President, obtaining 61.5% of the votes.

Following this election, the first Constitutional Government was formed and between July 1976 and December 1979, no fewer than six Constitutional governments came to power. Tragically, on 4th December 1980, the head of the then government, Sá Carneiro and members of his Social-Democratic party perished in an air crash which was later considered the result of sabotage. In January 1981, the Social Democrats again formed a government which lasted until 1983 when the April elections of that year gave a large share of the vote to the Socialist Party and it formed government with the social Democrats. It was this government which signed the agreement allowing Portugal to join the European Community in January 1986.

Independence for Portugal's Colonies

While the original revolt of the army was in favour of decolonisation and the withdrawal of armed forces from the colonies, the Portuguese people were behind this movement because many had lost relatives in the conflict. Bom Sucesso's gardener had lost his only son. In Angola, Mozambique and Portuguese Guinea, the soldiers simply laid down their arms. Angola and Mozambique in particular with developed administration, judiciary and culture had little need of Portugal. According to Oliveira Marques, 'Portugal was of little use to the colonies. Independence was, consequently, in the logic of the events.' [13]

The process of decolonisation lasted from 10th September 1974 to 11th November 1975. The first new State was Guinea-Bissau, 10th September 1974, followed by Mozambique, 25th June, 1975, Cape Verde, 5th July, São Tomé and Principe 12th July 1975. Angola's independence was not established until 11th November 1975. The most tragic was probably the situation of East Timor which was invaded and occupied by Indonesia in November 1975, and did not achieve independence until 2002

Bom Sucesso's Schools during the Revolution

The agitation which rocked Portugal following the Revolution of 1974 had its repercussions on Bom Sucesso's schools, especially the Senior Portuguese and Saint Dominic's International School. In the latter, many foreign families having to leave the country as embassies were closed, the classes were considerably reduced in the number of pupils. In the former, some of the senior students entertained leftist ideas. Students throughout the country were demanding the cancellation of examinations, claiming that this was customary in a year of Revolution. In imitation of communist courts set up to oust directors of businesses and banks, some of our students set up courts in the school to judge the sisters and the teachers. The teachers themselves joined syndicates and held meetings in the school until late into the night and the sisters were excluded from these. During the day no timetables were adhered to.

Many students had to leave as their parents were expelled from their work and could no longer afford the fees. The parents of some students were imprisoned or had to leave the country to settle in Spain or Brazil. It was a lonely time when sisters had to say goodbye to friends or colleagues and see them set sail from their own country. Some would never return.

The non-teaching personnel – supervisors and cleaners – turned against the sisters. 'Some left us, fortunately, but we were afraid to employ others in their place as the Communists were trying to infiltrate the schools. We had to clean all the classrooms ourselves with the help of some of the students whose parents stood by us. These students also helped us to prepare the school dinners and attend the doors as well as supervise recreation.' [14]

The most serious aspect of all the difficulties facing the community at the time was the infiltration of the Ministry of Education by Communists. History which had so much reference to Portugal's Christian past could not be taught. A new subject called Political Science was introduced and the teacher of this subject in Bom Sucesso, though a past-pupil, used Communist propaganda papers and booklets in the classroom. Fortunately, the principal was able to persuade her to leave.

Catholics were obliged to organise against anti-religious conflicts and the threat of Communism. On one occasion participants at a large Catholic rally in Lisbon were unable to leave the stadium for several hours because of Communist forces surrounding it. Many of our students with their parents were present at this rally.

Another very serious difficulty for all three schools was financial – the loss of pupils reducing the fees and the increase in teachers' salaries putting a great strain on resources. At the same time, sisters hesitated to increase the fees as many families were suffering a reversal of their fortune. 'We had a reduced number of students so there were too many teachers and we could not pay them all. Some had left of their own initiative and we asked others to leave but they refused and brought us to court – a communist court which ruled against us.' [15]

'We had begun to build St. Dominic's International School two years before the 25th April revolution. Loans had been arranged with the bank and construction companies contracted. About a month after the 25th, the construction company, a foreign one, was put out of the country. All building materials shot up by 10%. .... All costs went higher than our loan and the school was only half finished. The 'People's Commission` in the area wanted to take over the building. It was only with the help of some friends that they were dissuaded from doing so.' [16] Consequently, it became necessary to move the pupils into the new building before it was completed.

PROGRESS IN POLITICAL TURMOIL

What is surprising, when one reads the annals of those years, is the amount of normal activity taking place both within the convent and the schools in spite of the turmoil in society. In the Summer of 1974, the Community decided to open a secondary section to Saint Dominic's International School. The classes would be held in Bom Sucesso as the sisters qualified for 2nd level teaching were also teaching there. A Parents' Association was formed in order to collaborate with the sisters of the Portuguese College especially during the political crisis.

The annual *Lausperene,* (twenty-four hour Exposition of the Blessed Sacrament held in a different Church each day throughout the year to pray for the preservation of Lisbon from earthquakes) was held in our Church as usual. Community discussions on the renewal of Religious Life were regularly held while, from time to time, all-night vigils for peace in Portugal took place in the Bom Sucesso Church. These were very well attended by lay people.

One memorable prayer service was held in the Spring of 1975. During the Easter holidays, two sisters had gone to Fatima and there met Fr. Moore, a Canadian, whose mission in life was to carry a beautiful, large statue of Our Lady of Fatima on a world pilgrimage. He hoped to do this fifteen times in honour of the fifteen Mysteries of the Rosary. When he heard of the political agitation in Lisbon, he felt inspired to bring the statue there. While staying in Bom Sucesso he went out to bless the new school building nearing completion and in the evening, held a bilingual prayer service in Bom Sucesso Church. People from the surrounding district filled the Church and, though Fr. Moore spoke in English, they were moved by the simple sincerity of this priest and the spiritual presence which this beautiful statue inspired. There would be difficult days even years when atheism would threaten Portugal but there was no doubt, that evening, of the depth of faith among so many people.

On the day of elections, 25th April, 1975, the Rosary was said throughout the day by the sisters in rotation. Referring to this date, the annalist writes, 'prayer in many churches in Lisbon is non-stop to Our Lady of Fátima to save Portugal from Communism.' [17]

Another consoling event at this time was a short visit from the then Master of the Dominican Order, the late Fr. Couesnongle, a Frenchman. On 1st May, 1975, the Community was invited by the Portuguese Dominican Sisters to their Convent of São José in nearby Restelo where all Dominicans could meet the Master. Fifteen Sisters attended but on 3rd May, Fr. Couesnongle decided to pay a brief, un-scheduled visit to our convent. It was a very informal, friendly visit during which he spoke of his love for Brazil to our Brazilian sister and blessed the two invalids.

FINANCIAL HELP FROM IRELAND

The late seventies were years of extreme financial hardship for the Bom Sucesso community so that, at the General Chapter of the Congregation meeting in Dublin in July-August, 1977, an appeal for financial help was made and the communities in Ireland responded generously. The Acts of the General Chapter of Cabra Dominican Sisters simply state, 'The political upheaval in Portugal has had far reaching effects for our sisters in Lisbon. The prioresses showed their concern in a positive way and made plans to continue their support.'[18] This enabled the Bom Sucesso community to continue their work in Lisbon and again, phoenix-like, during the 1980s, the sisters not only continued their work in the schools but they began to diversify in other spheres of the educational apostolate.

13

Epilogue

THE FOUNDING OF SAINT ANNE'S

In 1983, a house on Avenida Salvador Allende, Oeiras, was purchased and a small community was established there on 20th November. The purpose of this foundation was to facilitate those sisters who were working in Saint Dominic's International School as the distance of this school from Bom Sucesso was considerable.

A new parish had been established in the area and during the year 1984-85, the parish priest asked if one sister could work full time in his parish. Because of their commitments in the school, this was not possible but two sisters gave part-time help. Prayer services were held in a Centre for cerebral palsy victims and two sisters became ministers of the Eucharist. For six years, they took part in the preparation for Confirmation of large groups of adults and were members of the Neo-Catechumenate in the parish. Gradually, they were able to withdraw as some parishioners were trained in pastoral work and began to assume responsibility within their parish. At the same time as two sisters worked in the Portuguese parish, the other two members of the Saint Anne's community helped in the parish of Saint Mary's, São Pedro do Estoril, for English-speaking families.

THE FOUNDING OF THE REGION OF PORTUGAL

At the Tenth General Chapter of the Irish Dominican Congregation, it was decided to divide the Congregation into regions and consequently, 'to set in motion arrangements for the election of Regional Vicars and Councillors in each of the Regions of Ireland, Argentina and Louisiana not later than the 31st December, 1977.'[1] Though culturally different from the other Regions, Portugal was not included because of a mere technicality. For the establishment of Regions, Rome required that there should be at least two houses in the area. This condition was fulfilled with the founding of Saint Anne's in 1983 and, thus, negotiations were begun for the establishment of the Region of Portugal, Dominican Cabra Congregation.

The first Chapter of the Region of Portugal was held from 27th February to 3rd March, 1987. The opening Mass of the Chapter was concelebrated by Cardinal D. António Ribeiro, Patriarch of Lisbon and four Irish Dominicans, Father Terence McLoughlin, Prior of Corpo Santo and Martin Hunter, together with visitors from Ireland, Fathers Tom Cleary and Gerard Gardiner.

In his homily, the Cardinal Patriarch emphasised three gifts of the Holy Spirit – Truth, Unity and Witness – and reminded the participants that the Chapter was not just for the Region of Portugal, nor even for the Congregation, but for the Church. He concluded by thanking the community for the service Bom Sucesso had rendered to education over the centuries and he looked forward to a future of growth and development.[2]

INVITATIONS TO MAKE FOUNDATIONS

In the late 1980s, the Bom Sucesso community was invited to found houses in other parts of the Portuguese world. In 1988, the Bishop of Angra in the Azores, wrote stating that in his diocese, there was a very great need for sisters in various areas of mission. Unfortunately, due to lack of personnel, this invitation had to be refused.

At about the same time, the Archbishop of Braga asked if sisters would take over a pastoral centre in his archdiocese. Two members of the Regional Council visited there but again they felt unable to undertake this work.

THE CELEBRATION OF 350 YEARS OF BOM SUCESSO: 1639-1989

On 12th November, 1989, Bom Sucesso celebrated the three hundred and fiftieth year of its foundation. The most important event of this celebration was the solemn Mass of Thanksgiving presided over by the auxiliary Bishop of the Lisbon Patriarchate, D. Albino Mamede Cleto. Concelebrating with him were Father Tom Cleary, Prior of Corpo Santo and Father Donal Mehigan, the Portuguese Dominican Provincial, Frei José Gallego Salvadores and Frei Alberto Maria Vieira from the Dominican priory in Fatima. Many representatives of the Dominican family in Portugal were also present.

A commemorative booklet which included a short history of Bom

Sucesso and many photographs of the convent and members of the community in different centuries was published. In the Introduction to this booklet, the Regional Vicar wrote, 'Throughout the centuries, the sisters have always succeeded in reading the signs of the times in the period in which they lived, always responding to them and becoming what we call today people of frontier missions.' [3]

THE SOCIAL CENTRE IN ALGÉS – *CENTRO DA SAGRADA FAMÍLIA*

In 1993, the sisters were again called upon to fulfil this vocation as people of frontier missions when they were advised to conform to new laws where the schools were concerned. On advice from the Patriarchate and Dominican as well as Franciscan legal experts they made a Trust/Foundation of Social Solidarity. One of the essential requisites for this Trust was a social centre. An already existing centre in Algés was offered to them by the Department for Social Security. This consisted of two prefabricated pavilions situated on stony ground in the middle of a crowded shantytown. Undeterred by this unpromising location, Sister Agnes undertook the organisation of the Centre and, with the help of a small staff as well as volunteers, transformed it into a beautiful establishment.

Today, this Centre offers a crèche for babies from four months, a nursery school, a pre-school and supervised after-school activities for young people. It also offers adult education classes both daytime and evening, especially for women. The latter courses are conducted in partnership with DGFV. (*Direcção Geral de Formação Vocacional*) and INOFOR (*Instituição, Inovação, Formação*). This Institution allows the Centre to give accreditation to those participants who complete a course.

The people who avail of these services are mainly Portuguese but many come from Africa, South America, even Asia and, more recently, Eastern Europe. The Department for Social Security pays a monthly subsidy for each child so that it is possible to accept a large percentage of children from underprivileged families. However, more fortunate families avail of the Centre's services also and parents pay according to their means. The Food Bank gives a monthly supply of food to supplement the food bought by the Centre at the Algés market.

Dona Teresa Pais Zambujo, President of the Town Council of Alges writes her appreciation of the cooperation between the sisters and the local authority, 'The institutional cooperation which, for several years, has been maintained between the Town council of Oeiras and the Irish Dominican Sisters' foundation of Social Work is the result of a basic common objective: to create opportunities so that families in the local community, especially those families that have less economic and cultural resources may enjoy conditions of wellbeing.

'It is to be remembered that it was within the ambit of a Projeito counter Poverty that this cooperation began in the creation of the Holy Family Centre. With the social responses available we can congratulate ourselves on the excellent relations of effective and constant partnership which has been maintained since then. The courage, generosity and affection which the Dominican Sisters radiate are a revitalising source of energy for us to continue in our own mission of advancing the development of the town.' [4] This is not only a tribute to the work of the sisters involved but it is also a reassuring expression of the humanitarian ideals of a modern Town Council

MINISTRY IN ZAMBUJAL

In 1993, in response to the call of the 1991 Regional Chapter, two sisters went to live in an underprivileged area of the city of Lisbon. They obtained a small apartment in Alfragide which they called Comunidade Dona Iria in memory of the foundress of Bom Sucesso. One of the sisters described this area as it was in 1993: 'We are in a parish of twenty-five thousand on the periphery of Lisbon. The parish which consists of a number of different units is served by just one priest. Our area of Zambujal has a population of four and a half thousand people who have, over the years, been gradually given housing accommodation. While the housing has been improved, many still live in extreme poverty.' [5]

The people again were mainly Portuguese but there were also many Africans, principally from the Cape Verde islands, who had had to leave their homeland because of drought. The *Ciganos* (nomadic people) were yet another ethnic group. In this maelstrom of cultures, while there were people of outstanding courage and enthusiasm there were also those who were disillusioned. Some years before, the boundaries of the parish had been changed so that many people had lost contact with the Church and were in danger of coming under the influence of sects.

The sisters began their ministry by walking around the *bairro* (the area) in order to come to know the people. Later, they organised English lessons and other educational activities including computer and guitar classes mainly for young people. Football practice was also included in the programme. As time passed, volunteers came to help with these activities.

In the religious sphere, a Bible group was started and what began as a very small group has grown in depth and numbers over the years. Recently, the Consolata Missionaries have chosen to work also in the *bairro*. Today, the sisters work in collaboration with the Consolata team and the Christian community in order to journey with the people of Zambujal.

CASINHA DE NOSSA SENHORA

In 1997, responding to another pastoral need the Bom Sucesso community founded a crèche for children from four months to three years of age. Dedicated to the Mother of God it has as its official name *Casinha de Nossa Senhora* (Our Lady's Little House). This is a service offered to mothers who have full-time or part-time employment and it caters for about twenty-two children.

It is housed in part of the building which was once the final home of Dr. Sleyne, the exiled Bishop of Cork and the meeting place for centuries of the members of the Holy Rosary Confraternity.

Initially, this service was conducted in conjunction with the local parish of Santa Maria de Belém but, since 2003, it functions independently of the parish. Formerly also, it was run with the financial support of *Santa Casa de Misericórdia de Lisboa*. More recently, it is subsidised by the Department of Social Services. As far as possible, preference is given to the most needy and to families from the locality.

The aim of all those engaged in this ministry is to offer care and early educational stimulation to the very young, thus supporting parents in their role as the primary educators of their children. A close relationship exists between staff members and the parents and, in every way possible, the spiritual dimension of human life is nurtured.

O COLÉGIO DO BOM SUCESSO

While all this enlargement of ministry was taking place, many of the other sisters have continued the tradition of pre-school, primary and secondary teaching in their schools – Colégio do Bom Sucesso and Saint Dominic's International School. The former is the oldest ministry of the Bom Sucesso community, dating from 1829 when the first child boarder, Mariana Russell Kennedy was entrusted to the care of the sisters. In 1860, with the arrival of four sisters from Cabra, Dublin, the school was formally organised into graded classes. In the school year of 2004-2005 it catered for six hundred and eighty-two pupils. Of these three hundred and seventy-five are girls and three hundred and seven boys. The age range is from pre-school to the third cycle (age sixteen) and the curriculum followed is that of the official State Education system.

The educational principles guiding the three sections of the school – pre-school, primary and secondary - are Christian and Dominican. The Dominican ideal of Truth inspires the whole pedagogical programme of the College so that its principal purpose is the integral development of the human person. Through the various educational activities, an effort is made to develop every pupil's potential in the intellectual, physical, social, emotional, moral, spiritual and cultural spheres so that each student may lead a fully human and Christian life.

In the moral sphere, the College's educational principles stress the development of the student's sense of her/his human dignity and the intelligent use of liberty. Respect for others and tolerance are important qualities. The pupil is also helped towards responsible and independent adult living by learning to take initiative and to be accountable for one's options

In the spiritual sphere, the aim is especially to help students experience and deepen a real living of the Christian Faith into which they were baptised. It is endeavoured to transmit to the young a sense of their mission to society by giving witness to Christian values. In order to achieve these principles, the collaboration of the whole educational community – sisters, teachers, students, parents and administrative staff - is considered essential.[6] Thus, the original ideals of the founding sisters are maintained and applied to modern needs.

SAINT DOMINIC'S INTERNATIONAL SCHOOL

The ethos of Saint Dominic's is defined in its Mission Statement, 'to offer an international education of the highest calibre, enriched and enlivened by the Dominican tradition of study and education, promoting the development of each student's potential....Dominicans value highly the commitment to the ongoing search for Truth which informs the belief that each student is an unique person with God-given rights and responsibilities.' [7]

Thus, an effort is made to have the Dominican ideal as an inspiration underlying the programme of the International Baccalaureate Organisation, a non-profit educational foundation based in Geneva. This organisation was registered as a foundation in 1968. Its purpose is to provide 'a common curriculum and a university entry credential'[8] for families who move from one country to another during the years of their children's basic education. The organisation has the further aim of intercultural understanding and acceptance of difference among young people.

At the turn of this century, there were 1,180 schools authorised by the International Baccalaureate Organisation in one hundred and one countries. At present, Saint Dominic's caters for six hundred and thirty-eight pupils aged between 3 and 18/19 years and forty-two nationalities. Classes are conducted in English but Portuguese, French, German and Swedish are also taught. Religious Studies incorporating study of the major religions of the world is part of the curriculum. Catholics have another programme while students of other faiths have instruction in their religion in their specific places of worship. The great feasts mainly of Hinduism, Judaism, Christianity and Islam are celebrated at school assemblies.

CONCLUSION

On 12th November, 2004, Bom Sucesso celebrated the three hundred and sixty-fifth year of its foundation completing almost four centuries of dedicated service to God and humanity in Portugal. In recent years many distinguished visitors, particularly from Ireland, have admired the beauty of the cloister and the church. Among these in 1991 was the then President of Ireland, Mrs. Mary Robinson. In 1995, the traditional relationship with the royal house of Bragança was renewed when D. Duarte, the present Duke of Bragança, left from Bom Sucesso for his wedding in the Church of Jerónimos. More recently, in November 2002, the present President of Ireland, Mrs. Mary Mc Aleese on a State visit to Portugal included Bom Sucesso in her itinerary.

This State visit to Portugal was a most important event for both countries as it highlighted the centuries old links between Portugal and Ireland. In her address at the reception for the Irish community and Portuguese friends of Ireland hosted by President Sampaio, Mrs Mc Aleese spoke of the many connections between the two peoples. 'The sea links our two nations. It haunts our music and our histories and echoes in the beautiful *Ceól na Mara* (the Music of the Sea) which we have just heard as it echoes too in Luís de Camões's great celebration of the Portuguese who "sailed through seas where none had sailed before."' [9] Portugal and Ireland are alike also in the impact that both countries have made worldwide, greater than 'our small size would lead one to expect.... With a small population and a land area not much bigger than our own, the Portuguese genius for exploration brought your language and culture to the far ends of the earth and infused Europe's Renaissance with much of its colour and depth. And in our contemporary world, Portugal has earned the support and respect of Ireland as a committed champion of independence in East Timor and as a champion of peace in Angola.' [10]

Referring to her visit to Bom Sucesso the President stated, 'I was educated by Dominican nuns in Belfast and so was thrilled to visit the Dominican convent of Bom Sucesso in Belém and to meet the Irish Dominican sisters and priests who continue the mission of care which their predecessors began in the seventeenth century.' [11] Thus, the President's speech encapsulated the long history of friendship between two peoples on the western seaboard of Europe and in this history Bom Sucesso has played its part. However, as Mrs. Mc Aleese stressed, it is important to develop the partnership into the future and in this Bom Sucesso has its role so that the light may continue undimmed for future generations.

Notes

Chapter 1: The Setting for our Story

1. Sanches, José Dias: *Belém do passado e do presente* (1964) p. 138, quoting the Cardinal Pariarch, D. Manuel G. Cerejeira on the occasion of the tercentenary of the Convent's foundation.
2. M.C.A. p.6
3. The body identified as that of the king had no royal insignia and this gave rise, during the years of the Spanish occupation of Portugal to the hope that D. Sebastião was not dead and would, one day, return to reclaim the throne of Portugal. This hope was known as *Sebastianismo*, one of the principal Portuguese myths
4. Sanches, op.cit. p.135
5. M.C.A. p.6
6. M. C.A.p.6
7. This story is also told in Frei Lucas de Santa Catarina's work, História *de São Domingos, IV parte*, cap. XXI (1767), Lisboa
8. Pe. Miguel de Oliveira, (1994), *História Ecclesiástica de Portugal*, p 184. Publicações Europa-América Lda
9. Saraiva, José, *História de Portugal*, (6a ed., Publicações Europa-América Lda, 1993) p.205-p.206
10. M.C.A. p.6
11. Sanches, José Dias, op.cit. p.135
12. I am indebted to Dona Isabel Napoles Sarmento for identifying the coat of arms over the Bom Sucesso entrance.
13. António Machado de Faria, *Armorial Lusitano, Genealogia e Heráldica*, 1961, dir.e coordinação DoutorAfonso E. Martins Zuguete, Editorial Enciclopédia, Lda., Lisboa, p.195-p.196
14. *Biblioteca Nacional da Ajuda*, 49-XII-40 p.49
15. M.C.A. p.5
16. BS12/3 Book of Investments, Indice no. 8
17. BS15/2 The will of the Countess, August 13th 1639
18. M.C.A. p.8
19. M.C.A. p.9
20. M.C.A. p.10
21. M.C.A. p.11

Chapter 2: Dominic O'Daly and the Foundation of Bom Sucesso

1. M.J. Culligan & P. Cherici, 2000, *The Wandering Irish in Europe*, Constable, London, p.178
2. *Armorial Lusitano*, op.cit., p.54
3. *The Book of Foundation*, cited in P. O'Connell, *the Irish College at Lisbon, 1590-1834*, Four Courts Press, Dublin, p.24
4. Margaret Mac Curtain, *Daniel O'Daly, 1595-1662, A Study of Irish European Relationships in the Seventeenth Century*, Thesis presented to the National University of Ireland, 1958, for degree of M.A., p.50

5. ibid., p.4
6. ibid., p.10
7. ibid., p.10-p.11
8. ibid., p.21-p.22
9. ibid., p.41
10. ibid., p.43
11. Frei Luís de Sousa, 1678, *História de São Domingos,* revised by M. Lopes de Almeida, 1977, Lello & Irmão ed. Porto, vol. II, cap.XVIII, p.1183
12. ibid., cap. XVIII, p.1182
13. ibid., p.1182
14. ibid., p.1183 (a cruzado was a gold coin of considerable value)
15. ibid., p.1183
16. ibid., p.1183
17. ibid., p.1184
18. ibid., p.1184
19. ibid., p.1184
20. ibid., p.1185
21. ibid., p. 1185 and M.C.A. p.72
22. M. Culligan & P. Cherici, *The Wandering Irish in Europe,* p.127-p.128
23. O'Neill and O'Donnell were earls in Ulster, in the north who resisted the English invasion of Ireland for nine years
24. Culligan & Cherici, op. cit., p.128-p.129
25. Frei Luís de Sousa, op. cit., cap. XIX, p.1186
26. M.C.A. p.20
27. Stone tablet in sacristy of Bom Sucesso
28. M.C.A. p.21
29. M.C.A. p.22
30. M.C.A. p.23
31. M.C.A. p. 24
32. Frei Luís de Sousa, op. cit., cap. XIX, p. 1189
33. Padre José de Vale Carvalheira, *Nossa Senhora na História e Devoção do Povo Português,* 1988, edições salesianas, p.147
34. I am indebted to Sister Bernadette Pakenham, O.P. for information on Our Lady of Aberdeen
35. This letter is also printed in Frei Luís de Sousa, vol. II, cap. XIX, p.1189-1190
36. Frei Luís de Sousa,op. cit. p.1197
37. Frei Luís de Sousa, op. cit., cap. XX, p.1190
38. ibid., p.1192
39. ibid., 1193
40. Margaret Mac Curtain, op. cit., p.2
41. ibid., p.2
42. Kieran Kavanagh, O.C.D., ed. , 1987, *John of the Cross, Selected Writings,* Paulist Press, NY, p. 10
43. E. Prestage, 1926, *Frei Domingos do Rosário, Diplomata e Político,* Imprensa da Universidade, Coímbra p.52
44. ibid., p. 52
45. ibid., p. 52

Chapter 3: The Early Years

1. M.C.A. p. 30
2. José H. Saraiva, *História Concisa de Portugal,* 7 edicão, Colecção Saber,

Publicacoes Europa-América, p.197
3. ibid., p.198
4. ibid., p.199
5. ibid., p.203
6. M.C.A., p.30
7. The surname of Saint Dominic is Gusman
8. Dominic O'Daly, *The Geraldines* quoted in M.C.A. p.31
9. John O'Heyne, *The Irish Dominicans of the Seventeenth Century,* trans.
(1902) Ambrose Coleman, W. Tempest, Dundalk, p.83
10. ibid., p. 83
11. ibid., p.83
12. The agreement made between Portugal and its ally England
13. Frei Luís de Sousa, op. cit., p.1103
14. M.C.A. p.32
15. ibid., p. 32.
16. ibid., p.33
17. Frei Luís de Sousa, op. cit., cap. XXIII, p.1206
18. ibid., p. 1206
19. ibid., p. 1206
20. ibid., p.1206
21. ibid., p. 1213
22. José Dias Sanches, 1940, *Belém e Arredores através dos tempos,* Livraria
Universal – Editora, Lisboa, p.93
23. Ana Cristina de Ayala B.M.F. Ferreira da Costa, *O Sacrário do Convento do
Bom Sucesso* (1997) Dissertação de M. em História de Arte, Universidade
Lusíada, Lisboa, p. 51
24. MCA, p.42
25. Ana.Cristina Ferreira da Costa, op.cit., p.79
26. José Dias Sanches, op.cit., p.94
27. ibid., p.94
28. ibid., p.94

Chapter 4: The Spirituality of the Community

1. Catherine Gibson, O.P., *The ambiguity of Bridal Imagery in Christian
Tradition,* thesis for M.Litt. (1990) Trinity College, Dublin, p.46
2. Rowan Williams, (1990) *The Wound of Knowledge,* Darton, Longman & todd,
London, p.40
3. Meister Eckhart, *Ave Gratia Plena,* German Sermon, no. 22 in *Meister
Eckhart, The Essential Sermons*, 1981, The Classics of Western Spirituality,
trans. E. Colledge & B. Mc Ginn, Paulist Press, NY, p. 196
4. Juan G. Arintero, O.P., *The Song of Songs, A Mystical Exposition,* first
published 1918, 1992 revised edition of a 1974 text, Tan Books & Publishers,
Rockford, Illinois, p.13
5. Arintero, p.379
6. Arintero, p. 451
7. Arintero, p.366-p.367
8. Arintero, p. 520-p.521
9. Arintero, p. 522
10. Saint Teresa cited in Arintero, p.254
11. Arintero, p. 250
12. Arintero, p. 239

13. Arintero, p.534-p.535
14. Arintero, p.494
15. Arintero, p.225-p.226
16. Arintero, p.134
17. Gregory of Nyssa, cited in Arintero, p.288 Sg..2:15 is the quotation identified.
18. Arintero, p. 276
19. Arintero, p. 276
20. Arintero, p. 533
21. Richard Woods, O.P., (1996) *Christian Spirituality*, p.279, Christian Classics, Texas
22. Frei Luís de Sousa, op. cit., p.1197
23. ibid., p. 1198
24. Frei Luís de Sousa, op. cit., p.1198
25. ibid., p. 1198
26. Frei Luís de Sousa, p.1208
27. Frei Luís de Sousa, p. 1205
28. Frei Luís de Sousa, vol. II, p.1199
29. ibid., p.1199-1200
30. ibid., p.1200
31. ibid., p.1200
32. ibid., p.1200
33. ibid., p.1202
34. ibid., p. 1212

Chapter 5: Other Ministries

1.Bolster, Evelyn, (1989) *A History of the Diocese of Cork*, vol. 3: from thePenal Era to the Famine, Tower Books p.15-16
2. APF. Fol. 512r (old pagination 486r)
3. APF. SOCG, vol 509 29/11/1694, n. 4
4. Bolster, op.cit., p.19
5. ibid., p.20
6. Quoted by Reginald Walsh,O.P. in *Glimpses of the Penal Times*, in *The Irish Ecclesiastical Record* September, 1906
7. Bolster, op.cit., p.22-p.23
8. R. Walsh op. cit., p.3
9. ibid p.3
10. Seán O'Callaghan, *To Hell or Barbados: The Ethnic Cleansing of Ireland*, Brandon Paperbacks, 2001.
11. R. Walsh, op. cit., Letter of Secretary of State Dawson to Mr. Whiting, Mayor of Corke, 9/1/1703
12. ibid., no.5
13. P.F. Moran (Bishop of Ossory), 1882, *The Conditions of Catholics in Ireland, One hundred years ago,* The Dublin Review
14. APF Letter of Dr. Sleyne, Bishop of Cork to Cardinal Giansone, 27th March, 1703
15. ibid.,
16. ibid.,
17. ibid.,
18. J. Hurley, *Dr. John Baptist Sleyne, Bishop of Cork and Cloyne, 1693-1712, (1893),* the Journal of the Cork Historical and Archaeological Society, vol. 2,p.200

19. MCA, p.53b
20. ibid., p.53b-p.54
21. ibid., p.53b
22. J. Hurley, op.cit., p.200
23. M.C.A. p.53b
24. BS1/1 *Livro da Confraria do Smo. Rosário do Mosteiro da N. Senhora do Bom Sucesso do Lugar de Bethelem,* erigida no anno de 1704, p.2
25. ibid., cap. 1, p.2
26. ibid., cap. 5, p.4
27. ibid., cap. 5, p.4
28. M.C.A. p.54
29. ibid., p.59-p.60
30. ibid., p.60
31. ibid., p.60
32. ibid., p.67
33. ibid., p.67

Chapter 6: Portugal in the Eighteenth Century

1. José Dias Sanches, (1964), *Belém do passado e do presente*, Sociedade de Geografia de Lisboa e Real Academia Golegã, Lisboa
2. M.J. Culligan & P.Cherici,2000, *The Wandering Irish in Europe, Their Influence from the Dark Ages to Modern Times.* Constable, London, p.187-p.189.
3. Ibid., citing a document in A.N.T.T.
4. A.H. de Oliveira Marques, *História da Maçonaria em Portugal,* vol I, *das Origens ao Triunfo,* Editorial Presença, p.122-p.124
5. M.C.A. p.55-p.56
6. ibid., p.59
7. ibid., p.62
8. M.C.A. p.61-p.62, quoting de Burgo, *Hibernia Dominicana*
9. M.C.A. p.56-p.57
10. ibid., p.57
11. José António Saraiva, *O Palácio de Belém,* 2da edição, Editorial Inquérito, p.38
12. M.C.A. p.55
13. ibid., p.54
14. ibid., p.61
15. ibid., p.63
16. ibid., p.64
17. P. Miguel de Oliveira, *História Eclesiástica de Portugal,* edição revista e actualizada, 1994, Publicações Europa-América, p.160
18. J.H. Saraiva, *História de Portugal,* 2da edição, 1993, Publicações Europa-América, p.254
19. ibid., p.254
20. de Burgo, *Hibernia Dominicana* quoted in M.C.A. p.65
21. M.C.A. p.65
22. ibid., p.66
23. ibid., p.66
24. S.S.A. XII43810, an account of the Brigittine sisters' experience in 1755, sent by Mother Teresa of Sion Abbey, Devon, England to Bom Sucesso in 1930, probably when the Bom Sucesso annals were being restored.
25. Ibid., page entitled *The Great Earthquake*

26. José António Saraiva, *O Palácio de Belém,* 2da edição, Editorial Inquérito, p.44

27. ibid., the queen's letter quoted in this book, p.44

28. ibid., p.44

29. ibid., p.45

30. M.C.A. p.66

31. S.S.A. XII43810

32. Data given to Père Mortier by Domingos Fructuoso O.P. (Portugal)

33. Père Mortier, *Histoire des Maîres Généraux*

34. *O Palácio de Belém,* op. cit., p.52

35. D. Birmingham, *A Concise History of Portugal,* 1999, Cambridge University Press, p.69

36. ibid., p.85

Chapter 7: Presence

1. M.C.A. p.69

2. Jac Weller, *Wellington in the Peninsula,* 1999, Greenhill Books, London, p. 20

3. J.H. Saraiva, *História Concisa de Portugal* 1981, 7° ed., Publicações Europa-América, p.262

4. ibid., p.262

5. M.C.A., p.69-p.70

6. Weller, op. cit., p. 25

7. ibid., p.21

8. S.S.A., account sent by Brigittine sisters in England.

9. ibid.,

10. ibid., and M.C.A. p.71

11. J. Weller, op.cit., p.63-p.64

12. J. Weller, op. cit., p.112

13. For a description of these lines cf. J. Weller, p.113

14. Weller, op. cit., p.114

15. ibid., p.122.

16. quoted from Brigittine annals in M.C.A., p.70

17. M.C.A., p. 71

18. S.S.A., Brigittine document already quoted.

19. M.C.A., p.73

20. J.H. Saraiva, op. cit., p. 270-p. 271

21. D. Birmingham, *A Concise History of Portugal* (1999) p. 108, Cambridge University Press.

22. B.S. 11/13 Relatório e documentação da suppressão dos Conventos do Bom Sucesso e São João Baptista, 1823, doc. 1 e doc. 2, p.4

23. M.C.A. p. 73

24. B S 11/13, p. 5 *Cópia da Consulta da Comissão encarregada de formar o Plano da Reforma das Ordens Regulares*

25. ibid., p. 5

26. M.C.A. p. 74

27. Requerimento que as 8 religiosas acima mencionadas entragarão à Sua Magestade em 16 de Maio de 1823. B.S. 11/13 p.7-p.9

28. ibid., p.8-p.9

29. M.C.A. p.76

30. J.H. Saraiva, op. cit., p.276

31. M.C.A., p.76
32. ibid., p.76
33. BS 11/13 Requerimento que as Religiosas Irlandesas fizerão entregar ao Embaizador Inglês, p.9-p.12
34. ibid., p. 12
35. M.C.A. p. 77
36. ibid., p.77
37. ibid., p.77-78
38. J.H. Saraiva, op. cit., p.279
39. ibid., p.279
40. B S 11/13 p.13–p.14
41. M.C.A., p. 81
42. Memoir, quoted in M.C.A., p.81
43. M.C.A. p.82-p.83
44. BS 11/13 p.2
45. BS 11/13 p.15

Chapter 8: The Foundation of the School

1. M.C.A. p.48
2. B.S.A. 2/29 Account given in 1941 by Mariana Kennedy's daughter, Dona Laura Cecília Kennedy d'Avelar Falcão
3. M.C.A., p.85
4. Dona Laura's account, op.cit., in B.S. archives
5. ibid.,
6. Tablet over her grave in the side garden of Bom Sucesso
7. B.S.A. 2/29, Alfredo de Kennedy Falcão's letter on his mother's death
8. David Birmingham, *A Concise History of Portugal*, 1999, Cambridge University Press, p.113-p.114
9. Manuel Clemente, 2002, *Igreja e Sociedade Portuguesa do Liberalismo à República*, Grifo. P.165
10. Clemente, ibid., p. 165, trans.
11. P. Miguel de Oliveira, *História Ecclesiástica de Potugal*, op.cit., p.245
12. Frei Raúl de Almeida Rolo, O.P., 1962, *Dominicanos em Portugal Lisboa, separata da revista Panorama*, tip. Da E.N.P. in B.S.A. 3/26
13. Clemente, op. cit., p.168
14. Oliveira, op.cit., p.246
15. ibid., p.246
16. B.S.A., 11/20
17. B.S.A., 11/21
18. B.S.A., 11/22
19. B.S.A., 11/24
20. Miguel de Oliveira, 1994, *História Ecclesiástica de Portugal*, op.cit., p.232
21. B.S.A., 11/29
22. Letters from Mr. Meagher, vice-consul British Embassy. B.S.A. 11/32
23. B.S.A. 11/31
24. M.C.A., p.87
25. M.C.A. p.87
26. ibid., p.88
27. ibid., p.88
28. Copy of Mother Teresa Staunton's letter to Mother de Ricci Maher, Cabra, dated 25th February, 1860, D.G.A.

29. ibid.,
30. ibid.,31. ibid.,
31. ibid.,
32. ibid.,
33. ibid., second section
34. ibid.,
35. D.G.A. Teresa Staunton's letter dated Feast of Saint Francis,
36. D.G.A. T. Staunton's first letter to Dr. Cullen, dated 15th April, 1860.
37. ibid.,
38. ibid.,
39. ibid.,
40. D.G.A. Copy of Dr. Cullen's letter to Mother de Ricci Maher re. Bom Sucesso.
41. M.C.A.p.88-p.89
42. T. Staunton's letter to Cabra, June 1860
43. ibid.,
44. ibid.,
45. ibid.,
46. ibid.,
47. ibid.,
48. ibid.,
49. ibid.,
50. ibid.,
51. ibid.,
52. ibid.,
53. ibid.,
54. T. Staunton's letter to Dr. Cullen, June 1860
55. ibid.,
56. ibid.,
57. ibid.,
58. Dr. Cullen's letter to Mother de Ricci Maher, dated 26th June, 1860. copy in D.G.A.

Chapter 9: A New Venture

1. José Hermano Saraiva, 1993, *História de Portugal,* Publicações Alfa, p.422, translation
2. Profession Book, D.C.C.A.
3. Edel Murphy, O.P., 1999, M.A., thesis presented to National University of Ireland: *The Contribution of Dominican Sisters to Education in the town of Dun Laoire,* p. 57
4. ibid., p.58. The annals of the Dominican Convent, Dun Laoire record this when noting her death, 5th October, 1862
5. Immaculata Boarding School records, 1845-1848
6. Profession Book, D.C.C.A
7. ibid.,
8. Teresa Staunton's letter to Dr. Cullen, 5th October, 1860. Copy in D.G.A.
9. ibid.,
10. Book of Professions, Cabra archives
11. BSA 11/48
12. BS A 2/4, no. 1, account written by V. Rev. T.J. Smyth, O.P.
13. ibid., p.2
14. BSA 2/4, *Mappa Estatística,* 1876-1877

15. BSA 2/4, no. 416. Sister Scholastica's letter, BSA 11/53
16. Sister Scholastica's letter, BSA 11/53
17. M.C.A. p.95 and archival record, p.4
18. *Diário de Notícias* 18th &25th 1876, from B.S. archives
19. M.C.A. p.95
20. Sister Augustine Begge's letter to Fr. Towers, August 18th 1880, D.G.A.
21. ibid.,
22. Sister Rose O'Neill, *A Rich Inheritance,* 1974, Connacht Tribune, Galway, p.111
23. Sister Augustine Begge's letter to the prioress of Taylor's Hill, September 4th, 1880, DGA
24. M.C.A. p.96, quoting the document
25. Sister Rose O'Neill, op.cit., p.112
26. D.G.A. p.209-p.210
27. M.C.A. p.98
28. ibid., p.98
29. BS11/61, letter no.2
30. BS11/61, letter no. 3
31. BS11/61, letter no. 4
32. ibid.
33. ibid.
34. BS11/61 no.5
35. BS3/23 Printed document in Bom Sucesso archives without date or name of author.

Chapter 10: The Third Centenary

1. M.C.A. p.99
2. ibid., p.101
3. ibid., p.102
4. ibid., p.103
5. BS3/12 Petition of the Master of the Dominican Order on behalf of Bom Sucesso, November, 1907.
6. ibid.
7. ibid.
8. ibid.
9. Letter of Pere Cormier, 30th December, 1907, Bom Sucesso archives
10. Saraiva, op.cit., p.482-483
11. A.H. Oliveira Marques, *Breve História de Portugal,* 4ta. ed., 2001, Editorial Presença p.464
12. ibid., p.466
13. A.H. Oliveira Marques, op.cit., p.467
14. ibid., p.467
15. Saraiva, op. cit.,p.486
16. *The Assassination of D. Carlos and the Principe Real,* by Joseph Degen, *The Lisbonian,* a quarterly review by students of the English College, Lisbon, February, 1908, p.76. copy D.G.A.
17. M.C.A p.105
18. ibid., p.105
19. Saraiva, op.cit., p.491-p.492
20. ibid., p.496
21. ibid., p.497

22. ibid., p.497
23. M.C.A p.108
24. ibid., p.108
25. ibid., p. 109
26. ibid., p.111
27. ibid., p.111-p.112
28. ibid., p.113
29. E.D.M (the nom de plume of Fr. Paul O'Sullivan), *A Thrilling Story of Fifty Years in Portugal,* p.55ff, published privately
30. ibid., p.54
31. Bom Sucesso archives, Letters of Bl. Hyacinth Cormier BS 3/12
32. M.C.A p.114
33. Decreto de 20 de Abril de 1911
34. Fr. Paul O'Sullivan's account of proceedings, from his book, *A Thrilling Story of Fifty Years in Portugal* p.56-p.57
35. M.C.A p.118
36. Saraiva, op.cit., p.500
37. M.C.A p.121
38. M.C.A p.127
39. ibid., p.516
40. ibid., p.519
41. M.C.A p.130
42 ibid., p.140
43. For this section I am indebted to Mother Cecilia's eye-witness account in M.C.A p.142
44. M.C.A p.143
45. M.C.A p.144-p.145
46. M.C.A p.146
47. ibid., p.146

Chapter 11: The 1940s

1. B.S.A.,Convent Annals, 1909-1949, p.123
2. ibid., p.123
3. ibid., p.125
4. ibid., p.125
5. ibid., p.128
6. The name given to the Salazar Government
7. BS Convent Annals, p. 131
8. ibid. p.138
9. C. Cleary, O.P., E. Mirphy, O.P., F. McGlynn, O.P., *Being Driven Forward*, Magicprint (Pty) Ltd., Johannesburg, South Africa, p.17
10. Bom Sucesso archives, Correspondence of Father Louis Nolan, O.P. with the prioress of Bom Sucesso, 1938-1942
11. BS 10/55, Copy of Prioress's letter to the Lisbon Câmara, not dated but probably July 1942
12. ibid.
13.BSA 10/55, *Dados sobre a mina das Religiosas Dominicanas Irlandesas do Convento do Bom Sucesso, fundado em 1639.* Copy of original dated 13th June, 1941
14. BS. 10/55 ibid., original document in the office of Dr. D. Pinto Coelho.
15. ibid.,
16. BS 10/55, Guy Wainewright, Letter of 26th November, 1952

17. BS 10/55, Guy Wainewright, Letter of 23rd June, 1953
18. BS 10/55, Guy Wainewright, Letter of 29th June, 1953
19. Sister Agnes, *Entering in Lisbon*, article in Weavings, 1988, p.49-p.55
20. ibid., p.55
21. BS Annals, 1909-1949, p.156
22. ibid., p.159
23. ibid., p.166
24. ibid., p.166
25. ibid., p.174
26. BS Annals, 1949-1955, p.2
27. ibid., p.14
28. ibid., p.19
29. BS 3/23, Fr. Garde's letter, dated 28/9/1952
30. BS 3/23, Fr. Garde's letter, dated 19/12/1952
31. BS 3/23letter dated, 29/1/1953
32. BS 3/23 letter dated, 14/3/1953
33. BS Annals, 1949-1955, p.32. Cutting from newspaper, name not given, date in handwriting, July. 1953
34. ibid., p.30
35. ibid., p.32
36. ibid., p. 33
37. ibid., p. 34
38. ibid., p. 44
39. Sister Frances Lally, letter dated 26th August, 2004
40. ibid.,
41. ibid.,
42. BS Annals, 1949-1953, p.46
43. BS 3/23, Fr. Garde, letter to Mother Gabriel, 20/12/1954
44. Note on the name, "The name Cabragh (says O'Halloran) is very ancient and deserves adverting to. In very remote times the Corybantes were the priests of the Irish, as well as the Greeks, and the Cabiri were the gods both invoked in sudden and dangerous emergencies. Hence Cabra would still retain the name from there having been there, a Seminary for the Corybantes." Lewis' Dublin Guide, 1787, cited in Dominican Convent Cabra Annals, 1647-1912, p.79
45. BS3/23 Father Garde's letter 20/12/1954
46. ibid.
47. ibid.
48. OPG/A 135 (1), 12th November, 1954
49. OPG/A 135 (3), 8th December, 1954
50. BS 3/23, Fr. Garde's letter to M. Benignus, 8th January, 1955
51. ibid.,
52. BS Annals, 1949-1955, p.50
53. ibid., p.51
54. BS 3/23 Fr. Garde's letter, 28th January, 1955
55. ibid.,
56. BS 3/23, Fr. Garde's letter, 5th April, 1955
57. Sister Frances, testimony
58. BS Annals, 1949-1955, p.53
59. BS 3/23 Fr. Garde's letter, 4th May,1955
60. ibid.
61. BS 3/23 Fr. Garde's letter, 9th August, 1955
62. BS 3/23 Fr. Garde's letter, 25th August, 1955

63. BS Annals, 1955-1964, p.6
64. ibid., p.6
65. BS 7/1, Mother Benignus Meenan, letter dated Rosary Sunday, 2nd October, 1955
66. BS 3/24,Fr. Michael Browne, letter, dated 27th September, 1955, Santa Sabina, Roma
67. BS Annals, 1955-1964, p. 18, special typed notice inserted
68. BS 3/23, Fr. Garde, letter dated 17th October, 1955
69. BS Annals, 1955-1964 p.8
70. ibid., p.8
71. ibid., p.12, 21st April, 1956
72. ibid., p.16,
73. ibid., p.16, 17th July, 1956
74. *Dicionário de História de Portugal*, vol.VIII, 1a edição, 1999, A. Barreto, M. F. Mónica (coordinadores), Figueirinhas
75. Joel Serrão & A.H. de Oliveira Marques (dircção), 1992, *Nova História de Portugal, Editorial Presença, 1ª edição*,p. 205, citing F. Nogueira, 1977, *Salazar*, vol. II, Atlântida, Coimbra, p. 9e11
76. ibid., p.205, citing Manuel Braga da Cruz, 1986, *Monárquicos e Republicanos no Estado Novo,* Lisboa, D. Quixote, p.91
77. ibid., p.215, referring to Prof. G. Braga da Cruz, 1955, *Problemas de Educação: direitos da família, da Igreja e do Estado.* Conferência na Sociedade de Geografia de Lisboa.

Chapter 12: Vatican II and Later

1. BS Annals, 1955-1964, p.36
2. ibid., p.36
3. BS 3/23, printed document, name of author not included.
4. BS Annals, 1955-1964, p.41
5. Padre Artur Roque de Almeida, *A Igreja na 2ª Metade do século XX* in *Padre Miguel de Oliveira*, 1994, Historia Ecclesiástica de Portugal, publiçoes Europe-America, p. 276
6. cited in Joel Serrão e A.H. de Oliveira Marques (dir), 1992, *Portugal e o Estado Novo*, vol. XII, Editorial Presença, p. 215.
7. ibid., p. 216
8. cited ibid., p. 216-217
9. A.H. Oliveira Marques, *Breve Historia de Portugal*, 4ª eidçao, 2001
10. ibid., p. 639
11. ibid., p. 640
12. Saraiva, op. cit., p. 544-545
13. Oliveira Marques, op.cit., p.717
14. Sister Aedris's Account of 1975/6
15. ibid.
16. ibid.
17. BS Annals, 1975-1976, p.17
18.Acts of the 10th Chapter of the Cabra Dominican Congregation, Ireland, 12 July-6 August 1977, Art.13, p.12

Epilogue

1.Acts of the 10th Chapter of the Cabra Dominican Congregation, Ireland, 12 July-6 August 1977, Art.13, p.12

2. Minutes of the First Chapter of the Region of Portugal, p.1
3. *Convento do Bom Sucesso*, 1639-1989. Introduction
4. Letter from A President da Camara Municipal de Oeiras, 22 September 2004
5. Teresa Wade,O.P., *Christmas Letter,* 1993, p.1/2
6. Colégio do Bom Sucesso, *Princípios Educativos*
7. Mission Statement of St. Dominic's International School, Portugal, revised, October, 2004
8. *Education for Life*, brochure of the International Baccalaureate Organisation, Geneva , Switzerland, 2001.
9. President Mary Mc Aleese, Address to Irish Community and Friends of Ireland, at the Hotel Ritz, Lisbon, 6th November, 2002
10. ibid.
11. ibid.

Chronology

218 B.C.	Roman legions invade Iberian peninsula in second Punic war
61 B.C.	Julius Caesar arrives in Lusitania
27 B.C.	Olisipons (the future Lisbon) becomes a Roman municipality
589 A.D.	Beginning of religious unity in the peninsula with the Visigothic king's conversion to Christianity
711	Invasion of the peninsula by Islamic forces
844	The Normans attack Lisbon
867	The reconquest of Coimbra by Afonso II
1037	Fernando, king of León and Castile assumes title of overlord/emperor
1085	Conquest of Toledo which becomes the capital of León and Castile
1086	Defeat of Christian forces at battle of Zalaca near Badajoz
1092-1107	Galecia governed by Count Raymund, son-in-law of AfonsoVI of León
1094	Count Raymund suffers defeat near Lisbon as Yusuf controls Spain
1096	Count D. Henrique marries Teresa, daughter of Afonso VI. The country of Portucale is founded and a bishop nominated to Braga
1112	The death of D. Henrique. Dona Teresa governs Portucale until 1128
1128-1185	The reign of her son D. Afonso Henriques.
114 3	D. Afonso Henriques uses the title of king of Portucale for first time
1147	Conquest of Santarém. Conquest of Lisbon with help from crusaders
1153	Grant of the site for Alcobaça Abbey given to Bernard of Clairvaux
1179	Pope Alexander III recognises the independence of Portugal
1185	The death of D. Afonso Henriques, the first king of Portugal
1185-1211	The reign of D.Sancho I of Portugal
1189	D. Sancho with help from crusaders gains control of Silves
1190	Caliph Abu-Yacub takes control of Southern Portugal as far as Évora
1191	Yacub Almansor reconquers the Algarve, Alcácer do Sal and Palmela
1211	Death of D.Sancho I
1211-1223	Reign of D. Afonso II. Beginning of Parliament and written laws
1217	Definitive reconquest of Alcácer do Sal
1223-1245	Reign of D. Sancho II. Complaints made to Rome about inefficiency of the king
1229	Reconquest of Elvas and neighbouring area
1245	Pope Innocent IV deposes D. Sancho II as *rex inutilis* His brother D. Afonso nominated as governor of kingdom Civil war until 1247
1248-1279	Reign of D. Afonso III. Period of peace and development
1249	Final expulsion of Moors in the Algarve
1250-1252	Conflict with king of Castile over control of the Algarve
1267	Afonso X of Castile cedes dominion of the Algarve to Portugal
1279-1325	The reign of D. Dinis. Social and economic progress
1297	Treaty of Alcanizes defines frontier between Portugal and Castile
1319	Founding of the Order of Christ
1320	The heir to the throne revolts
1324	The king yields to the future D. Afonso IV
1325-1357	Reign of D. Afonso IV
1336	Conflict between Portugal and Castile. Portuguese fleet routed

1340	Battle of Salado. Portugal and Castile defeat the Sultan of Morroco
1348-1349	The Black Death
1353	Commercial treaty between Edward III of England and Portuguese traders
1357-1367	Reign of D. Pedro I
1367-1383	Reign of D. Fernando
	Portugal involved from time to time in Hundred Years War
1369-1371	First war with Castile. Peace of Alcoutim
1372	Treaty between king of Portugal and Duke of Lancaster
	Second war with Castile
1373	Treaty of alliance between king of Portugal and Edward III of England
1381	Third war with Castile. Help from England
1383	The Infanta Dona Beatriz, heiress to throne marries D. João I of Castile
	The king dies and his widow, Dona Leonor becomes regent
	The people revolt against the queen
	João, the Master of Avis, illegitimate son of the king nominated *Regedor*
1384	The king of Castile invades Portugal. He lays siege to Lisbon
	He withdraws as his army is decimated by a plague
1385	The Master of Avis proclaimed king in Coimbra
	Battle of Aljubarrota. Portugal defeats Castile
1385-1433	Reign of D. João I. Beginning of military expansion in N. Africa
	Beginning of maritime expansion in the Atlantic
1386	Treaty of Windsor between João I and Richard II of England
1387	Marriage of D. João I and Philippa, daughter of John of Gaunt of Lancaster
1411	Treaty of peace and perpetual alliance with Castile
1415	Conquest of the city of Ceuta in N.Africa
1420	The Infante D. Henrique is nominated apostolic administrator of the Order of Christ. The purpose of this military Order is to fight the Moors
1424	Naval expedition to occupy Canary Islands
1427	Discovery of the Azores
1433	Death of João I
1433-1438	Reign of D. Duarte.
	Gift to the Infante D. Henrique of the islands of Madeira, Porto Santo and Desertas.
1434	Gil Eanes reaches Cabo Bojador-the first specific voyage of discovery
1435	Gil Eanes and Afonso Baldaio sail to Angra dos Ruivos, fifty leagues further
1436	The gold Coast explored
1437	Military expedition to conquer Tanger. The Infante D. Fernando captured
	D. Fernando, the Infante Santo remains hostage in the power of the Moors
1438	Decision not to surrender Ceuta in exchange for the Infante D. Fernando
	Death of the king D. Duarte. His son, D. Afonso V aged six becomes king
	His mother assumes the regency. Opposed by D. Pedro, she leaves Portugal

1439-1449	Regency of D. Pedro. Opposition between him and the king
1438-1481	Reign of D. Afonso V. He assumes power in1449
1440	Naval expedition to the Canary Islands
1441	The navigator Antão Gonçalves goes beyond the Gold River and reaches Cabo Branco (Ras Nouadhibou)
1443	Nuno Tristão voyages twenty-five leagues beyond Cabo Branco
1444	Voyage of Dinis Dias to Cape Verde
1449	Conflict between the king and former regent, D. Pedro D. Pedro is killed by royal forces at battle of Alfarrobeira
1455-1456	Discovery of the islands of Cape Verde arquipelago.
1456	A cargo of sugar from Madeira is sold in England Diogo Gomes explores the rivers of Guinea
1458	D. Afonso V conquers the city of Alcacer Ceguer in N. Africa
1460	Discovery of western islands of Cape Verde arquipelago Pedro Sintra reaches Sierra Leone The Infante D. Henrique, the Navigator, dies
1462	The desert island of Santiago in Cape Verde receives the first inhabitants
1469	The crown arranges with the merchant Fernão Gomes to explore one hundred leagues of African coast every year
1471	Control by Portuguese of Tangier abandoned by the Moors
1471-1472	Discovery of the islands of Sao Tomé and Príncipe
1476	War with Castile
1479	Treaty with Castile. Portugal renounces its claim to the Canaries
1481-1495	Reign of D. João II. Construction of outpost for the gold trade in Guinea
1482	Diogo Cão's first voyage. Contact with kingdom of the Congo
1488-1488	Diogo Cão's second voyage. He dies at Cape Cross
1487	Bartolomeu Dias rounds the Cape of Good Hope. First time link is made between Atlantic and Indian oceans The king orders Afonso Paiva and Pero Covilha to go overland to India with a view to obtaining information about India and sea-route there
1492	Jews expelled from Spain. Many settle in Portugal
1492	Columbus discovers the Americas for Spain
1492-1498	Portuguese voyages to Greenland and Newfoundland
1494	The Treaty of Tordesilhas whereby Portugal and Spain divide the lands to be discovered between them at an imaginary line 370 leagues west of the Cape Verde islands
1495-1521	The reign of D. Manuel I, *o Venturoso*.
1496	Expulsion of Jews from Portugal at demand of Spain. Forced conversions
1497-1499	Vasco da Gama's expedition to India by the sea-route
1498	He reaches the Indian city of Calecute
1500	The fleet commanded by Pedro Álvares Cabral on its way to India deviates west and discovers Brazil
1501	João da Nova discovers Ascension Island
1502	Vasco da Gama establishes a Portuguese warehouse for the spice trade in Cochin on the coast of Malabar The building of the Monastery of Jerónimos is begun
1505	D. Francisco de Almeida nominated first Portuguese viceroy of India
1506	The *custódia* (monstrance) de Belém is made from gold given in

	tribute by a king on the East African coast
1507	Conquest of Ormuz by Afonso de Albuquerdue
1510	Afonso de Albuquerque conquers Goa. It becomes seat of Portuguese administration in India until 1961
1511	Conquest of Malacca. The Portuguese explore Pacific ocean
	Discovery of the island of Ternate in Moluccas archipelago
1513	Portuguese naval expedition to the Red Sea
	Jorge Álvares journeys to China
1514	Building of Torre de Belém
1521-1557	The reign of D. João III. Deficit in Oriental trade
	The introduction of the Inquisition causes withdrawal of capital from Portugal
1533	Henry VIII of England breaks with Rome
1537	Founding of Jesuits
1543	The Portuguese make first contacts with Japan
1553	Foundation of São Paulo in Brazil
1557	Death of D. João III. Throne inherited by his three-year old grandson, D.Sebastião. His grandmother, Queen D. Catarina is regent
1562	Queen Dona Catarina retires from being regent. Cardinal Henrique, son of D. Manuel I becomes regent
1566	Dona Iria de Brito, future foundress of Bom Sucesso is born
1568-1578	Reign of D. Sebastião
1572	Publication of *Os Lusíadas,* Luís de Camões' epic poem of the discoveries
1575	At the request of King D. Sebastião, Pope Gregory XIII creates diocese of Macau which includes China and Japan
	Foundation of Luanda
1578	Battle of Alcácer Quibir. Death of King D. Sebastião
1580	Spain invades Portugal. The Portuguese are defeated.
1581	Phillip II of Spain, grandson of Manuel I becomes Phillip I of Portugal, thus uniting the two countries. The new king promises to respect autonomy of Portugal
1582	The Portuguese pretender to the throne, D. António, prior do Crato, is defeated at the naval battle near the island of São Miguel
1588	At the request of the Portuguese, Pope Sixtus V creates the diocese of Japan
1589	D. António, pretender to the throne arrives in Portugal with English help.
	The people do not support him and he returns to England
1598	Death of Phillip II of Spain and I of Portugal. Reign of Phillip III
1609	The Dutch capture Ceylon/Sri Lanka and establish a trading post in Japan
1615	Corpo Santo church and priory founded by Dominic O'Daly.
	The Portuguese conquer Maranhão, Brazil
1617	Benguela in Angola is established
1622	Persians with English help capture Portuguese fortress of Ormuz
1624	The Portuguese Jesuit, António de Andrade explores Tibet
1630	The Dutch conquer Pernambuco in Brazil
1637	Popular insurrection against Spain in several regions of Portugal
1639	Foundation of Convento do Bom Sucesso
1640	A Restauração – Portuguese nobles declare the Duke of Bragança king of Portugal. He becomes King D. João IV

1641	The Dutch capture Angola. The Dutch conquer Malaca
1648	Portuguese forces from Brazil re-conquer Luanda
1650	Serious incident caused by English refugees from Cromwell's England
1654	Treaty between João IV of Portugal and Cromwell of England
1656	The death of João IV. Queen Luisa de Gusmão becomes Regent
1662	Marriage of the Infanta Dona Catarina de Bragança to Charles II of England
1668	Treaty of peace with Spain
1670	Bom Sucesso Church is completed
1697	Discovery of gold in Brazil
1703	Portugal intervenes in Spanish war of succession, supporting Archduke Carlos. The Methuen trade agreement between Portugal and England
1706-1750	Reign of João V. Prosperity due to gold from Brazil
1715	Treaty of Utrecht ending Spanish war of succession
1717	At request of pope, Portuguese fight the Turkish fleet
1729	Discovery of diamonds in Cerro Frio, Minas Gerais, Brazil
1731	Construction of the Lisbon aqueduct is begun
1748	King João V of Portugal receives title *Fidelíssimo* from pope
1750-1777	Reign of D. José I. Reign is characterised by initiatives of the future Marquês de Pombal to modernise administration and develop State control
1755	The Lisbon earthquake
1758	Assassination attempt of King D. José I
1759	Execution of several members of the nobility accused of regicide attempt
	Expulsion of the Jesuits from Portuguese territory
1761	First law against slavery. All slaves entering Portugal are declared free
1763	Rio de Janeiro chosen as seat of government of Brazil
1767	Exportation of Brazilian cotton to England is begun
1768	The Portuguese abandon their last outpost in Morocco – Mazagão. Its people go to Brazil and found city of Mazagão
1769	The Portuguese abandon their last outpost in Morocco – Mazagão. Its people go to Brazil and found city of Mazagão
1777	Death of King D. José. The end of the power of the Marquês de Pombal
1777-1816	Reign of Queen Dona Maria I
1782	In Moçambique, the foundation of Lorenço Marques/Maputo
1789	The French Revolution
1792	D. João, heir to the throne becomes Regent because of Queen's illness
1806	Napoleon tells Portugal to close its ports to English ships
1807	The French commanded by General Junot invade Portugal
1808	Popular revolt against the French. The English arrive in Portugal. The battles of Roliça and Vimeiro. The Sintra Convention. The French leave
1809	Second French invasion under the command of General Soult
1810	Third French invasion under the command of General Massena Construction of the Lines of Torres Vedras
1811	The French leave Portugal
1815	Defeat of Napoleon. Brazil raised to category of a kingdom. In Portugal
	Political power in the hands of the English under Beresford

1816-1826	The reign of João VI
1817	Anti-English conspiracy led by General Gomes Freire de Andrade Conspirators executed in Lisbon
1820	A provisional Junta of Government initiated in Oporto. Lisbon adheres to Movement
1821	3rd July, King D. João VI returns from Brazil. His son and heir D. Pedro remains in Brazil as regent there
1822	7th September, the Prince Regent, D. Pedro proclaims the independence of Brazil.
	23rd September the first Constitution of Portugal is promulgated
	1st December, the first session of parliament/National Congress
1823	Nuns expelled from Bom Sucesso for one month.
1823	*Vilafrancada*, a reactionary movement to suspend Constitution
1824	30th April – *Abrilada*. Failed anti-liberal revolt of D. Miguel, the king's younger son
1826-1853	Reign of Queen Dona Maria II. D. Pedro authorises The Constitutional Charter
	He abdicates in favour of his seven-year old daughter, Maria II
1828	D. Miguel is regent but claims the throne of Portugal
1831	D. Pedro abdicates the throne of Brazil and becomes leader of liberal movement to ensure the throne of Portugal for his daughter
1832	Siege of Oporto. Civil war
	Another liberal force arrives in the Algarve and marches without resistance on Lisbon.
1834	Triumph of liberal movement. Suppression of religious Orders of men
	Confiscation of their property
1836	Constitution of 1822 re-established
1842	The Constitutional Charter restored. Government of Costa Cabral
1846	*Maria da Fonte*, popular movement against government of Costa Cabral
1851	Marshal Saldanha causes the fall of the government
1853-1861	Reign of D. Pedro V
1861-1889	Reign of his brother, D. Luís I
1867	Abolition of death penalty
1875-1876	The Socialis and Republican parties are founded
1876	Founding of Geography Society to protect Portuguese interests in Africa
1884	Three Portuguese on scientific exploration of the interior of Africa
1886	Portuguese occupation of regions between Angola and Moçambique
1889-1908	Reign of D. Carlos I. Republican movement progresses
1890	English ultimatum for Portugal to withdraw from regions between Angola and Moçambique
1891	Republican revolt in Oporto
1895	Campaigns in Africa. Negative effect of these on public opinion
1901	The *Partido Regenerador-Liberal* founded. João Franco is its president
1908	The King D. Carlos and his son, D. Luís Filipe, heir to the throne are assassinated. His second son, D. Manuel becomes king
1910	The Republic is established. The king D. Manuel II leaves Portugal
1911	The first Republican Constitution is approved
1915	The dictatorship of Pimenta de Castro
1916	Germany declares war on Portugal

1917	A contingent of Portuguese soldiers sent to France
	The revolution of Sidónio Pais
1918	Assassination of Sidónio Pais
1921	Several politicians are assassinated in one night
1922	Gago Coutinho and Sacadura Cabral cross the Atlantic by plane
1926	A military revolt. A military dictatorship begins
1927	Revolts against military dictatorship
1928	António de Oliveira Salazar becomes minister for finance.
	General Carmona becomes president
	End of military dictatorship and beginning of *Estado Novo*
1935	Political parties prohibited. The *União Nacional founded*
1939	Portugal recognises the government of General Franco in Spain
1939-1945	The Second World War. Portugal is neutral
1940	Celebration of eighth centenary of Portugal.
	Exhibition of *O Mundo Português*
1943	Secret agreement with Allies for the use of an airport in the Azores
1949	Re-election of General Carmona as president
1955	Portugal becomes a member of the United Nations
1958	Presidential election. General Humberto Delgado, popular candidate but Admiral Américo Thomás, government's candidate becomes president
1961	India occupies Portuguese territories in India.
	Beginning of rebellion in Angola
1963	Beginning of guerrilla warfare in Portuguese Guinea
1964	Beginning of guerrilla warfare in Moçambique
1966	Opening of bridge over the Tagus at Lisbon
1974	The Revolution of 25th April. A military Junta in power
	General Spínola is president. Then General Costa Gomes
1975	Four provisional governments led by General Vasco Gonçalves, a communist
1976	Third Republican Constitution. It is socialist and democratic
	General Ramalho Eanes elected President
1985	Portugal joins the European Union
1992	The Maastrict agreement is ratified in Portugal
2004	Portugal's prime minister, Manuel Durão Barroso, becomes president of the European Union.

Appendices

Appendix 1

List of some documents in Archives of Bom Sucesso Convent

1. A double document relating to a royal donation to the Bom Sucesso community. The first document is dated, Madrid, 21st March, 1639, the date when the King of Spain granted the licence for the foundation. The second document is dated, Lisbon, 16th January, 1641. The royal donation is being given by the King of Portugal only a few weeks after the Restoration of Portuguese independence.

2. A legal document, dated 19th July, 1642, on the taking possession of the estate and olive grove in Golegã, named Casal de Baralha, by the Born Sucesso Community's representative – a preacher. As part of the legal proceedings, earth and olive branches are symbolically offered. It is one of the earliest documents still extant indicating the title of the Convent. (see page...

3. An ordination by the Master of the Dominican Order, Fr. John Baptist de Marinis, dated 1655, that the College of the Holy Rosary and the Monastery of Bom Sucesso were founded for Irish Religious. He ordains that these two foundations remain for Irish Religious in perpetuity.

4. Two documents relating to Dr Sleyne, Bishop of Cloyne in Ireland:-

   a) 1705. A letter from the Nuncio in Lisbon to Cardinal Palucci informing him that Bishop Sleyne had arrived in Lisbon and that the prior of the Dominicans in Cork had left Lisbon to take care of the bishop's diocese in Cork.

   b) 1712. A letter to the Secretary of State in the Vatican, announcing the death of Dr. Sleyne and informing that the funeral ceremony was conducted by the Dominicans of Corpo Santo.

Appendix 2

List of Sisters Professed in Bom Sucesso
1639–1955

Name	Professed	Died
Antónia Theresa de Jesús	in Setúbal	13-10-1649
Catherina do Rosário de Burgho	08-12-1641	25-03-1651
Luíza de Mello Sampayo	20-11-1640	28-03-1651
Cecília do Rosário	03-1641	07-1652
Isabel da Paixão	1651	28-12-1659
Marianna Smapayo de Mello	03-1641	04-05-1668
Leonor de Santa Margarida	20-11-1640	21-03-1669
Maria Menezes Mendonça,		
sister of Magdalena	1670	
Magdalena de Silva Menezes	20-11-1640	07-05-16720
Ursula de Butgho	08-12-1641	26-02-1673
Jacinta de Jesús e Maria	20-11-1640	09-08-1674
Leonor do Calvário Tancos	02-02-1643	04-12-1676
Brigid of St. Patrick	1660	27-08- 1689
Anna Joachim,		
daughter of Countess of Fingal	c.1692	
Joanna da S. Trindade White	03-1641	09-01-1694
Angélica das Chagas de Mello	03-1641	03-1694
Maria da Encarnação	1661	19-07-1694
Agnes do Rosário Shanly	1650	c. 1695
Felicia	1668	15-12-1697
Iria de S. António Muscry &		05-12-1701
BarryMarianna da S. Trindade	1651	1706
Francisca das Cinco Chagas	1643	06-01-1708
Maria Gertrudes	c.1686	
Elena da Cruz		
Catharina da Coluna		10-1726
Thereza Maria da Assumpção		
Anna Maria of Jesus Plunket 1726		1726
Marianna do Sacramento		
Catharina of St. Thomas		
Joanna Baptista		
Thomazia dos Anjos		09-1727
Catherine Theresa of Jesus		02-1728

Name	Professed	Died
Joanna da Encarnação		08-1728
Catharina de Cristo		09-1728
Leonor de São José		10-1728
Thereza Josepha de Atalaya (13 yrs)	10-1731	
Margaret of Saint Joseph		
Eufrazia Maria		12-1731
Joanna Evangelista		
Catherine of St. Joseph	c. 1680	
Mary Baptist of Jesus		01-1732
Catherine of Jesus		04-1733
Mary of Jesus		12-1733
Francisca Maria da Purificação		06-1734
Antónia do Sacramento		12-1734
Anne of Jesus, Mary & Joseph	1734	
Marianna das Chagas		30-12-1734
Madalena de Jesus O'Daly, grand-niece of Dominic O'Daly		01-1737
Mary Josepha		03-1737
Catherina da Conceição		11-1737
Thereza of Jesus & Mary		06-1739
Julianna		12-1741
Margarida da S. Trindade		12-1741
Margarida da Bondade		01-1742
Antónia Frances dos Reis		1744
Catherina Rosa		01-1745
Thereza Maria da Purificação	c. 1726	1746
Anna Maria de Santa Thereza	c. 1726	1748
Theresa Micaella de Jesús		1751
Anna Maria da Cruz	c. 1726	1752
Anna da Conceição		1752
Angélica of Jesus and Mary	1729	1752
Anna Bernarda	c. 1730	1753
Joanna Maria de São José	c. 1727	1753
Thereza de Jesús	1712	1754
Thereza de Madre de Deus		1755
Joanna do Rosário		1756
Francisca Manuela, daughter of VI Count Atalaia	1742	1756
Thereza Joaquina de Jesús	c. 1729	1757
Anna Maria de Jesús		1758
Catherina Thereza de Jesús	c. 1726	1759
Margaret Tuite	1742	11-1764
Thereza de Jesús	1712	03-1765
Iria Victoria Tuomy	1713	12-1766
Antónia de S. Clara, daughter of Count of Atalaia	1703	12-1766

Name	Professed	Died
Thomazia de Santa Rosa	1711	06-1767
Eugenia Mac Carthy	1698	12-1767
Anna Bernarda Mac Crohan	1743	01-1769
Marianna Theresa Fanning	1729	08-1769
Mary of the Assumption French	1730	01-1771
Antónia Lycet	1724	09-1771
Maria Magdalena Van Zellar	1737	07-1772
Joseph of St. Anna Plunkett	1717	06-1774
Rita Marianna do Menino Jesús	1765	1774
Maria de São José	1770	1775
Marianna Francisca Faro	1749	1777
Catherine O'Carroll	1714	10-1778
Elizabeth Baptist Scurlog	1725	02-1780
Anna Joachina O'Kennedy	1742	06-1780
Inez Antunes	1721	08-1780
Marianna Rosa O'Kennedy	1715	11-1781
Mary Cleary	1748	06-1782
Brigid O'Ferrall	1739	1783
Thereza de Jesús	1777	04-1784
Francisca Angélica de Sta. Clara	1720	10-1784
Scholástica Maria de Campos	1721	09-1786
Marianna Josepha da Cruce	1726	10-1786
Anne Rosa Lycet	1727	01-1787
Maria Jerónima	1749	03-1789
Thereza Rita Faro,daughter of 3rd Count Vimieiro	1748	08-1789
Barbara Maria Rosa	1769	1789
Magdalena of the Trinity Fox	1753	11-1790
Maria Rosa	1730	12-1790
Thomasia Rita	1756	01-1791
Michaella Antunes	1720	01-1793
Maria da Graça Archdeacon	1751	08-1793
Marianna O'Byrne	1745	08-1795
Barbara Springler	1725	12-1795
Maria Josefa da Presentação	1764	11-1798
Mary of the Incarnation O'Thomas	1728	1799
Thereza Murrough	1756	08-1799
Matilda (Americana)	1727	10-1800
Maria Honoria	1769	1802
Cecilia of St. Dominic Concannon	1773	1804
Marianna do Carmo Oates	1757	02-1806
Osanna Rosa	1777	08-1806
Iria de Cristo	1776	09-1806
Marianna do Rosário	1796	1806

Brigid of St. Patrick Egan	1773	1807
Maria da Piedade Msc Donnell	1761	01-1808
Maria da Piedade Msc Donnell	1753	11-1811
Isabel Maria de São José	1803	1815
Anna Vitória	1777	02-1816
Maria Margarida	1779	04-1816
Engrácia de Jesús	1785	1817
Catherine of Jesus Egan	1785	06-1817
Anna Thereza Baptist Brett	1773	07-1818
Anna Maria de São Domingos	1768	09-1818
Mary Rita	1764	01-1820
Teresa Silva	1820	
Eugénia Josefa	1769	1825
Helena da Cruz	1789	02-1826
Anna O'Neill	1775	16-03-
Catherine of Siena Concannon	1777	1830
Margaret Theresa Dorran	1803	1831
M. Gertrudes da Conceição		1836
Albuquerque	1806	
Maria Honoria O'Flynn	1794	1843
Cecilia do Carmo O'Neill	1775	1843
Brigid Theresa Staunton	1803	02-1845
Mary of Jesus de Cunha	1777	1846
Anna Rita de São José	1785	
Gertrudes Rita da Santa Anna	1785	
Eugénia Marianna de Jesús	1795	
Júlia of St. Joseph Joyce	1803	04-1849
Ana Maria do Carmo	1804	1854
Mary Magdalena	1835	1856
Mary of St. Joseph Joyce	1803	1857
Maria Theresa Silva	1815	
Catherine Butler	1826	1859
Anna Maria Hay	1832	01-1860
Isidoria	1803	1860

In August 1860, at Mother Teresa Staunton's request, nuns from Saint Mary's Dominican Convent, Cabra, Dublin, came to help the depleted community.

Mary Bernardine Bodkin	1852 (in Cabra)	06-1868
Theresa Monica Staunton	1805	24-08 1870
Mary Dominic Butler	1827	04-1871
Iria Quinlan	1826	1872
Rose Dunne	1867 (in Spain)	1873
Osanna Kent		12-03 1880

Novitiate re-opened in 1865

Name	Professed	Died
Mary Catherine de Ricci Mc Auley	1869 (in Bom Sucesso)	26-04-1890
Mary Martha Lynch	1872	09-09-1890
Hyacinth Phelan	1869	1892
Mary Immaculate Conception Magalhães	1891	19-12-1893
Eliza Brown	1827	1894
Mary Thomas Tarrant	1848 (in Cabra)	01-06-1896
Mary Aquinas Moloney	1883 (Galway)	27-07-1896
Mary Petronilla Francis O'Reilly	1841 (in Cabra)	07-03-1900
Elisa de Sá (Madeira)	1897	14-05-1900
Margaret Murphy	1847 (in Cabra)	19-09-1903
Mary Antoninus Evans	1860 (in Cabra)	12-01-1904
Mary Scholástica Guitar	1850 (in Cabra)	08-07-1905
Mary Patricia Hegarty	1869	10-08-1905
Mary Thecla Murtagh	1858 (in Cabra)	06-02-1909
Mary Columba Mathews	1858 (in Cabra)	13-06-1909
Mary Joseph Masterson	1883 (Galway)	26-02-1911
Mary Veronica Sheridan	1852 (in Cabra)	27-07-1911
Mary Columba Haidy	1912 (received)	22-10-1912
Mary Imelda Timmons	1853 (in Cabra)	17-01-1913
Mary Thomas Prendergast	1903	02-06-1915
Mary Vincent de Paul Coghlan	1862 (in Cabra)	13-06-1916
Mary Magdalen Mac Donnell	1868 (in Spain)	25-09-1916
Mary Rose Richardson	1875	21-07-1917
Mary Stephana Farrel	1871	21-10-1917
Catherine Harrison	1867 (in Spain)	03-11-1917
Mary Pius O'Carroll	1873	08-03-1920
Bridget Murphy	1868 (in Spain)	13-02-1921
Mary Anthony Carvalho	1885	29-12-1923
Martha d'Olival (Madeira)	1897	19-04-1924
Mary Pius Hollanda (Brazil)	1909	31-07-1924
Mary Agnes Byrne	1869	28-12-1925
Mary Augustine Begge	1870	(in Galway) 09-02-1926
Joseph Murphy	1868 (in Spain)	15-03-1928
Mary Peter Geraghty	1919	01-01-1930
Mary Cecilia Francis Bretschneider	1872	03-02-1935
Mary Vincent Murray	1873	14-10-1935
Mary Austin Cheevers	1874	12-11-1936
Mary Dominic Higgs	04-09-1873	16-03-1938
Mary Raymond Farrelly	1893	19-06-1938

Name	Professed	Died
Mary Alberta Teresa Claffey	1883	09-11-1938
Mary Alberta Elcock	1899 (Drogheda)	05-03-1946
Agnes (Catherine de Ricci) Birkbeck	1904	30-01-1947
Mary Bernard Grunling	1906	12-02-1948
Mary Osanna Fernandes	1896	12-03-1948
Mary Joanna Mary Rafferty	1904	19-11-1957
Mary Inez Faria	1898	03-07-1958
Mary Angela Dunne	1903	31-08-1958
Mary Louis Murray	1912	13-01-1967
Mary Veronica Hand	1926	24-07-1969
Mary Dominica de Sá Nogueira	1903	09-09-1969
Mary Reginald Hayden	1905	23-05-1970
Mary Imelda Warner	1925	21-07-1972
Mary Cecilia Murray	1905	10-08-1972
Mary Catherine Walsh	1925	14-08-1974
Mary Joseph Dorr	1932	23-12-1974
Mary Baptist Reilly	1905	12-01-1976
Mary Finbar O'Driscoll	1925	23-11-1978
Mary Gabriel da Costa Cunha	1908	18-11-1982
Mary Antoninus O'Rourke	1930	06-03-1982
Mary Hyacinth White	1927	10-04-1986
Mary Alphonsus Davis	1929	31-07-1987
Mary Emmanuel Davis	1927	11-04-1994
Mary Rose Niall	1927	09-08-1998
Mary Philomena Sisk	1936	26-04-2000
Mary Thomas Kennedy	1925	27-02-2003
Mary Agnes Talty	1945	
Mary Teresa Faherty	1945	
Mary Francis Lally	1955	

Appendix 3

Sisters Assigned from Cabra to Bom Sucesso, 1955-2006

Imelda Joseph Mc Evoy	1955-1958
Brid Trant	1955-1968, 1984-1988
Feighin Gilhooly	1956-1962
Jeanne Mc Loughlin	1956-1965
Isabel Duggan	1957-1965
Michelle Forde 1962	1962-
Aedris Coates 1962	1962-
Una Dempsey 1962-1973	1962-1973
Honor (Aimee) Mc Cabe	1963-1976, 1984-1985
Margaret (Vitalis) Hegarty	1964-1966
Deirdre (Cletus) O'Neill	1964-1975
Lazerian Lynch	1965-1966
Maureen (Jude) Flanagan	1966-1966
Maura (Cosmas) Corbett	1966-1973
Teresa (Pia) Owens	1966-1969
Ena (Gonzales) Looby	1966-1972
Mary (Benita) O'Brien	1968-1971
Kate (Berchmans) Mc Glynn	1969-1971
Ignatius Gorman	1970-1971, 1973-1976
Margaret Purcell	1972-1977
Mary Daly	1972-1976
Christina Greene	1973-1976
Joan O'Shanahan	1973-1988
Teresa Wade	1974-
Marcoline Lawler	1975-1982, 1983-1992
Alicia Mooney	1975-
Marie Humbert Kennedy	1975-1979
Bernadette Pakenham	1976-
Catherine de Ricci O'Connor	1977-1990
Una Rodgers	1977-1978
Helena Marion Mc Intyre	1977-1978
Colm Mc Cool	1978-
Marie (Yvonne) Mc Hugh	1978-1989
Lua Tuohy	1979-1981
Mary Isabel Gutierrez Rodellar	1981-
Cécile Diamond	1981-1984
Maureen Hawkshaw	1982-1984
Patricia Fitzsimons	1982-1983

Mary Brannigan	1984-1993
Marie de Lourdes Lynch	1985-1987
Finbar Lawler	1986-1988
Anne Patricia Morgan	1986-1991
Ursula Bastow	1987-1988
Martinez Murphy	1989-
Nuala Mary Mc Kinstry	1992-
Elizabeth Delaney	1994-
Patricia O'Reilly	1998-2004
Laura Peelo	2001-2004

Appendix 4

The Life and Adventures of Mrs.Tarrant, Miss Guitar, Mrs. Bodkin and Miss Evans during their nine days residence in the world! 1860*

They were driven with great spirit from poor dear Saint Mary's and for escort they had Francis Granville who kept up with the cab until they came near Saint Peter's. On their arrival there Father Mc Namara came out and received them …inviting them in as it was ascertained the Packet was not to sail until a later hour….A second cab was called and Fr. Mc Namara said to Mrs. Bodkin, "Take care of these two children and Mrs. Tarrant and I will go together". Off they started and then really began to feel they had launched into the world.

At the North Wall, the noise, bustle and confusion, with the weight of dress, the encumbrance of gloves (which all through was the most oppressive part of the load) overpowered the poor travellers….They found the stewardess well prepared to pay them all attention. They were placed together in a cabin between two others well filled. The great thought was how they should escape observation and consequent detection for they were looked in upon on all sides …. After more than an hour's delay, they moved off after taking one last farewell of poor old Ireland!

The sunset was grand that evening and was fully admired in its reflection on Howth. Not a ruffle on the water and the vessel steadily went its course being well freighted - a number of passengers of all classes, nine hundred cows and a great number of sheep. The time passed very agreeably until past 11 o'clock, the revered and kind guardian doing everything to make the time pass pleasantly and prevent them from thinking of self or their concerns….Poor Mrs. Bodkin felt great inconvenience from the world's vanity (a hoop) – it was catching in everyone and everything to her great humiliation. …. Mrs. Tarrant and she, at length, retired and the restraint of so many hours and the strange appearance of each in the others' eyes had the effect of setting all four laughing.

After a struggle and a little time they were obliged to become well behaved for the stewardess was most officious and under the circumstance perhaps too attentive. She recognised Fr. Mc Namara and her curiosity was excited to know our object in travelling with him. At last, she whispered to Mrs. Tarrant "I think, Ma'am, you are all going to retire from the world." Poor woman! If she knew they were only entering it! …,

* An account of the journey of four Cabra sisters who travelled in 1860 to join the Bom Sucesso community in Lisbon.(page 144).
Original account in D.C.C.A. Copy made by Maura Kealy, O.P., from which this is taken. The original is without full stops and paragraphs.

Such a sleepless night! At break of day, the cows began to low and Mrs. Bodkin started up thinking they were answering Frank's familiar voice and that she had slept beyond the time. At 7 o'clock, The Windsor neared the pier at Liverpool and after some delay, the travellers found themselves comfortably settled in the Grecian Hotel. Mary Joseph, "the little girl" of the party was so knocked up she was obliged to go down and the others after making themselves tidy (which caused some delay on many occasions) they started off walking for Saint Mary's Church which was near the hotel. Fancy a walk through the streets!

The good Father said Mass at a side altar at which they assisted. The Church is Pugin with good stained windows and High Altar of the same kind as dear Saint Mary's but…all as unlike what had been known and seen – brought the painful recollection to the mind of all the good and holy things which had been left behind with the uncertain future with all its fears and doubts. However, these were only passing thoughts for the deep-seated feeling of all four was to make the best of everything.

Breakfast being over, Fr. Mc Namara went to engage the berths and leaving the ladies to write their letters until 1 o'clock. They first took a look at all the grandeur that surrounded them…. Then the dress took some time to arrange for the front on one was sure to come loose, the cap on another did not always conceal the cropped head and poor Mrs. Tarrant was so out of the way grand with her Barege that she had to pay well for it for it was sure to tear and catch in everything and at all moments she was obliged to have her needle and thread in hand….

At 1 o'clock, the Father returned with the intelligence that the Lisbon boat was not to sail until Thursday. Started for a drive, were surprised to find the town so pretty – passed several churches and the Town Hall, a beautiful building of the Corinthian order (as well as I remember) and considered one of the finest in Europe….

Visited the Convent of Notre Dame, received by a very pleasing religious to whom Fr. Mc Namara introduced the party as a "Community of Dominican Nuns"…. The object of the Institute is to educate teachers who will be able to conduct schools through the country. Religious sometimes go from their communities for a few months to learn the system….

On hearing of the difficulties of Bom Sucesso they said their congregation had suffered much in the same way. It was instituted in France and something being demanded by those in power, which would be an infracture of the rule, they refused and, in consequence, were obliged to leave the country and took refuge in Belgium…. These good Sisters expressed so much sympathy and surprise at the missionaries' undertaking that they could not help feeling a little awe at what was before them. The worldly dress particularly amused them and of all Mrs. Bodkin's bonnet because it was "so very worldly"….

Returned to the hotel, had dinner at 4 o'clock, had to submit to course after course with all sorts of grand things and were not sorry when the waiter retired and left all at liberty. Wondered if he remarked no name was mentioned for, up to this, the assumed name had not become familiar. The conversation that evening was all of Cabra…. M. Joseph obliged to retire early but, though sick, was gay and able to enjoy a laugh, which never failed when all four got together. Separated at 8 o'clock to perform devotions and got to bed about the usual time but not to sleep.

On the Assumption, went early to Saint Mary's and had the same great happiness of receiving our Divine Lord. The Father celebrated at a side altar, which must have made them pass as some special class of persons – the Congregation always going to the High Altar…. started in a cab to visit Mount Vernon outside the town. Graciously received by the Reverend Mother who said she had been expecting the party from the steamer all the morning. The good Sisters who lately visited at Cabra appeared and were most affectionate. All appeared quite interested in the mission but wondered at the undertaking and had the humility to say they never would have courage for it. …. The altar is in the choir where the community Mass is daily said. The choir opens into the Church where is the High Altar at which Mass is celebrated at a later hour on Sunday for the inmates of the "House of Mercy" and the public. The choir is very nice, rather small. Nothing remarkable about the decoration of the Altar, a crown (gift) was suspended over the Most Holy from which descended white silk drapery…. Found three letters and little souvenirs from the Reverend Mother of Dundalk, Sisters de Sales and Malachy. Returned to the hotel which we were fortunate in finding quiet and respectable. M. Joseph better but yet not able to move. The heat and the noise were too much for her, poor thing, yet we could do nothing to make it better.

Drove to Crosby, five miles distant. Arrived at the convent (a tidy small house by the roadside consisting of six rooms and also small school rooms) as Vespers were commencing. The superioress, an old friend of Father Mc Namara was sent for…. Her story was interesting. She joined eight years ago (under his advice) and was sent to a French seaport, one of the largest establishments where she had a great deal of employment. On an hour's notice she was ordered to Paris and when there was told to start for her post of superiority in Crosby. She had arrived a week or two before we saw her and, poor thing, was overpowered at her charge, a community of thirty-two. During her residence in France, she forgot her native tongue and gave us no little amusement by trying to relate her sorrows in broken English….

Dinner at 6 o'clock which passed off pleasantly. At 8, separated, the Father proposing all remaining in the sitting-room to say the Office, on which each took possession of a corner. And we were getting on very well when in came the waiter to ask the arrangements for the morning, looking with surprise (it is supposed) at each keeping a respectful distance. Mrs. Tarrant, fortunately, preserved composure to give him an answer. It is not necessary to say what the others did – packed up all the loose things and made ready for an early start….

The morning being wet, a cab was called but, as there was a delay, the Father went on to save time. On the ladies saying "to Saint Mary's…the driver asked the way (so little is anything Catholic known in this land of plenty). One of the party had to guide the native to the Church! Enjoyed the drive as yesterday. Breakfast seasoned by welcome notes from Cabra; had not time to read them. M. Joseph much better at the prospect of getting out of the noisy town (she knew not what was before her). Mrs. Bodkin came to the resolution of leaving the hoop (as if accidentally) behind her – it would have never lived through the "Braganza". Had a long drive to the docks and so came to the end of the letters.

Arrived in time but found the boat was not to sail for an hour. Settled all comfortably – Mrs. Tarrant and Mary Joseph on one side of the saloon and the other two on the other and the Father engaged the berth between. It was all very small but very clean. Remained on deck to see all that was going on. At last moved off, and to see the vessel on all sides surrounded by masts, appeared as if it never could be extricated. However, the English have a way of doing things well and an experienced pilot steered it through and after fifty minutes it cleared the dock. Nothing interesting on the shore, constantly threatened rain but at last brightened. All were struggling to keep up.

At last, M. Joseph retired and took possession of the top berth…. where she was comfortably concealed by the newest crimson moreen curtains Enquired if there were a stewardess on board, was answered in the negative by the steward who was the picture of good humour and benevolence. Shortly after, M. Guitar gave up, making choice of the underneath which was without curtains. The passengers were a Brazilian who could only speak his own language, a native of Lisbon who spoke English well and an Englishman who was going in search of employment as an engine driver to Lisbon. Tried getting up, Mrs. Bodkin struggled on not to leave Mrs. Tarrant alone but, at last, could do so no longer and she, Mrs. Tarrant, was left all the honour of being at the captain's side at 3 o'clock dinner. He was a blunt, civil, good man who would give an answer but could not spare another word.

The sick people knew no more of public life on that day or the next. Mrs. Tarrant kept up and charitably looked to the wants of all but, indeed, these wants were few. They only desired what they could not have – rest. The vessel heaved and tossed incessantly and shook and trembled at every moment and the heat was oppressive – at least for those in the curtained berth for they were close to the engine and the others were fanned by a breeze. A day and two nights passed on the same – a word could only be now and again exchanged. Poor Miss Evans would sometimes say, "Are we in danger?" and she would get an answer from one who knew as little as herself, "Oh, Please God, No" and she was satisfied.

On Saturday, the storm continued and all were more ill – Mrs. Tarrant even could not stir. At last, the good Father came to look after the sufferers…. Mrs. Tarrant and Miss Guitar had great adventures their side. The window blew in once and Miss Guitar could lend no help. So, the steward had to settle it. Again, she was thrown from the berth to the floor and could not move until Mrs. Tarrant came to her aid. The night the same. Oh! The six precious nights on the "Braganza"! Some thought that perhaps they might never know again the sweets of sleep.

Sunday morning came. It became calmer but the vessel still heaved greatly…. Mrs. Tarrant and Mrs. Bodkin appeared at dinner – a dinner on board which under such circumstances was not the most enviable. However, the motto was "to make the best of everything". The captain did the honours of the table in real, laconic style and the mate graced the foot. The ladies were put on a bench covered with red, on one side, and each in turn had the honour (made up between themselves) of occupying the place near the captain

Remained on deck the remainder of the evening and was well repaid for the effort, by hearing the good Father's opinion on so many subjects – what nice things he said of religious life and what instructions he gave for the future. He saw many things in the distance and spoke of them as they have since been proved. How often did he repeat during the different conversations, "Remember no good can be done without the practice of virtue". Another time, he was full of anecdote and so entertaining on his travels.

In the evening, the sea became calm and we were going steadily, the captain said, at eight miles an hour. The passengers had the politeness not to interest themselves in us. On Monday, Miss Guitar joined the party at breakfast. The good steward was all attention to get us everything. Tea without milk was the great luxury for the rest of the time. The Father said, "Why don't you keep a goat on board?" "It is hard enough to keep ourselves alive without minding a goat", said he. It was most enjoyable all day. Miss Evans came up and was put lying on a cushion on deck. There was a very heavy sea but, as the wind was favourable, it did not increase the motion. The dolphins were playing and jumping all round the vessel, which kept all eyes engaged for some time.... Talked and laughed all day. Dinner as usual. At the close of the second course, it was the custom to put a glass on the table, well filled with what appeared to some matches and which made it be expected that the fumes of cigars would follow. Miss Guitar thought they were a particular kind of vegetable peculiar to the country of her adoption. After all the conjectures, it was discovered they were toothpicks and the custom prevails amongst all classes in Portugal, even the nobility.

A long conversation on the state of religion in Spain and Portugal. It was melancholy and a good subject for meditation for the night – that four weak beings could be of any use or hold on in such a torrent of impiety. Separated on deck to say the Office. It was very devotional – the great expanse of ocean so beautifully blue except when one great breaker dashed over another. It was very rough, which added to the beauty but the "Braganza" made her way steadily and there was no inconvenience – she was so heavily laden. All retired to our cabin for a little to talk and laugh. Mary Joseph better but not able for any exertion. The steward came to ask so kindly, "How is the little girl this evening?" and the Father, when ordering her dinner, always said, "Keep this for the child upstairs".

Tuesday was very enjoyable – it was so fine and rough and grand. The sun was very hot. So, it was proposed getting up an awning. It gave a little more than the captain cared for and he exclaimed, "If Job were alive now, he would find something to try his patience". The captain became much more civil and explained the compass.... When parting, the Father said, "Tomorrow will be an eventful day". Each felt that but left all solicitude to the loving care of

257

Providence. Expected to land at 7 o'clock on Wednesday.

Set about early preparations for the great day. All tried to make themselves as smart as they could, concealing, at the same time, habit, belt, beads etc., which made it no easy matter to move. Got on deck in time to see the Tagus and its banks. The villages looked pretty but the want of vegetation and burnt up look of the land was remarkable. A number of windmills was to be seen. Passed the "Bom Sucesso" without knowing it. Got up to Lisbon and had a great delay waiting for the Custom House officers to visé the passports. They were very slow even when they came on board, which attracted Mrs. Tarrant and Mrs. Bodkin's attention and put them really in a fright which they only made known to each other. In vain, they looked out for the promised consul.

After near an hour's delay, it was announced they should land in a boat and then they left the poor "Braganza" in fear and joy. On landing they were conducted to the Douane which was close by. The ladies were standing within the Hall while the luggage was being brought in when a polite gentleman having a connection with the place made signs to them to enter the office and conducted them to chairs placed behind a table, evidently the post of honour of the great man of the office. They were too glad to be seated and, at the same time, too anxious to appear too grand to mind or care where they were placed.

They bowed and seated themselves quite at their ease, when, after a few minutes, appeared a gentleman the look of whom was enough to make them think if he could catch anything about them he would be sure to pay them off. He looked English from being unlike the pleasing, smiling natives. He was short and fat without a smile to be seen on his visage, giving such a look as he passed on anyone thinking of taking possession of anything he had to do with…and to assist his vision he had a glass fastened in one eye. He conducted all in intense silence, making signs to have everything as he wished. He should have locked trunk opened and looked through. Mrs. Tarrant as she was key-bearer, had to stand up and assist him in his efforts. The glass eye fastened on the writing desks. He thought he had a prize, there was such difficulty in unlocking one but that made him more patient. However, he could find nothing. So, he nodded that they might all be locked again.

The consul had sent his clerk as he could not come himself…. The luggage was all tied together and each end of the rope fastened to pieces of board which were fastened on to two men's shoulders and then they carried the heavy load up hill and down hill. There were no carriages to be had, so, we followed on foot and with the great heat, heavy clothes and hilly way, we were pretty well done up when we got into the "Braganza", the best hotel in Lisbon. It is nicely fitted up with painted, panelled walls, matting on the floor and richly covered sofas and chairs.

Had breakfast of fish, figs, tea, coffee etc. Shortly after, Mr. Munroe, the American consul was announced. He spoke very agreeably about the State of Portugal as to religion, education etc. Praised the people and said by kindness they can be won. Made many excuses for the state of things in consequence of civil war and oppression. Praised the king who is of a literary, studious temper. Proposed our visiting some churches on the way but said he was sure every moment would be an hour to Mrs. Staunton until she had us within her walls. On hearing our fears as to our safe arrival, said they were groundless but since, we have heard there was reason to be uneasy for, if it had transpired there is a strong party who surely would have prevented the entrance. He also said there was no circumspection necessary about letters. They were always sure to go safe and unopened by the authorities. (The letters from this house are merely sent to England as a favour, to save postage).

He (the consul) having ordered the two carriages, the party started for Belém, three miles from Lisbon where the Convent is situated. It is like a connecting street the entire way – pavements in use. The carriage drawn by mules that went at a brisk pace. There is a look of poverty about the people, perhaps it is because the men go barefooted. On the way, stopped at the Church of Saint Rock – a fine one. The different chapels beautifully decorated with gold, the altars very rich. One chapel exquisite and the great object of admiration to all travellers though small (about the size of the Infirmary). It has cost half a million of money. It was originally set up in Saint Peter's in Rome when the Holy Sacrifice was celebrated at it, was afterwards removed. The altar is principally of lapis lazuli – set in with different kinds of Italian marble; the walls are all mosaic and are ornamented with three large subjects from the life of Our Lord, representing painting but done in the same beautiful mosaic. It was a great pleasure to see such a sight. The kind Father would have wished the party to have seen many other grand things but they were so keyed up, feeling they would not have enjoyed it. At 11 o'clock, the goal was gained! The enclosure passed! May they rest in peace! (written in hurried moments at Bom Sucesso, in the hope of giving a few minutes interest).

Bibliography

Archives

Archives of Bom Sucesso Convent, Belém, Lisboa

Arquivo Nacional da Torre do Tombo, Lisboa

Arquivo do Palácio da Ajuda, Belém, Lisboa

Archives of the Dominican Order, Santa Sabina, Rome

Arquivium Propaganda Fide, Roma

General Archives of the Dominican, Cabra, Congregation, Dublin

Archives of the Dominican Convent, Taylor's Hill, Galway

Archives of the Dominican Convent, Cabra, Dublin

Theses

Ferreira da Costa, Ana Cristina de Ayala Botto Mariz Fernandes, *O Sacrário do Convento do Bom Sucesso,* 1997, dissertação de M.A., Universidade Lusíada, Lisboa

Gibson, Catherine, 1990, *The Ambiguity of Bridal Imagery in Christian Tradition,* thesis for M.Litt., Trinity College, Dublin

Mac Curtain, Margaret, *Daniel O'Daly 1595-1662, A Study of Irish-European Relationships in the Seventeenth Century,* thesis presented to the National University of Ireland, 1958, for degree of M.A.

Murphy, Edel, *The Contribution of Dominican Sisters to Education in the Town of Dun Laoire.*

Histories

Birmingham, David, 1993, *A Concise History of Portugal,* Cambridge University Press, Cambridge, England.

Bolster, Evelyn, 1989, *A History of the Diocese of Cork,* vol. 3, Tower Books

Chartrand, R., 2001, *Bussaco, 1810, Wellington defeats Napoleon's Marshals,* Osprey Publishing Ltd., Oxford, U.K.

Clemente, Manuel, 2002, *Igreja e Sociedade Portuguesa do Liberalismo a República,* Grifo – Editores e Livreiros, Lisboa.

Connolly, S.J. ed., 1999, *The Oxford Companion to Irish History,* Oxford University Press.

Culligan, M.J., & Cherici, P., 1999, *The Wandering Irish in Europe, Their Influence from the Dark Ages to Modern Times,* Constable, London.

Klein, H. S., 1999, *The Atlantic Slave Trade,* Cambridge University Press, Cambridge, England.

Lydon, J., 1998, *The Making of Ireland, from Ancient Times to the Present,* Routledge, London.

Machado de Faria, A., 1961, *Armorial Lusitano,* direcção e coordinação – Dr. A.E. Martins Zuguete, Editorial Enciclopédia Lda., Lisboa.

O'Callaghan, S., 2001, *To Hell or Barbados, The Ethnic Cleansing of Ireland,* Brandon Paperback, Mount Eagle Publications, Dingle, Co. Kerry.

O'Connell, P., *The Irish College at Lisbon, 1590-1834,* Four Courts Press, Dublin.

O'Heyne, J., *The Irish Dominicans of the Seventeenth Century,* trans. 1902, A. Coleman & W. Tempest, Dundalk, Ireland.

Oliveira, M. de, 1994, *História Eclesiástica de Portugal,* edição revista e actualizada, Publicações Europa-América, Portugal.

Oliveira Marques, A.H. de, 2001, *Breve História de Portugal,* Editorial Presença, Lisboa.

Oliveira Marques, A.H. de, *História de Maçonaria em Portugal, das Origens ao Triunfo,* vol.1, Editorial Presença, Lisboa.

O'Neill, R., 1994, *A Rich Inheritance,* Published by Dominican Sisters, Galway.

Prestage. E., 1926, *Frei Domingos do Rosário, Diplomata e Político (1595-1662),* Coímbra, Imprensa da Universidade.

Sanches, J.D., 1940, *Belém e Arredores através dos tempos,* Livraria Univeral, Lisboa.

Sanches, J.D., 1964, *Belém do Passado e do Presente*

Saraiva, A.J., 2da edição, *O Palácio de Belém* Editorial Inquérito, Lisboa.

Saraiva, J.H., 2001, 6ta edição, *Histtória de Portugal,* Publicações Europa – América.

Serrão, J. e Oliveira Marques, A.H. de, direcção, 1992, 1a edição, *Nova História de Portugal,* vol.11, Editorial Presença, Lisboa.

Texto Editora Lda., ed., 2000, *História de Portugal das Origens à Actualidade,* Colecção Universal.

Weller, J., 1999, *Wellington in the Peninsula,* Greenhill Books, London.

Archaeological and Historical Societies

The British Historical Society of Portugal, 1986, A.H. Norris & R. W. Bremner, *The Lines of Torres Vedras, the First Three Lines and Fortifications South of the Tagus.*

New Lights on the Peninsular War, 1989, International Congress on the Iberian Peninsula, Selected Papers, 1780-1840, Lisbon.

Cloyne Literary and Historical Society, 1996, P. Mac Cotter & K. Nichols ed., *The Pipe Roll of Cloyne,* Collectors' edition, no. 363.

Cork Historical & Archaeological Society, 1893, *Biographical Sketches of Persons remarkable in Local History,* vol. VII.

Other Books

Arintero, J. G., 1992, *The Song of Songs, A Mystical Exposition,* trans. J. Valender & J. L. Morales, Tan Books & Publishers, Inc., Rockford, Illinois.

Kavanagh, K., 1987, *John of the Cross, Selected Writings,* Paulist Press, NY, USA.

Williams, R., 1990, *The Wound of Knowledge, Christian Spirituality from the New Testament to St. John of the Cross,* Darton, Longman & Todd, London.

Index